THE ART OF TEACHING CHRISTIAN DOCTRINE、

The Good News and Its Proclamation

JOHANNES HOFINGER, S.J.

UNIVERSITY OF NOTRE DAME PRESS

IMPRIMI POTEST: Joseph Onate, S.J., Provincial

Manila, P. I., April 27, 1957

IMPRIMI POTEST: Theodore J. Mehling, C.S.C., Provincial

NIHIL OBSTAT: Eugene P. Burke, C.S.C., Censor Deputatus

IMPRIMATUR: ✠ Leo A. Pursley, D.D., Bishop of Fort Wayne

April 16, 1957

FIRST EDITION 1957
  SECOND PRINTING 1958
  THIRD PRINTING 1959

Library of Congress Catalog Card Number 57—11224

© 1957 BY UNIVERSITY OF NOTRE DAME PRESS

NOTRE DAME, INDIANA

Preface

This book is largely the fruit of my work and experience, especially during the last few summers in the United States. I have learned much myself by this experience and have been particularly impressed both by the wide-spread interest in the field of religious education as well as by the apostolic spirit of so many thousands of Christ's heralds.

It gives me pleasure to take this occasion to thank the Rev. Josef Andreas Jungmann, S.J., Rector of the Canisianum in Innsbruck, Austria, my most esteemed Master. The book owes much in all its parts to his guidance and inspiration. Thanks to Father Michael A. Mathis, C.S.C., who first invited me to the United States, to lecture in the Liturgy Program of the Summer Sessions (1954 and 1955), and now again in 1957, at the University of Notre Dame; and also to Father Robert R. Henle, S.J., for his invitation to lecture at St. Louis University last summer. Special gratitude is due Father Bernard Schuerman, S.J. of the same University, because, besides translating my booklet *Nuntius Noster,* he persuaded me to prepare this book. Sincere thanks also are due to two of my confreres of the Institute for Mission Apologetics in Manila, P. I.: Father Joseph Kellner, S.J., who contributed the Instruction on Matrimony in Part III of this book, and Father Joseph Ramsauer, S.J., who wrote the summary of "Our Message" in the beginning of Part III. And last, but not least, I want to thank Mrs. Mary Perkins Ryan not only for polishing my poor English, but also, I am happy to say, for improving the ideas themselves of many portions.

Johannes Hofinger, S.J.

Manila, Philippine Islands
Low Sunday, 1957

Table of Contents

vi

PART IV—THE HERALDS OF CHRIST—THEIR PERSONALITY AND FORMATION

APPENDIX

Part 1

Our Task

CHAPTER ONE

Towards a Better Understanding
Of Our Catechetical Task

A most promising catechetical movement has been in existence in the Catholic world for more than fifty years. And especially during the last twenty-five years, its progress has been most successful, not only in its expansion to nearly every country in the world—we find countries today showing an intensive interest in a thorough catechetical revival which were in no way influenced by such tendencies twenty years ago—but even more in the deeper understanding and clarification of its program. For the great improvement in religious education which has been brought about by the catechetical movement has been due chiefly, in the final analysis, to a deeper and more accurate understanding of the work of catechetics.

ON THE TRACK OF A BETTER METHOD

During the first few decades of its existence, the catechetical movement stressed methods above all. It sought to improve religious instruction by relating it more closely to daily life, and by introducing more of what are now called "visual aids". That this should have been the first step is quite understandable in relation to the circumstances existing at that time in the countries in which the catechetical movement arose. In Germany, France, Austria and Belgium especially, great advances had been made in the teaching of secular subjects by the application of the findings of applied psychology. But in the field of religion, before the beginning of the catechetical movement, teachers had for far too long held complacently to the time-worn dry method of analyzing and so explaining the text of the catechism.

To realize what this meant in the concrete, let us recall the lengthy, difficult and picture-less catechisms of those days, splendid models no doubt of precise formulation of the Church's doctrine, but equally splendid models of a completely unpsychological presentation of that

1

doctrine. To make matters worse, children were generally required to learn these unchildlike catechisms by heart, word for word. We do not need to say that the result in many cases was mere mechanical memorizing of abstract texts, the meaning of which was often grasped in part or perhaps not at all; and that these memorized texts offered the well-meaning but helpless child next to no nourishment for his religious life.

But how was it possible for so many catechists to be content with such an unsuitable method for such a long time—and that in an era when secular subjects were already being taught by far more attractive methods? One of the most important reasons surely was that these teachers lacked an adequate comprehension of their catechetical task. How could a teacher who realizes that in giving religious instruction he is the living instrument of the Divine Catechist ever acquiesce in the use of such an un-Christ-like method?

The better catechists of the time, animated by a genuine priestly spirit, recognized, it is true, the great danger of this situation. In earlier times, the children of good Christian parents had grown up naturally, as it were, into good Christian living. Religious instruction in the schools had only a supplementary role; it organized and deepened the religious knowledge already acquired by the children in their homes and in their parish church. But now, particularly in the great industrial centers where the great mass of the people were rapidly becoming more and more estranged from religion, a Christian milieu for the children's formative years could no longer be presupposed. Cases multiplied in which children were found to have brought next to nothing from their homes in the way of religious instruction. The school, therefore, had to furnish everything which had formerly been supplied by the Christian home, both in the way of an example of Christian living, and of direct instruction. Under such circumstances, abstract teaching, divorced from the realities of daily life, was foredoomed to failure, since it went over the heads of the children and past their hearts. In fact, such instruction not infrequently did more harm than good, for, far from overcoming the religious indifference brought by the children from their homes, it succeeded only in boring them to the point of rebellion against the catechism class, and, ultimately, against religion itself. Obviously, only a method of instruction which was concrete, lively, and interesting could be expected to cope with this difficult problem.

This was the situation in central and western Europe at the beginning of the century when the catechetical movement began its work. And it is not difficult to show that the situation in other countries was not very different, and that it soon became almost identical, owing to the ceaseless improvement in secular teaching methods, together with the equally ceaseless spreading of the problems brought by expanding industrialism. The same was true in the United States also, especially with regard to the situation of the Catholic children attending public grade schools (according to reliable statistics, now more than 50% of the total number). These millions of children could be kept and formed for Catholic living only by additional religious instruction of a high level both from the didactic and from the religious point of view.

The principal postulates of the first period of the catechetical renewal in Europe may, then, be summarized as follows:

1. Religious instruction must adapt itself to the child's psychology: it must, therefore, begin with the visual and the concrete. Accordingly, during the first years of school, the biblical-historical approach should take precedence over the systematic order of the catechism.

2. Religious instruction on the school level should not only communicate religious knowledge, but also and above all, it should establish religious dispositions and convictions. It should, therefore, as a matter of principle, address itself to the whole human being: it is his heart and will, above all, that must be formed to the image of Christ. The question, then, is one not only of clear, intelligible instruction, but primarily of effective education that forms the young person and equips him for Christian living. In this program, this stressing of religious *education* rather than religious *instruction* alone, was the result not so much of a timely adaptation of modern teaching-methods, but rather of a clearer and deeper insight into the nature of our catechetical task.

It may be that in this first period, the importance of methods was sometimes overestimated, and, in fact, considered to be the only thing needed for a good and effective kind of catechesis. Such a view is of course wrong and has fatal consequences. But we should not forget that these efforts toward finding better methods came, in the final analysis, from a renewed and deepened sense of the great responsibility of catechists, and that the discovery of such methods was absolutely necessary in those days of old-fashioned lifeless teaching.

Moreover, since the end of the thirties, a deeply religious examination of the nature of our catechetical apostolate has been undertaken, and this has done away with the exaggerations of the first phase of the movement. Such has been the case, at least, in central and western Europe, where, in the last years before the second world war, a second phase of the catechetical renewal was inaugurated.

RECOVERING THE CHRISTIAN MESSAGE

Beginning with this second period of the catechetical movement, however, the realization became ever more widespread that a true catechetical renewal must also concern itself with the *content of religious instruction*. This does not mean, of course, that traditional Catholic doctrine be changed in order to conform with modern fashions of thought, nor that it be watered down to suit the secularized outlook of modern society. Far from it. But quite apart from anything like this, legitimate problems do exist concerning the content of religious instruction.

For teaching to be successful, it is of the utmost importance that the teacher know how to select the most significant points in the abundance of material at hand. He must be able to present the subject-matter to his students from the angles which have the greatest formative value, from the angles which will cause the students to welcome this teaching. He must arrange the topics so that dominant ideas stand out unmistakeably, so that the most important things are recognized as such by the children, while less important matters are used to serve as illustrations, or to bring to life the basic themes.

A catechetical movement sincerely intent on more than a superficial success had to ask itself sooner or later whether these things were being done; and an honest facing of facts led to a clear realization that religious teaching was not being carried out in this way. Nor was it a question merely of the qualifications of individual teachers; it was recognized that there were widespread and significant deficiencies in the religious instruction generally customary, deficiencies which urgently demanded that the catechetical renewal give its attention also to the question of the content of religious instruction.

This change of outlook on the part of catechetical leaders was occasioned particularly by a book by the famous liturgist, Rev. Joseph A. Jungmann, S.J. of Innsbruck: *Die Frohbotschaft und unsere Glaubensverkündigung* (The Glad Tidings and our Proclamation of the Faith) (Pustet, Regensburg, 1936). This book demonstrated convincingly the fact that our teaching of the truths of the faith, in spite of all the advances of theology during the centuries, and in spite of the improvements that had taken place in the previous decades in catechetical methods, as a whole sadly lacked the inspirational power and the perspective of value which characterized the ancient manner of teaching found in the classical Roman liturgy and in the religious writings of the patristic era. Our teaching of the faith, both in catechetics and in sermons, does not sufficiently stress what is essential and central in Christian doctrine. Above all, it does not adequately communicate the truths of the faith from that point of view which is intrinsically proper to the proclamation of the Christian message. Christian doctrine, after all, claims to be a "gospel", a glad tidings. It must therefore succeed primarily in presenting the Christian religion as something desirable and valuable, as something to be received with joy and to be experienced as joyful.

One may not, of course, minimize the hard demands of Christian morality. Nor did the early Church do so. On the contrary she insisted on them boldly, without compromise or sugar-coating. But the difficult demands were not in the forefront of Christians' consciousness. "Gospel" means "good news". The ideal teaching of Christian truth must, therefore, result above all in grateful recognition of those incomparable gifts that we have received from our loving Father through Christ: the divine life to which we were re-born in Baptism, which increases and grows strong in us by means of the sacraments; membership in the family of God which we enjoy by grace in the community of the Church; and the pledge of eternal happiness to which we look forward in hope. Viewed against such a background, the rigorous demands of Christian morality themselves share in the beauty and glory of the new order of things given to us in Christ.

Fr. Jungmann further pointed out in this same book that, in earlier centuries when Christian doctrine and Christian life were still a dominating force in the West, it was not so imperative as it is now to emphasize clearly and forcefully what is central and most valuable in Christianity. But today we must not shut our eyes to the fact that, even in so-called Catholic countries, the Christian religion itself is in danger among the masses of the people; it must fight for its very existence against extraordinarily vital and powerful foes. No longer is one or other doctrine questioned—as was the case with former heresies—but Christianity as a whole. For this reason, it is all the more necessary today to bring out, as powerfully and attractively as possible, its essential content and worth.

The improvement of religious instruction as to its content, called for by Fr. Jungmann, accordingly entails the right selection of matter, its right ordering, and the right emphasis or "spotlight" put on the individual truths of the faith. And this selection, ordering and emphasis must be clearly oriented to the goal of Christian instruction, which is nothing other than the building up and fostering of Christian life. And while it is true, of course, that the entire Christian revelation must without exception be at least implicitly believed, this does not mean that all the data of revelation must be "proclaimed" in the same way.

Since the appearance of Fr. Jungmann's book, the name *kerygma* (a publicly announced message) has come to be more and more generally given to those aspects of revelation which were meant to be explicitly and emphatically proclaimed. The Greek word is used seven times in the New Testament, especially to refer to the core of the apostolic preaching. See, for example 1 Cor. 1:21; 1 Cor. 2:43; 1 Cor. 15:14. The corresponding verb *kerysso* (to proclaim, to preach) is found sixty-one times in the New Testament, and is also used to describe Christ's preaching and that of St. John the Baptist. It designates the action of a herald, particularly of one who announces an event and summons his hearers to action.[1] The message, then, which St. Paul as the herald, *keryx,* of the eternal King is to proclaim to fallen humanity is none other than that bedrock of Christian truths which constitute the essential content of the Christian glad tidings. This message must bring the inner nature and worth of Christianity into as clear focus as possible. It consists in the incomparable good news of the eternal love of God, Who, through His only-begotten Son, has called us to Himself and enables us to reach our true home. In brief, it is the good news of our salvation in Christ.

It is in this sense, accordingly, that modern catechetical writing more and more generally refers to the contemporary concern for the content of religious instruction as *the kerygmatic renewal.*

From what has been said, it is obvious that the scope of the kerygmatic renewal cannot validly be restricted to religious instruction given in school. It is concerned with all the various forms in which the Christian message is to be proclaimed, including its preaching in church as well as catechetical instruction in schools, the dissemination of this message through the press as well as the theological formation given in seminaries and universities. But it might be well to call attention to the fact that the kerygmatic renewal involves questions pertaining to teaching even on the grade school level, and in the chapters that follow, we hope to prove this beyond doubt.

But however strongly we wish to stress the value of the kerygmatic approach, we in no way mean to imply thereby that the hard-won achievements of the first period of the catechetical movement are no longer important or to be neglected. In this respect too, Fr. Jungmann's recent work *Katechetik* (2nd ed. Herder, Freiburg, 1955) gives sound

---

1.   On the meaning of the word *kerygma* in the New Testament, see A. Rétif, *Qu'est-ce que le kérygma?,* in *Nouvelle Revue théol.,* 1949: 910-922; A. Rétif, *Foi au Christ et mission d'après les Actes des Apôtres,* Paris, 1953, 11 ff.; Kr. Stendahl, *Kerygma-Kerygmatisch,* in *Theol. Literaturzeitung,* 1952, 715-720. On the sacred and profane use of the words, *keryx, kerysso, kerygma,* and *prokerysso,* in connection with the New Testament, see G. Friedrich in Kittel, *Theologisches Wörterbuch zum Neuen Testament,* 3, 682-717. A. Rétif overemphasizes, perhaps the difference between *kerygma* as first used for preaching the Kingdom of God to unbelievers, and the subsequent instruction of catechumens and the faithful, for which the words *didache* and *didascalia* are more customary.

advice. No other manual today, to our knowledge, succeeds so perfectly in making use of the principles of the methodological and of the kerygmatic renewal to form a well-ordered, harmonious whole.

And also, the kerygmatic renewal leads not only to a better understanding of the message, *kerygma,* which we are to proclaim, but also, most happily, into a more searching insight into the nature of our catechetical apostolate. Far more clearly and consciously than before, we now consider ourselves as the privileged instruments of Christ, instruments by which, in our own times, He continues His great catechetical apostolate as the Herald of the heavenly Father. We know ourselves to be sent by Christ, we believe that He works with us and through us. "As the Father has sent me, I also send you (John 20: 21). "Go, and make disciples . . . and behold, I am with you all days" (Matt. 28: 19 ff). These great words of Christ are spoken to us also.

HERALDING WITH CHRIST

Whoever is sent to teach religion by ecclesiastical Superiors—and this, obviously, is the case not only with priests, but with hundreds of thousands of Sisters and lay teachers teaching religion in Catholic schools and Confraternity classes—participates in the apostolate of the Church which proclaims Christ's message to all nations until the end of the world. Because of the canonical mission (commission given by the bishop), a Christian participates in a special way in the teaching apostolate of Christ Himself, Who now and always until the end of the world is teaching through and in His Church. It is obvious that the authority of the teacher varies in the different classes of teachers used by Christ as His instruments. And this is true also of the teaching clergy. Is there not a great difference between the teaching authority of the Holy Father and that of a simple priest? Yet are not both of them instruments of Christ the Teacher? Furthermore, it would be wrong to evaluate Christ's instruments exclusively from the point of view of their authority. What is the final purpose of Christ's teaching? Is it merely to make some authoritative statements in the name of His Father? Or is it not, rather, to beget and to form perfect children for His Father, who will adore Him in Spirit and in Truth (John 4:24)? Should we not, then, above all evaluate the instruments of the teaching Christ according to their formative influence?

If we are to understand our catechetical task rightly and fulfill it properly, nothing is so important as the deep conviction, born of faith, that we are sent by Christ, that we have to let Him work through us, that we have to adapt ourselves as completely as possible to Him. This basic attitude of a fully "Christian" catechist will, without further ado, give us the right attitude toward the message that we, as Christ's mouth-pieces, are to proclaim. It will give us the right attitude to the goal toward which we are working, and the right attitude to the students whom we are to address in Christ's name. As instruments of Christ, we desire, naturally, to teach only what He would teach these actual students in these concrete circumstances; we desire to carry out our teaching with Our Lord's own deep love for and personal interest in each of these students.

This radically "Christian" view of our catechetical apostolate will also provide us with the right attitude as to catechetical methods. As soon as we desire to be nothing but instruments of Christ—but to be His perfect instruments—clearly we shall want to do our work as well as possible. And therefore we shall be eager to use every means that may help to perfect our teaching. But at the same time, we shall never become the slaves of methods.[2] We shall consider it much more important to strive for a deeply religious understanding of our message than to use the "latest" achievement of methodology. Methods, then, will become for us what they should be: means to bring out our message in all its richness. And we shall therefore be more concerned with the message itself than with the methods of its proclamation. We shall study particularly the basic questions of the kerygmatic renewal: what are we to teach; what is the central core of the message we are to proclaim; what are the essential doctrines we should stress; from what viewpoint should we present this message so that it becomes truly the "gospel" of Our Lord; what would be the best arrangement of the catechetical material for the purpose of leading our pupils to understand it in a rightly religious way and to make use of it in their daily Christian lives?

These are also the questions which we shall try to answer in this book. First, in part I, we shall show how our catechetical task is, more particularly, one of progressive initiation into the mystery of Christ. Thus we must not only proclaim His message with Christ, we must *proclaim Christ*. For Christ, the great Gift of the Father's love and our Way to the Father is Himself the central theme of our message, just as participation in Christ's life is the proper goal of our apostolate. Then in Part II, we shall answer the question of how the catechetical material must be ordered so that this central theme will shine out as clearly as possible, and so that the individual doctrines will most fully contribute

2. Still less shall we become slaves of marks and tests. These may be necessary as part of class-room procedure, but what, finally, can they test? Not the student's religious attitude, but, at best, only his knowledge of religion. And even this, in any more than a quite superficial sense, cannot be tested by the "true-false" or "objective" tests so much in use.

to the attainment of the proper goal of all catechetical activity. Then we shall be prepared more specifically to consider, in Part III, the longest section of this book, the actual content of our message. What are, in the final analysis, the essential doctrines of Christianity; what should we stress most especially in these particular doctrines; from what viewpoint should we present them? And, obviously, in order fittingly to proclaim this divine message, we must have well-trained heralds. And so the fourth and final section of this book will be concerned with the important question of the appropriate formation of the catechist.

CHAPTER TWO

The Central Theme
Of Our Message

Obviously, no efficient heralding of our message is possible without a proper understanding of this message we are to proclaim. Therefore we who are heralds of Christ must first of all face the question: What is, actually, the message Christ wishes to proclaim through us? In particular, what is the core, the central theme of this message, and what are the interrelations of this central theme with the other fundamentals of Christian doctrine?

OUR CENTRAL THEME: THE MYSTERY OF CHRIST

The message entrusted to us is made up of many different doctrines, but it is, by its very nature, far more than a list of truths. It is *a wonderful unity with one central idea* which we must bring out as clearly as we can.

What would you think of a guardian who was to hand over to his ward a beautiful palace; but instead of presenting him with the palace, gave him only the mass of stones, beams and planks that once went to make up the building itself? Would it not be a catechetical crime to transmit to our students only some incoherent fragments instead of the organic divine message?

The first heralds of Christ, the Apostles, were already aware of the catechetical problem we are now dealing with. St. Paul the great catechist of the ancient Church, in particular, was perfectly aware of the necessity of catechetical concentration on the real heart of the Christian message. His letters excel in richness of doctrine and, at the same time, they are outstanding in their luminous unity. Again and again, he returns to the fact that, ultimately, his teaching is one all-comprehensive doctrine, a central mystery. As he sees it, his special vocation lies in the fact that to him, "the very least of all saints, there was

10

given this grace, to announce among the Gentiles the good tidings of the unfathomable riches of Christ, and to enlighten all men as to what is the dispensation of the mystery which has been hidden from eternity in God" (Eph. 3:8).

Clearly, this central mystery which is to be proclaimed to the whole world is the message of the unfathomable riches that are given to us in Christ. The same idea is brought out in similar language toward the end of his Epistle to the Romans which, more than any other, contains "his Gospel" (Rom. 16:25). And in the Epistle to the Colossians, St. Paul again speaks of this mystery, that forms the essence of his whole catechesis, as, simply, "the mystery of Christ" (Col. 4:3), or, more fully and precisely, "the mystery of God the Father, which is Christ" (Col. 2:2),[1] or "Christ in you, your hope of glory" (Col. 1:27). In other words, the Apostle's message presents Christ as the great Gift of the Father's love, proclaiming how the Father reveals and gives Himself in Christ, and how He invites us to share in the life and glory of His only-begotten Son. "He (the Father) has called you, by our preaching, to gain the glory of our Lord Jesus Christ" (2 Thess. 2:14). Among many other texts, see especially Eph. 1:9 ff.; 1 Cor. 2:7; 1 Cor. 1:9; 1 Tim. 3:16). Thus the actual content of his apostolic message is simply Christ. He resumes his whole preaching in the classical formula: "We proclaim Jesus Christ" (2 Cor. 4:5. See also 1 Cor. 2:2; 2 Cor. 1:19; Gal. 1:16). His apostolate essentially consists in heralding the good tidings of Christ: "My own work has been to complete the preaching of Christ's gospel" (Rom. 15:19; 1 Cor. 9:12; 2 Cor. 2:12; 2 Cor. 9:13; 2 Cor. 10:14; Gal. 1:7; Phil. 1:27; 1 Thess. 3:2; Rom. 1:9).

In all of this, the great catechist of the ancient Church is only expressing very clearly what is also revealed in the Gospels, which are the most magnificent documents of Apostolic preaching. *The mystery of Christ is the fundamental theme and unifying principle of all Christian religious instruction*. It is the good tidings of of our salvation in Christ: the divine Father reveals Himself to us in His Son; He has, in the exact sense of the world, *visited* us, given Himself to us and taken us home to Himself,—not only each of us individually, but all of us together in the wonderful unity which we form through our living connection with Christ in His Mystical Body.

Seen in this light, our message of the mystery of Christ is truly "a message of salvation", it is the good tidings of Jesus Christ, our Redeemer. Christ appears clearly as the blessed self-revelation and self-communica-

---

1. An inexact translation of this important text is found in the Latin text of the Vulgate and in most English translations.

tion of the Father, and as our only way to the Father. This is how Our Lord Himself understood His own mission and message to mankind, and, in His farewell discourse to His Apostles at the Last Supper, He gave it this classic formulation: "I am the way, and the truth, and the life. No one comes to the Father but through Me" (John 14:6). Christ's message is clearly centered in the Father. Christ Himself is the most excellent gift of the Father's love to us (John 3:16; Rom. 8:32; 1 John 4:9).

It is true that Christ is the center of our message, but only because He is "the Christ", the messenger of God, the great Gift of the Father to us and our leader in the journey home to the Father. Only in this way can we clearly see the essential aspects of our teaching, which are *theocentricity* (centered in God, that is, God the Father, the beginning and end of our salvation) and *Christocentricity* (centered in Christ, the only way to the Father). This is exactly what Christ means when He said that He and the Father are the two poles of Christian faith, and, therefore, of Christian teaching: "This is everlasting life, that they may know Thee, the only true God, and Him Whom Thou hast sent, Jesus Christ." (John 17:3).

Naturally, no Catholic catechist would ever deny these basic truths of Christian teaching. But are these truths always brought out clearly and emphasized strongly in our catechetical instructions? Do we bring them out in all our teaching from the very beginning? Does the danger not sometimes exist that catechists, overly concerned with the techniques of teaching children at various age-levels, do not point out these fundamental truths with sufficient clarity and emphasis? Yet it is these truths which should, at every moment, be the luminous center of religious instruction in order properly to form the religious life of Christians becoming aware of their faith. It is for this reason that we do not think it advisable, for example, to entitle a course for beginners "Jesus-Mary",[2] since this cannot help giving the child the impression that Jesus and Mary are the two poles of our religion. It is wrong to think that concessions of this kind are the inevitable corollary of a method of instruction suited to the child's mentality. Should any good method of teaching alter the essential structure of doctrine? Rightly understood, methods of teaching are servants. They assist the teacher in making his teaching understood as accurately and easily as possible. But methods must never be allowed to tyrannize over the meaning of what is taught. The objection might be made that the children have to be helped to learn by such means, and that the necessary corrections can be made

2. *Jesus-Maria Course of Religion,* by Alexander Schorsch, C.M. (Archdiocese of Chicago School Board, Chicago, Ill., 1955.).

later on. But what efficient architect would allow himself to be guided by considerations of "easiness" when laying the foundations, in the hope of making essential alterations later? Obviously this would result in innumerable difficulties. As we shall show in Chapter 4, it is not so difficult to instruct children properly in the mystery of Christ from the very beginning. But we must first understand the supreme importance of this basic necessity. Of course, although the mystery of Christ should be from the very beginning the center of our catechetical instruction, this does not mean that we should use the term itself. It is not a question of the *term,* but of the *matter.* The expression "mystery of Christ" does not occur once in the Gospels, and yet it is their center. We should never, then, use the term "mystery of Christ" in the lower grades.[3]

Once the catechist has undersood what the mystery of Christ really means: God's redemptive plan with Christ as its center—and not simply the "life of Jesus" from Bethlehem to Calvary—then it will be relatively easy to see the other fundamental teachings of Christianity in their right order, and to put them into their proper place in our teaching. And so all the doctrines of the faith can be easily and organically included in this holy ordering.

CENTRAL THEME AND FUNDAMENTAL DOCTRINES

For example, the place and importance in our catechetical instruction of our teaching on Mary, the mother of our Redeemer, should be entirely determined by her unique share in the mystery of Christ. And this does not mean only her share in the temporal birth of the Son of God, the fact that in her womb the "mystery that from eternity has been hidden in God" (Eph. 3:9) became man and dwelt amongst us, full of grace and truth. We have also to teach her great work in the unfolding of this mystery among men, since she is the mother of the redeemed, and, at the same time, the most perfect member of the Mystical Body of Christ. Just as Our Lady's loftiest and most basic claim to our veneration is the fact of her supreme service to the mystery of Christ, so our teaching of Marian dogma and devotion must serve first of all, to lead our students to a fuller understanding of the mystery of Christ and of our participation in it. In order to attain this goal of Marian catechesis, it is not, of course, enough to mention continually the beautiful principle: "to Christ through Mary". The doctrine

3. A good example of how the "Mystery of Christ" may be presented to small children without using unchildlike terminology, may be found in the remarkable course *On Our Way* worked out by Sister Maria de la Cruz, H.H.S., for teachers of the Confraternity of Christian Doctrine (Sadlier, New York).

behind this principle must be explained in such a way as fully to indicate its significance. Have we as yet succeeded in doing this?

In a similar way, the most important topic of *grace* can only be properly understood and taught in relation to the mystery of Christ. For this doctrine refers entirely to our unmerited share in the mystery of the incarnate Word, and to the fact that only through our living relationship with Christ, only in Him and through Him, can we share in His divine life, can we obtain the gift of becoming God's children. Since grace is, in its essence, Christ's life in His members, this doctrine cannot, without serious dangers, be taught in isolation from Christ. For this aspect of the mystery of Christ, St. Paul coined the classic expression: "Christ in you" (Col. 1:27). Do we not sometimes endanger our students' understanding of this truth by imitating the teaching of theologians who have enlarged and complicated the tract on grace with many specialized questions, and at the same time have isolated it from its essential relation to Christ? Is the center of our catechesis of the "grace of Christ" really "Christ and His Mystery"? It is certainly not enough repeatedly to point out that every grace is granted to us through the merits of Christ. Grace is not only merited for us *by* Christ; it is a living community of life *with* Christ, the new and wonderful life that comes to us and fills our being thanks to our vital connection with the True Vine. It is, therefore, only in the light of Christ that the grace of Christ can properly be understood and explained.[4]

The same is true, of course, concerning the teaching about *the Church and her worship*. If our consideration of the Church amounts to a mere statement and description of her social and juridical structure, have we not miserably failed to teach the truth that the kingdom has become a joyful reality in our midst? The character of the Church, her final meaning, her tasks, her power, her mystery can, again, be understood only in the light of the Mystery of Christ: she is His Mystical Body in which the divine life, brought to us by Him from heaven, is to be developed and perfected.

4. A tendency exists today to consider "grace" or divine life as "the" central idea of Christian revelation, and, in consequence, as the central theme of our catechetical instruction. See especially the booklet by Rev. Paul M. Baier, *Supernatural Life* (2nd ed. 1955, published by the author himself, 225 Blackman St., Wilkes-Barre, Pa.). See also Fr. Baier's article "Supernatural Life—Central Idea" in the *Catholic Educational Review,* May, 1956. Although the doctrine on the divine life communicated to us in Christ holds a very important place in Christian teaching, we should not say that "supernatural life" is the central idea. For the central idea cannot be a gift of God, but only God Himself Who has called us in Christ to share in His life. Cf. on this important point, Joseph A. Jungmann, S.J., *Christus als Mittelpunkt religiöser Erziehung* (Herder, Freiburg, 1939). See also Franz Schreibmayr, *Ist das Reich Gottes oder Christus der Mittelpunkt des neuen Katechismus?* in *Katechetische Blätter,* 1953, 444-445.

For it is through the sacraments and sacrifices of the Church that we are brought into the mystery of Christ in the most living and effective way. The sacraments allow us to share in His life: the Mystery of His life-giving redemption becomes effective in us. In the Eucharistic Sacrifice, we share in the mystery of Christ's sacrifice on Calvary; in the sacrifice of the Church, the mysterious sacrifice of Calvary is completed. On Calvary, Christ offered His sacrifice alone; in the Church's Eucharistic sacrifice, He lets His Bride share in His sacrifice, conferring on her the honor of sacrificing with Him, and allowing her to become the sacrifice with Him. Thus the sacrifice of the Head offered on Calvary is completed in the sacrifice of the whole Christ, including Head and members, on our altars.

And, finally, the new divine life which Christ gives us in the sacraments also demands of us *a new way of life according to the image of Christ*: "For we were buried with Him by means of Baptism into death, in order that, just as Christ has risen from the dead through the glory of the Father, so we also may walk in newness of life" (Rom. 6:4). Our sacramental participation in the mystery of Christ must lead to a new Christian way of life in the spirit of Christ; thus also our moral task as Christians can be understood and pondered only through the central idea of the mystery of Christ and our participation it it.

Obviously, then, this comprehensive view of our good tidings is of the utmost importance for the success of our catechetical instruction. Here is the heart of our Christian teaching which must be thoroughly taught and forcefully emphasized in all forms of catechetical teaching. Let us not deceive ourselves by thinking that we have as yet been completely successful. And why have we not been as successful as we should like to be? Certainly there has not been even a single catechist who lacked good will. In the United States especially, a foreigner is continually edified by the exemplary zeal of innumerable catechists, Sisters and laypeople as well as those in Orders. If some of these eager catechists have not as yet succeeded in placing Christ and His mystery in the center of all their teaching, this is to be explained only by the insufficiency of their training.

Catechists need not so much detailed and exhaustive explanations of doctrine—although, of course, this is necessary to some degree. Experience shows, however, that our catechetical instructors, especially the Sisters, already possess a thorough knowledge of the different dogmas. But what they need, first of all, is a magnificent, joyful and comprehensive view of the different aspects of the mystery of Christ. We know from experience how eager and grateful they are for this service, which is one that we really owe them.

But is it Sisters and lay catechists only who need to be given this view? It would seem to be required also in the seminaries. And therefore, the special purpose of kerygmatically oriented theological teaching is to allow the mystery of Christ to become evident in all the theses that the students must master, so that they do not become lost or side-tracked among a collection of isolated topics, losing the vision of the whole. For true theology is, finally, a systematic effort to understand as well as possible the plan which God has made known to us in Christian revelation, and which He is realizing in our salvation. And this plan consists in "gathering all creation both in heaven and on earth under one head, Christ" (Eph. 1:10).

Chapter Three

The Proper Goal of Our Catechetical Apostolate

The modern catechetical movement originated chiefly as a much-needed reaction against the intellectualism which, toward the end of the nineteenth century, was severely endangering the teaching of religion. While the importance of religious knowledge was over-emphasized, religious formation and religious living were unintentionally neglected. Teachers all too often were content to have their students merely memorize the catechism, sacrificing true understanding to mechanical drill. But even where true understanding was the aim, and an aim which was achieved to a high degree, the heart and its education were still neglected. In contrast, the catechetical movement has emphasized what is the true educational function of our catechetical activity: we not only have to give our students a thorough knowledge of their faith, but we must also form true Christians who truly live their Christianity. Religious knowledge in itself is not the real goal of our teaching, it is only a means. The goal of religious instruction is religious living.

The catechetical movement would contradict itself if it were ever to question, or to turn away from, this, which is the only true interpretation of our catechetical task. Yet does it not seem to be doing precisely this in the most recent catechetical efforts? Are not "teaching" and "instructing" again being too strongly emphasized, the more so when scholarly expressions, such as "kerygma" and "kerygmatic renewal" are being used?

Such is certainly the reaction of many people deeply concerned with the success of catechetics to our preoccupation with "kerygmatics". But the answer to this difficulty may be easily seen if we clarify our concern for the proper "heralding" of the Good News by reference to the central mystery of our catechetical teaching, "the mystery of Christ". Like the Apostles, we too must above all *preach Christ*. As we pointed out in the last chapter, the "mystery of Christ" is not only the heart of our instructions, but the theme which embraces, penetrates and unifies all the other Christian doctrines. What, then, do we wish to achieve by teaching the mystery of Christ, and how do we attain this goal?

NOT ONLY KNOWLEDGE OF, BUT PARTICIPATION IN THE MYSTERY OF CHRIST.

We must try very hard, it is true, to explain the mystery of Christ to the students entrusted to us. But, as we all know, mere knowledge of this mystery is by no means enough. Knowledge of the mystery of Christ should be, primarily, the spring of holy action, of a mysterious occurrence to which we must consent in our hearts with lively faith, and with which we must cooperate with generous devotion.

St. Paul saw this truth very clearly. According to him, the teacher's true vocation is "In order to perfect the saints for a work of ministry, for building up the body of Christ, until we all attain the unity of the faith and of the deep knowledge of the Son of God, to a perfect manhood, to the mature measure of the fullness of Christ" (Eph. 4:11–13). This holy knowledge of God's Son must induce us to practice "the truth in love, and so grow up in all things in him who is the head, Christ" (Eph. 4:15). When he speakes of the mystery of Christ in the Epistle to the Colossians, he stresses the same truth very strongly: "Him (i.e. Christ) we preach, admonishing every man and teaching every man in all wisdom that we may present every man perfect in Christ Jesus" (Col. 1:28). But, as St. Paul knows very well, this is not accomplished by a single effort. It is hard labor requiring much patience. And what is the goal of this educational process? "My dear children, with whom I am in labor again, *until Christ is formed in you*" (Gal. 4:19).

Christ has Himself explained His mission in the same way: "I came that they may have life and have it more abundantly" (John 10:10). All His messianic work, and especially His catechesis, is directed toward this goal. Christ does not recognize a religious knowledge sufficient in itself; each of His words is clearly concerned with a religious *life*. This is the heart of the incomparable message that He, the great Herald of the divine Father, has brought to us; the call to a new life, or, more precisely, the invitation to participate in His own life which He, the divine Vine, communicates to us, His brothers and members. Our catechetical task essentially consists in communicating this message of our divine Master to the students entrusted to us. We should actually betray our apostolate if we were ever to content ourselves with mere knowledge. As Christ's messengers, we must communicate His life, we must lead people to effective participation in His mystery.

Therefore, if we are to understand our wonderful task more perfectly and to carry it out more fruitfully, we must understand explicitly what "participation in the mystery of Christ" should mean to us. Since this is the ultimate goal of all our catechetical efforts, we cannot be contented to be vague about it.

What Does Participation in the Mystery of Christ Mean?

We must realize clearly, first of all, that this participation is not brought about perfectly by a single event with an instantaneous effect. It is true, of course, that, all at once, by Baptism we receive Christ's life and become His members for ever. Through the unmerited grace of God, we have, by Baptism, been made partakers in the mystery of the life-giving death of Christ. "Do you not know that all we who have been baptized into Christ Jesus have been baptized into His death? For we were buried together with Him by means of Baptism into death, in order that, just as Christ has arisen from the dead through the glory of the Father, so we also may walk in newness of life" (Rom. 6:3–4). But the life that we receive at Baptism as a holy gift must be fully developed in our life as Christians; it has to mature in the organically progressive growth in Christ which St. Paul calls the goal of Christian instruction (Eph. 4:15). The question is, then, what are the main phases of this growth, and how can we foster it by religious instruction and training.

Through the special kindness of God, most of us were made members of the divine Vine before we came to the use of reason. When we were baptized, we could not even begin to understand what a wonderful gift God was giving us, nor could we realize that it brings with it the vocation to a life in Christ. We could not, therefore, accept this task by a free decision of our own. But God does not want to force His gift upon us; when our reasoning powers have begun to develop, we are to accept this gift with our own free will, and to cooperate willingly in the development of this new life. This development is essentially God's work, but we are called upon to play our part in it also.

So we see clearly the fundamental task of all catechetical teaching: we are to help the maturing Christian gradually to become aware of the magnificence of his vocation and of the greatness of his task in life as a Christian. As God's heralds, we are to present Christian doctrine to him, but not merely as something that he must "study" and "know". We are to make him aware of God's personal invitation to him, first given at Baptism. From the first lesson, then, the child should realize that he is personally addressed and personally invited, not merely by the teacher, but by God. And he should also realize that God is waiting for his answer to this invitation, for his "yes" arising from his Christian *faith,* for his "yes" gratefully given to Christ, and to a life to be lived in and with Christ. We do not mean, obviously, a "yes" that is given by the intellect alone; we mean the full response of Christian faith, consisting essentially in the honest will to follow unreservedly God's loving invitation to a life in Christ. Such faith is our fundamental answer to God's gift. Our Lord Himself expressed this gift in the words: "God so loved the world that He gave His only-begotten Son, that those who believe in Him may not perish, but may have life everlasting" (John 3:16).

Our catechetical instruction, then, from the very beginning must be directed toward this full faith in Christ and willingness to follow Him. Our first and fundamental task is to awaken, deepen, and gradually to perfect this willing faith. Catholic religious instruction is, above all, instruction in *faith.* But the term "instruction" must not be understood too narrowly. Here it means not only "teaching", but from the beginning, obviously "practical guidance", "exercise". The principle "learning by doing" is very applicable here, but it must be "doing" from the heart. And by far the most important expressions of faith are not more or less isolated "acts of faith", but rather *truly Christian prayer.* In prayer we thank the divine Father for His gift of love; in prayer we reaffirm our willingness to follow Christ faithfully; in prayer we humbly ask for God's help that our life may correspond to our faith. Do we truly try to develop our students in this kind of prayer, or are we satisfied with their mechanical repetition of prayer-forms?

Faith and its expression in prayer are, then, the first step toward growth in Christ—and even this step is possible only through grace. If this faith is sincere, then the student will himself begin to take the second step: a life growing from faith. And since all our faith is centered in Christ, this means a life in and with Christ. Such a life is our vocation: this is what we accept in making our profession of faith. We teachers, then, must show the young Christian what this "in and with Christ" means. We must first of all bring home to him the beauty of this life with Christ. Next we must not only "teach" but also guide him to good and Christlike action. For the pupil has to learn from his own experience that this life with Christ, in spite of the many sacrifices that it demands, is a wonderful and enviable life, the only life truly worth living.

In this life based on faith, reception of the Sacraments and participation in the Eucharistic Sacrifice play an immensely important role. It is through these means that, during our pilgrimage on earth, we come closest to Christ. Here we are honored by God with an objective participation in the mystery of His only-begotten Son, a participation which, by ourselves, through our own religious efforts, even though these are aided by grace, we could never obtain. Undeserved by us, Christ is more and more perfectly given to us. But our own cooperation when we receive the Sacraments and take part in the Mass, differs greatly from our part in the reception of Baptism, before we had the use of reason. At that time, we personally could not contribute anything. But now that we have the use of our reason and free will, we must prepare ourselves to receive the grace of the sacraments. And the more carefully we prepare ourselves, the more effective their grace will be in us. Hence, *proper guidance in receiving the Sacraments is extremely important.*

In the light of these clarifications, our catechetical task begins to seem more and more momentous. We need to ask, then, can this task always be realized in each day's catechetical instruction in every class? What are the chief ways by which our catechetical goal may truly be reached, not only in the more advanced religious instruction given in high-school, but as early as the basic teaching given in the grades?

What Are the Chief Means of Introduction to the Mystery of Christ?

Modern catechists all agree on the means whereby children—particularly in the grades—are best introduced to the mystery of Christ: the Bible, the Liturgy, Doctrine and Christian Living.

By "the Bible", we here mean the simple historical-biblical catechesis which, through the telling of the good tidings, introduces children for the first time to the mystery of Christ. Guidance in living the sacramental life of the Church and elementary instruction about the Church's worship come under the heading of "Liturgy". "Doctrine" means systematic catechesis following the order of a catechism and presenting the good tidings as a logical structure. And the fourth means frequently added to this triad of Bible, Liturgy, Doctrine, that of *Christian Living,* means that we must not content ourselves at any time with mere "instruction" but that by means of practise in prayer and right action, we must guide our students into living the mystery of Christ.

This "Christian Living" is not, obviously, a course by itself. And the triad of Bible, Liturgy, Doctrine does not mean three independent ways of teaching, but rather a trinitarian order forming one organic whole. In order to achieve an initiation that is progressive and effective, each one of these ways must be followed, and each one at the fitting time.

Since this basic triad is of such supreme importance in religious instruction, we shall treat of each of these means in a separate chapter, showing the special function of each in progressive initiation into the Mystery of Christ, and the way in which each is to be taught so that its full fruit may be gained.

Initiation Into the Mystery of Christ Through Bible History

A glorious task confronts our catechetical apostolate. Not only must we give our students a sound knowledge of their religion; we must also initiate them, step by step, into the Mystery of Christ. They are to enter more and more completely into a living union with Our Lord; they are to be more and more filled with Him. Beginning with the teaching given in the first school grade, we must consistently aim at this goal, and gradually realize it. How is this to be carried out, first of all, in the lower grades of grammar-school? Primarily through a biblical-historical catechesis that leads to Christ through the telling of the history of salvation.

WHY BEGIN WITH A BIBLICAL-HISTORICAL CATECHESIS?

The reasons seem convincing. First of all, the Apostles themselves led their catechumens, both from Judaism and paganism, to Christianity by this method. In the New Testament, we find the written expression of their historical catechesis, and this leaves no doubt that the *kerygma* of the ancient Church consisted above all in the joyful proclamation of all the great things that God had realized among men through His Son. "I write of what was from the beginning, what we have heard, what we have seen with our eyes, what we have looked upon and our hands have handled: of the Word of Life . . . What we have seen and have heard we announce to you, in order that you also may have fellowship (the Greek word *koinonia* means *participation*) with us, and that our fellowship may be with the Father, and with His Son Jesus Christ" (1 John 1-3; cf. Luke 1:1-4). In these words of his first Epistle, how strongly the favorite disciple of the Lord introduces his Gospel, stating that it is through the narrative of the historical life of Christ that he wishes to lead his readers to this union with the Father and the Son!

23

This historical catechesis of the primitive Church proclaimed those "wonderful works of God" (Acts 2:11) which the Apostles had already enthusiastically announced to the Jews gathered together on the first Pentecost, and which St. Peter, chief of the Apostles, then summed up in condensed catechetical form (Acts 2:14–40). St. Peter proceeds in a similar manner when he is confronted for the first time with the task of preparing pagans for their reception into the Church. Here, too, he gives a historical survey of God's works among men, from the baptism preached by St. John to the glorification of God's Son (Acts 10:34–43).

St. Paul followed this same method in his systematic catechesis, as we can see for example in the draft of the catechetical speech which he gave in the synagogue in Antioch of Pisidia. He speaks of the blessings God had showered on His chosen people, blessings which find their climax in the redemptive work of the true Messias (Acts 13:16–41). It is interesting to see also how, in his famous speech in the Areopagus, which is not so much a catechesis as an attempt to make contact with his pagan listeners, he tries to return from his philosophical introduction to a proclamation of the historical fact of Christ, before his audience interrupts him (Acts 17:22–31).

Furthermore, we all know the principle concerning basic catechetical instruction, established by St. Augustine, the outstanding catechist of the ancient Church: "When anyone is to receive his first catechetical instruction, he shall be given the complete history (of salvation), starting from the place where it is written: 'In the beginning God created heaven and earth' down to the present period of the Church." (*De catechizandis rudibus,* cap. 3 n. 5.)

But such catechesis in the form of historical narration is recommended to us, not only because of this most ancient and venerable tradition but also for intrinsic reasons both theological and didactic. *Theologically—* it is obvious that the method of historical catechesis is especially suited to the particular character of Christian revelation which is of its very nature above all the "story of redemption", the incomparable news of what God, the loving Father, has done for our salvation. This "good news" centers around Christ Who was sent into the world as the greatest proof of the Father's communicative love, and Who is, at the same time, our only way to the Father out of a world remote from God.

From the viewpoint of *psychological method* also, modern catechists have long agreed that the historical-narrative catechesis is indeed the simplest, most adequate and most effective method of initiation into the Christian religion.

The great precursors of the modern catechetical movement clearly realized and strongly supported the principle that primary catechetical teaching is not to be presented as a systematically ordered catechesis, but as the narrative of our salvation. For example, Archbishop Augustin Gruber of Salzburg stressed this principle as enunciated by St. Augustine, and gave sound reasons for using this approach.[1]

The catechetical movement in our century has from the beginning made this principle one of its basic demands, and it quickly received general agreement, at least in theory. At the first catechetical Congress (Vienna, 1912), Wilhelm Pichler presented the first draft of a *Katholisches Religionsbüchlein* (A Booklet on the Catholic Religion), which is, in its way, a classic. It has been translated into fifty-four languages and is quite widely used in missionary countries. Numerous adaptations have followed.[2] With this masterpiece, Pichler presented, against the objections raised by his opponents, irrefutable proof that by means of the story of salvation it was possible to teach the child the substance of the Christian religion and, at the same time, to make this a spiritual experience. Catechists and spiritual advisors belonging to the long-standing school of teaching had, until then, continually objected that the stories of the Bible were doubtless beautiful and edifying, and should be valuable as additional material in catechesis, but that, in the end, the purpose of religious instruction was simply to impart to the child solid and accurate religious knowledge. This being so, a real catechism was absolutely necessary in order to bring due order and clarity into religious instruction. But now Pichler had demonstrated that this "solid and accurate" knowledge could actually be more perfectly and easily imparted by means of a properly handled historical catechesis than by the "traditional" method.

But it took several decades, unfortunately, before this theory was fully translated into catechetical practice. Even today, and even in catechetically progressive countries, one can find places in which a small catechism, such as the *Catechism for First Communicants,* is used in instructing the children, and "biblical stories" are told only incidentally if time permits, more or less as a relaxation or reward for attention

1. Archbishop Augustin Gruber: *Katechetische Vorlesungen über des heiligen Augustinus Buch:* Von der Unterweisung der Unwissenden in der Religion (Salzburg, 1830). Rev. Gustav Mey, *Vollständige Katechesen,* Einleitung, Freiburg, 1871). And long before this time, some advanced catechists had already recommended the same method, and had prepared "historical catechisms" of which the most famous is the biblical catechism of Claude Fleury: *Catéchisme historique.* Contenant en abrêge l'Histoire Sainte et la doctrine Chrétienne. (2 tomes, Paris, 1683.) The first edition of these booklets contained the explicit approbation of Bossuet and Pirot. But the booklets were put on the Index because of the Gallican tendencies of the author, although these tendencies scarcely appear in his catechism.

2. *Jesus and I,* by A. Heeg, S.J. seems to be the booklet of this kind best known in the United States.

during the rather dry catechism instructions. In contrast to this, modern catechists say that *it is biblical-historical instructions which deserve the predominance and unlimited authority in the first grades of school, together with the self-evident and absolutely essential introduction to and practice of Christian life and prayer.* And, of course, the proper techniques and procedures are most important in achieving complete success with such a biblical-historical course.

How Do We Lead Children to the Mystery of Christ through Bible History?

In order that we may really guide the student to Christ by means of Bible history, it is necessary above all that Christ, and even more, the *Mystery of Christ,* be the radiant center of this history. How easy has the divine Father made this task for us! His only-begotten Son is the center of His redemptive plan, which He has accomplished in spite of all human failures. Seen from God's point of view, the classic formula of St. Paul is fully true: "Jesus Christ, yesterday—today—forever" (Hebrews 13:8). From the beginning to the end, everything is centered in Him. By the eternal ordinance of the Father, Christ must bring everything together in one wonderful unity (Eph. 1:11). Until His blessed coming, everything is preparatory. All nations await Him (Agg. 2:8). In Him the Old Testament finds its fulfillment and perfection (cf. Rom. 10:4; Gal. 3-4; Matt. 5:17). With Him comes the fullness of time (Gal. 4:4; Eph. 1:10). And since the coming of Christ, the history of salvation shows us in essence the growth of the kingdom of God established among us, the unfolding of the truth He has made known to us, the development of the divine life that He gave to us, and which, in His Church, He continues to communicate to us, to nourish in us, and to bring to perfection.

The objection might be made that, from the theological point of view, this fact of the centrality of Christ is certainly true, and that such a Christocentric view of the total history of redemption can probably be given in later years, and should be seriously aimed at in the religious instructions at the high school level. But can we really hope for any results in trying to communicate this view to children in the first grades of grammar school? Will not this theological view of the plan of redemption be even more difficult for small children to understand than is the catechism?

In answer to this, we must first of all admit that, in the course of his religious training, the young Christian must comprehend and live the Mystery of Christ more and more deeply and fully. It is the *progressive* initiation into this Mystery which is important. Therefore, obviously, *we should expect understanding of and participation in this central mystery of our religion only to the degree corresponding to the child's age.* In other words, we should look for no scientific, abstractly formulated reflections, but for simple, childlike understanding and experience. And it is not difficult to achieve this by means of a childlike presentation of the story of redemption. Let us, then, now call attention to some particularly important aspects of such a presentation.

Since we do not expect the children in the lower grades to gain abstract knowledge of or to make abstract reflections on the Mystery of Christ, we should *omit all abstractions from the instruction in the first grades.* Everything in its proper time. In the beginning, it is quite enough to show Christ to the children in such a way that He stands radiantly before them as the Savior sent us from the divine Father out of His incomparable love. He is God the Father's own Son. He is putting in order again what our first parents upset by their sin. He has made us all God's children. He has taught us and shown us how a good child of God must live. His strongest desire is to take us home, some day, to the Father in heaven. There is our true home. There He has prepared an eternal paradise for us, incomparably more beautiful than the one He made for our first parents.

Even first graders can easily understand these truths, especially if they are presented by means of an appealing narrative, well illustrated. Thus beginners' catechisms, according to the principles of modern catechesis, consciously omit *all abstract formulations* and should *concentrate on those basic truths* of our religion which flow of themselves from a simple and childlike proclamation of the history of redemption. But we must try our utmost to let these basic truths shine out in their proper radiance. We should lift them from their historical frame and take great care that the children become perfectly familiar with them.

And if we follow the main phases of the history of Redemption, and present them at all fittingly, Christ will naturally be shown as the center of divine revelation, as the incomparable gift of the Father, our leader and way to the Father. In this way, we will run no danger of giving the children that false and sentimental "Jesus piety" which seems rather to forget the divine Father and to put the "little Jesus" in His place. Thus while, on the one hand, we should omit all abstract formulations in these first grades, on the other hand, we should make every effort to present Bible history from the very beginning in such a way that its theocentricity and Christocentricity stand out as impressively as possible, and gradually permeate the life and prayer of our children.

In this way, we shall indirectly avoid two forms of onesidedness which might well endanger the success of this biblical-historical instruction. First of all, we obviously have to avoid that kind of instruction which contents itself with a purely entertaining narration of the Bible stories, and does not take the trouble to elaborate the content of truth contained in the holy story. Bible history, even in the very first grades, is far more than a series of beautiful stories about Christ, far more than the life of Christ told in a childlike way. It is the introduction into the Christian religion by way of Bible history. The hesitation still felt by some ecclesiastical superiors about the use of this Biblical narrative method is usually the result of some unfortunate experience along these lines. Just as formerly an "explanatory" analysis of a catechism was too easily considered to be sufficient, today it may sometimes happen that Bible stories are told beautifully but *the doctrine is overlooked*. It is certainly to the interest of the catechetical movement to be aware of this danger and to meet it effectively by providing solid catechetical outlines for the catechists.

And we must also guard against the opposite danger: that of trying to develop *too much* doctrine from the historical presentation. Let us stress again that doctrine at this level should be limited to essentials. From the point of view of method, this warning might be formulated in this way: *in the first grades, the narrative presentation must predominate, not the resulting explanation.* The story must be presented in such a way that only very little special explanation of the doctrine it contains is necessary, and the effect of the instruction should be further deepened by such activity on the children's part as drawings, dramatizations, etc.

Another task to be carried out by the narration is the communication of, or at least laying the groundwork for, *true religious feeling*. This task is especially important, of course, with regard to the Person Who is the center of sacred history. What a glorious task we have to carry out in our first instructions—to win our students' hearts for Christ! Even in the first grades, the children should begin to gain a true, though childlike devotedness to Christ. Love for Him must now be solidly rooted in the children's hearts, and must be fed continually so that it will grow. How can we accomplish this most easily and effectively? Certainly not by means of many details of dogma which children of this age cannot understand or value, but by a proper presentation of sacred history. From such a presentation, the greatness and attractiveness of Christ should shine out to the children, and fill them with enthusiasm for Him and for His work.

Thus, with due regard for our students' age, we must from the beginning present a picture of Christ which harmoniously unites His awe-inspiring greatness and His loveable attractiveness, His tender intimacy with each of us, and His worshipful majesty. In the lowest grade, as well as everywhere else, sweet sentimentality is of absolutely no use.

In this context, we might also point out the catechetical importance of the way in which Our Lord and also the other figures of sacred history, are pictorially represented to the children. These pictures should, especially in the first grade, accompany, facilitate and deepen the effects of the biblical narrative catechesis. Pictures should be adapted, as far as possible, to the particular instructions that they are to assist. For the first grades, therefore, we should have simple pictures, with true religious feeling, which clearly present the catechetical meaning of their subject. These pictorial representations must be of a kind which can create and bring to life the image of Christ in the children's imaginations and so in their hearts. And this can never be achieved by sentimental pictures, even in the lower grades. True childlikeness in religious representation certainly does not consist in adding as many flowers and flying angels' heads as there is room for. And the fact that in our schools can be found so many religious pictures that are the products of poor taste and poor art is certainly not a good sign of a high level of catechetical instruction. For it indicates not only a lack of that sound aesthetic feeling which is of more than a little importance in education, but it indicates also a certain watering-down and cheapening of the religious substance. But, of course, in warning against sentimentality in pictures used in catechetical work, we do not wish in any way to recommend those abstruse "modern" pictures which, at least in grammar school, have no place in our teaching.

Finally, we should draw attention to a misunderstanding that might arise from this strong emphasis on "history" in elementary instruction. History generally means the story of the past which we contemplate from the standpoint of the present. And in Bible history also we tell of events that happened a long time ago. But we must not forget that, with this particularly "history", it is always a question of the present. What the loving Father has done for us from the beginning of creation up to today is the basis of our present life and actions. The Mystery of Christ must never be approached or presented as something past. It must include and be directed toward our present life. Beginning with the very first grade, *not "Christ in Juda", but "Christ in you"* (Col. 1:27) *is the actual theme of our good tidings.* In this light, religious instruction is, from the very beginning, not so much history as "mystagogy", that is, an introduction into the Mystery of Christ, the holy knowledge of our vocation to a new life in and with Christ, instruction in the practice and development of this life. In this central task of religious education, the proper training in Christian worship, that is, *the liturgy,* takes an important part, which will be discussed in the following chapter.

Up to this point, we have been speaking only of the teaching of Bible history in the lower grades. But it is obvious that, in the higher levels as well, biblical instruction should play an important part. But here the catechetical function, and hence the method, will be different. Space does not permit us to give detailed instructions as to instruction on the Bible in the higher grades. Let it suffice to summarize the leading principles.

In the upper grades, we need special Bible classes to accompany the systematic catechesis given from a catechism (see chapter six). The syllabus must provide the suitable coordination of the subject matter in the catchism and the Bible classes, so that they are interrelated and aid each other. The task of these Bible classes should be to help students from year to year to become better acquainted not only with sacred history and with the themes of the Bible, but with the inspired text itself. The students must learn to find in the Bible the answers to their problems and the nourishment of their spiritual life. They need above all to find inspiration and nourishment for their prayer-life in the use made of the Word of God in the liturgy and in diligent private reading as well. Bible classes in which we read the sacred text with the students and show them its inexhaustible riches for their own lives, need, in a special way, a thoroughly religious atmosphere. The more perfectly the teacher knows how to stand back and to let God speak to the students Himself through His inspired word, the better. And in this way, the teacher will, at the same time, prepare the students for the right liturgical reception of God's Word.

In the upper grades of grammar school, the easy parts of the Bible—that is, many narratives of the Old Testament, some simple and prayable Psalms, the synoptic Gospels, the Acts of the Apostles and some of the easiest Epistles—should be read by the students themselves. Later on, in high school, the students should become familiar with the whole New Testament and with all the essential parts of the Old Testament. For many reasons, it is not advisable to wait until the college level to give a thorough knowledge of the Bible, and at that time to focus religious instruction on Holy Scripture.[3] But, of course, if a solid knowledge of the Bible has been previously neglected, it must be provided in a college course in Religion.

3. See, for example, *A Course for College Students,* by Rev. John J. Fernan, S.J. (4 vols. Jesuit Educational Association, N. Y., 1953-1955).

In the Bible classes of the grade school and high school level, one of the chief principles to be used in selecting the texts for study should certainly be their liturgical use. Since the Mystery of Christ is in fact the central theme of the Bible, it goes without saying that Bible classes throughout all the years of religious instruction must always serve the students' progressive initiation into the Mystery of Christ.

It is relatively easy to provide sufficient and efficient instruction in the Bible in Catholic schools, which, especially in the United States, usually set aside a large number of hours for religious instruction. The case is completely different for Catholic students attending public schools. These students must also be led to the Bible; they also have to be taught how to nourish their spiritual life and their prayer from the Word of God. But classes for such students should not try to provide Bible classes running parallel with the catechism classes. The problem should rather be solved by spending a full year on the Old Testament and another on the New. And since there is so little time in these classes, it is of special importance to stimulate the students to a fruitful private study of the Bible and to show them how to develop a better understanding and more fruitful use of the biblical treasures provided by our Mother the Church in the liturgy.

Generally speaking, biblical instruction is still one of the weak points in our religious teaching. How many Catholic pupils have received religious instruction for twelve or even sixteen years and have not been given any close or personal contact with the Bible in all that time! At the end of their long schooling, many have not even read the whole New Testament. Evidently, something is wrong. And one of the reasons for this undeniable fact seems to be the insufficient and too formalistic biblical formation given in seminaries and motherhouses. During their own time of spiritual and theological formation, future catechists have never been given the right understanding of the religious wealth of the Bible.

CHAPTER FIVE

Progressive Initiation Through the Liturgy

The proper goal of our catechetical apostolate is not a theoretic knowledge of Christ and His mystery, but as perfect a living union with Him as possible. Bible history in the early grades, therefore, must bring the past into the present. The mystery of Christ reaches from the past into the present; it embraces all centuries, and we live and share in it as did Christ's first disciples in Palestine. The Christ to Whom the Biblical narratives lead us is not merely a great figure of the past, the subject of historical narration. He is the Christ Who now continues and perfects His work in us, and Who invites and enables us to cooperate actively in His holy work. He lives and is active among us. Through our personal contact with Him here and now, we receive a share in His divine life. Where and when is this especially brought about? Obviously, above all in the sacramental life of the Church, in her Eucharistic Sacrifice and her sacraments—in other words, in her *liturgy*.

We can readily understand, therefore, why liturgy should play such an important part in religious instruction even in the primary grades. Leading representatives of modern catechesis have agreed upon this principle for many years, and have stressed it repeatedly. Yet we must admit that in this case theory is far ahead of practice, even in countries such as the United States which excel in catechetical activity. How can we explain this inconsistency? The reason is, in part at least, that some catechists do not as yet have a clear understanding of the outstanding catechetical value of the liturgy, and in part also because some catechists do not as yet know how to make the best use of the liturgy in their teaching.

How the Liturgy Presents the Mystery of Christ

The unique catechetical value of the Liturgy essentially derives from the way in which it contains and makes us familiar with the heart of Christian religion—the mystery of Christ.

It may be true to say that, in the beginning of the catechetical movement, many catechists perceived the great catechetical value of the liturgy *from the point of view of methods only.* The main concern of that era was the problem of methods, and so this limited vision is quite understandable. And even from this point of view, there was every reason to ask for a more intensive utilization of the liturgy in catechetics. The worship of the Church, after all, certainly offers an excellent catechetical object lesson. And this is still true today, even in this age of highly-developed teaching techniques. Even today, a real chalice that the child can observe closely is more illustrative, and more formative in a religious sense, than is a painted one. Even today, a priest who, before the children's eyes, approaches the altar and begins the Mass, attracts the child's attention in a higher degree than would the same scene presented in a movie or on television. The truths of our faith find an impressive, concrete and even dramatic expression in the house of God with its furnishings, in the liturgical objects and actions. The liturgy is a tremendously versatile catechetical picture book which makes the children familiar by means of their senses with the majestic mysteries of our faith.

Moreover, the liturgy directs us to express our response to those holy mysteries again and again in prayer, and so to take a personal positive attitude toward them, and to assimilate them through participation in them (learning by doing). This teaching function of the liturgy is enhanced by the rich diversity in the seasons of the Church's year, by the religious atmosphere, and by the impressive religious experience from the very beginning associated with worship.

But however much we agree upon, and want to utilize fully all these values, we must realize that by themselves they do not represent the decisive catechetical value of the liturgy. The essence of this value consists in teaching us—in this concrete and educational manner—*the substance of Christian faith and life.* The catechetical concentration on essentials, so often lacking in our religious instruction, here finds exemplary realization. Again and again, Mother Church has us pray and sing the basic mysteries of our faith. And the keynote is always the mystery of all mysteries—the mystery of Christ—which we celebrate, and renew in celebrating, and which represents the central theme of the entire liturgy.

This concentration is particularly impressive in the two liturgical subjects which are of decisive importance in the lower grades, that is, the Mass and the liturgical year. In both, we find the same admirable fullness of doctrine combined with an exemplary concentration on the basic theme of all Christian revelation: our salvation through Christ, or, in other words, our participation in the mystery of Christ. How clearly both the Mass and the liturgical year express the theocentricity and the Christocentricity which are so essential to our religion: Christ, the great gift of the Father, Christ, our way to the Father. Anyone who participates in the liturgy with an open heart will not long be wanting in the necessary religious knowledge, and he will acquire even more quickly the basic Christian attitude which is far more important than a precise knowledge of details.

The same is true, of course, concerning a third unit of the liturgy, the sacraments. But these are not as easily understood by the children of the lower grades. By themselves, they do not unfold the entire mystery of Christ in the same fullness as do the Mass and the liturgical year. And they are not experienced as a unit in actual practice— even a mature convert does not receive all the sacraments in succession during an easily surveyed period of time. While we do not deny that the liturgy of the sacraments also tells us impressively of the mystery of Christ, yet the significance of the sacraments lies more in what they give than in what they reveal.[1]

And here is the last and most decisive reason why teaching through worship is superior to all other forms of Christian teaching. *The liturgy gives what it teaches.* It not only presents the mystery of Christ concretely; it also lets us immediately participate in this mystery. If there is anywhere in Christianity that a true initiation into the mystery of Christ takes place, it is here. How clearly has Christ Himself expressed this truth concerning the central sacrament, the Holy Eucharist, which in its sacramental sign demonstrates most impressively our participation in the life and the mystery of Christ. "He who eats My flesh and drinks My blood, abides in Me and I in Him. As the living Father has sent Me, and as I live because of the Father, so he who eats Me, he also shall live because of Me" (John 6:57-59). St. Paul uses equally forceful words to impress upon us the principle of our actual participation in the mystery of Christ by the fundamental sacrament, Baptism. "Do you not know that all we who have been baptized into Christ Jesus have been baptized into His death? For we were buried with Him

1. But valuable catechetical instruction can and should be given by means of proper explanations of the true significance of the sacramental rites, especially when such explanations accompany a demonstration of the rites. For an aid in giving such explanations, see *A Commentary on the Ritual*, by the Liturgical Committee of the University of Notre Dame, (Liturgical Press, Collegeville, Minn.).

by means of baptism into death, in order that, just as Christ has arisen from the dead through the glory of the Father, so we also may walk in newness of life" (Rom. 6:3 ff., see vv. 3–14, likewise Col. 2:12; Gal. 3:28; 1 Cor. 12:13). For all the other sacraments, something similar is true, marriage being no exception (Eph. 5:32).

The Eucharistic Sacrifice, above all, offers us a real participation in the mystery of Christ: the Lord includes His Bride, the Church; He includes all His mystical members in His Sacrifice, sacrificing with them, and they with Him. There may be different views among theologians as to the way in which Christ's redemption is present and constantly active in the Church's worship. But Catholic theologians have always agreed that it offers a mysterious participation in the redemption through Christ, that we not only receive the sanctifying fruits of His redemption, but also are enabled to participate actively in His mystery and His worship. This is true first of all and in the highest degree of the Eucharistic Sacrifice. And it is also true of the sacraments, and, though to a much lesser degree, of the other divine services of the Church. This participation comes about simply because, on the one hand, the mystical Christ, the Head with His members, is the actual active subject of any liturgical celebration, and, on the other hand, the actions of the mystical Christ form an indissoluble inner unity with Christ's redemptive work.

The Church's worship, accordingly, is a veritable catechetical treasure-house. Since true participation in the mystery of Christ is the final goal of all catechetical effort, the liturgy takes the first place among means of achieving that goal, and it cannot be replaced by anything else. Obviously, we want to open these riches to our students as early and as fully as possible.

How to Unlock the Liturgy.

As we have just seen, the liturgy has two important purposes, so far as our present topic is concerned: it must effectively reveal the mystery of Christ, and it must actually communicate it. As daily experience shows us, not every liturgical celebration fulfills this twofold task perfectly, or even adequately. Are there not Catholics who have attended hundreds, perhaps even thousands of Masses, and yet understand very little about the actual meaning of the celebration. Their mere *attendance* does not help them greatly to understand their religion better, nor does it result in an adequate participation in the mystery of Christ. To "unlock" the liturgy means, therefore: first, to conduct our liturgical services in such a way as to guide our students to a proper understanding of the mystery of Christ; and, second, to train our students to take part in the holy mysteries in such a way as to grow in participation in the mystery of Christ. Whatever means truly serves one of these purposes will necessarily help to attain the other also, since they form an organic unity. They should be recognized clearly as two aspects, but they should never be separated in our intention as teachers. For this reason, we shall treat them together during the rest of this chapter.

Beginning in the first grade, the introductory Biblical instructions are, if this is at all possible, to be given in such a way that *the course of the stories follows the course of the liturgical year.* We should prepare the children, in a way suited to their age, for the great feasts, and we should celebrate these feasts with them, especially Christmas and Easter (with Holy Week preceding it). The mysteries celebrated in these feasts should also form the high points of our Biblical catechesis, and thus the effect of the biblical catechesis will be deepened by liturgical experience. Long before the child can clearly understand, his taking part in the liturgical celebrations of the mysteries of Christ enables him to experience these mysteries not merely as historical narratives, but as present religious values.

From the very beginning, then, we should try, after careful preparation, to celebrate the main feasts of the Church with the children, in such a way that they are made familiar by experience with the present reality of these feasts. Of course we should begin with the historical work of the redemption; and, for this reason, the biblical-narrative catechesis must precede the direct preparation for a liturgical celebration. But we should not stop at the history; the mystery of the past serves to make us understand and value what Christ is now effecting in us. Both are gifts of divine love; in the mystery of the feast, we celebrate and give thanks for both together. Our Christian feast days are, essentially, feasts of thanksgiving for the "wonderful works of God" (Acts 2:11), which, in their totality, form the mystery of Christ. The fact that the Eucharistic Sacrifice is the climax of the celebration of these feasts clearly shows their "thanksgiving" character. Especially on feast days, then, the Holy Sacrifice is to be seen and celebrated as our communal thanksgiving to the Father, and, starting in the primary grades, we must help the children to offer their thanks above all through this Sacrifice.

All this must be done, of course, in the simplest and most childlike manner, but *childlike in the best sense.* In connection with Christmas, for example, certainly any average pupil in the lower grades, to whom we have spoken of the fall of man, of the promise of the Savior to come, of the long awaiting of mankind, and of the fulfillment of God's promise and plan, will understand that "with the Child of Bethlehem, something of heaven has fallen upon earth" (Jungmann). The Child has been given to us by the divine Father as His greatest gift; since then, Christ has been our Brother, Who wants to lead us all, without exception, home to the Father in heaven. Thus the children's holy Christmas joy develops into a heart-felt thanksgiving to the divine Father. We thank Him for His Son Whom He gave to us as our Brother and Redeemer, we thank Him for the fact that He has made us children of God and called us to heaven through this Child of Heaven. Over a hundred years ago, a great friend of children, Christopher von Schmid, expressed this truth in a truly childlike way in the well-known carol:

> O come, little children, come all of you come,
> O come to the crib, to the stable, O come,
> And see what great joy in this night, out of love
> The Father has sent us from heaven above.

We must not think that any sentimentality is needed in order to open the mystery of Christmas to the children, but we also should not forget that, in the first grades, the child has a holy right not to be burdened with such theological terms as "grace", "supernatural", etc., or with a precise theological explanation of "vicarious satisfaction". To the children, "Savior" should simply mean He Who has freed us from sin and reopened to us the gate of heaven. The liturgy itself gives us irrefutable proof that a simple telling of the holy mysteries is quite consistent with religious depth, with no need for theological terms and abstract expressions.

In the higher grades also we should not disregard the Church year, but rather, as far as possible, try to harmonize our subject matter with the rhythm of the liturgy, and we should try to accomplish this without artificiality. Special feasts still need and deserve preparation of the students. Help to a fuller understanding of the texts of the Propers of the Masses of the feasts should certainly be given, and also, on the last school day of each week, a short introduction to the Mass of the following Sunday.

In addition to this elementary introduction to the Church's year, closely connected with Bible history, we should, beginning again in the primary grades, make the children familiar with the practice of Christian prayer, with the Church's worship and with the Sacraments which are of the most immediate significance to the children. For the first grade, an explanation of Baptism, the Eucharist, and, perhaps, Confession, are quite sufficient. And here again the principle holds true: let the child, whenever possible, learn by direct observation and by doing: be sparing with theoretical explanations. Offer this first introduction to the sacraments as simply as possible, but, from the very beginning with the proper catechetical view: meeting Christ, participation in His life and in His devotedness to the divine Father.

Liturgy is the Church's worship, and this means, above all, prayer—the Church's prayer. To lead our students to the liturgy means, first of all, therefore, to lead them to *liturgical prayer*. One of the most common reasons why so many people, even very devout Catholics, cannot find their way to liturgical prayer, or can do so only with great difficulty, is, certainly, a faulty training in their early youth which has lead them to an unliturgical spirituality that they find it very hard to change in later life. But proper guidance in such prayer does not consist in using liturgical prayers for the children's own prayer life too early or too exclusively. We should always remain aware of the fact that liturgical prayer is essentially community prayer, and that, for the personal prayer of the individual and its formulation, certain important modifications have to be made. Nor should these modifications be overlooked in the first intructions which are to awaken and to develop spontaneous Christian prayer in each child. Again, obviously, the language of liturgical prayer rarely corresponds to the child's individuality. Our aim is prayer arising truly and unartificially from the children's hearts to the Father in heaven. And, certainly, we should not be too narrow-minded on this point. Once we have sufficiently developed the meaning of individual prayer and its expression, it is not detrimental if prayer texts are used which the child cannot fully understand (and far better than giving him artificially constructed "children's prayers" to memorize). Children act like adults in many ways, even though their minds do not fully grasp what they are doing; and they grow in understanding by being given something above them to make their own.

In our introduction to Christian prayer, we owe the child some adaptation to his own individuality. But this does not mean that we should make any concessions with regard to the basic attitude of Christian prayer. In the child's prayer, as in the adult's, the divine Father must predominate, and not, for instance, the Guardian Angel. As in our religious instruction, we must first tell of the Father in heaven, of His power and His love, so we must begin our training in prayer with the divine Father and always refer to Him. Of course, we must also lead the praying child to Christ. But since Christ has been presented from the outset as the gift of the Father, as our leader to the Father, there will be no difficulty for the child in praying in this way also. The child finds, after all, the same situation in his prayer as in his family; he goes with his brothers to the father. And again, any good family training should stress "thank you" rather than "please", and so the child should begin with no psychological obstacles to an early training in the prayer of praise and thanksgiving.

Nor shall we in any way injure the child's personality if we begin very soon to teach him to respond in prayer to the wonderful mysteries of our faith, in other words, to pray "dogmatically" (which of course does not mean dogmatic terminology, but content, as the liturgy itself is "dogmatic"). Such a response will develop by itself if in our instructions, we stress above all the religious values of what we teach, and if the individual instructions generally culminate in prayer. This may be carried out by a spontaneous prayer, or by an appropriate formal prayer, or by a good hymn, or by some suggestions as to how the students can turn the subject just studied into the object of a prayer. And if the instructions really elaborate the mystery of Christ and make the children familiar with it, their prayers will certainly be directed towards this central mystery. Children so trained will easily find their own way in liturgical prayer. They will not need to readjust themselves, for they already possess the right attitude. In liturgical prayer, too, it is "the spirit that gives life" (John 6:64).

Between the Bible history in the primary grades and the systematic catechesis in the higher grades, it might be advisable to give the children a kind of survey of the most significant doctrines of the faith, a survey of which the Mass and the sacraments are the center. This course would involve not merely an explanation of the liturgy of the Mass and the sacraments, but also a survey of the entire mystery of Christ. But this should, in accordance with the children's age, be developed from the easily perceptible forms of worship, leading to their deep meaning. And this course should allow the relationship of this central mystery to the other basic doctrines to appear in its full light.[2]

But in such a course, we should, of course, be on our guard against the danger of going into too great liturgical detail. The understanding of the whole is what is important, and the individual ceremonies of the Mass, for instance, should always be explained with regard to their function in the whole. But what is of supreme importance here, however, is intelligent and devoted liturgical action. Here, above all, knowledge should be completely at the service of right doing. As Fr. Jungmann has said so well: "Not much liturgics, but much liturgy" (*Katechetik,*

2. The *Christ Life Series* (Macmillan, N. Y.) might offer valuable stimulus in this respect. And for such a course to be given in Confraternity classes, we refer again to the series *On Our Way,* by Sister Maria de la Cruz, now being published by Sadlier, New York. This course includes on the sixth-grade level a survey of Christian doctrine carried out by means of a study of the liturgical year. Such a special course in liturgy could be of great value. Rightly given, it would be an excellent and organic transition from the biblical narratives of the first grades to the systematic catechesis to be given later. But we should be clear that liturgical education should by no means be restricted to such an intermediate course in liturgy. The right liturgical attitude, approach, and practice from the very first religion class up to religious teaching on the college level is much more important.

p. 65). He explains this in more detail in the following words: "Much practical living of religion at home, in school, in church . . . Needed explanations can, in most cases, be given in occasional instructions by connecting a related topic of liturgical life with the subject of the current lesson, or by using such a topic as a conclusion."

We could formulate these principles as follows: in liturgical training the leading and active role should be taken by *meaningful active participation in the Church's worship,* not by the religious instruction courses in school. Certainly, the classes are important, but, in the end, they are only preparatory. The actual and decisive values of the liturgy cannot be acquired through study, but only through proper participation.

And it is because we appreciate these values so highly that we should strive to attain an exterior form of worship that fully expresses them. We must not think that a catechetically valuable worship is simply impossible under the present laws. Our goal may be quite easily attained in a well-organized dialogue Mass which properly combines prayer and song, and which clearly brings out the main parts of the Mass. From the standpoint of religious pedagogy—since it is a question of guidance to the liturgy, and through the liturgy to the mystery of Christ—a dialogue Mass is preferable even to a sung or solemn high Mass. This is not a question of the highest form of celebration, objectively speaking, but of the form of Mass most fitted to give our children and young people a proper understanding of the teaching and the meaning of the Mass, and one which will help them to participate as intensively and actively as possible.[3]

But, although a properly conducted Mass is the center of liturgical training, we must carefully guard against *liturgical isolationism.* Proper participation requires preparation and explanation of the liturgy, and, what is even more important, proper participation must show its effects in daily Christian life. We must try to impress the children quite early in their training that Christian worship is not an expression of religious experience with no consequent obligations. Worship must be "religious", that is, it must bind us to God, it must stand the test of daily life, it must form our lives. We must not only celebrate Mass through the ministry of the priest, we must also live the Mass. The promise of full self-surrender which we made with Christ to the Father during the Holy Sacrifice has to be realized in our lives, and so we shall truly live the mystery of Christ.

3. As an aid, remarkable for its great catechetical and liturgical value, for the celebration of the most fruitful form of Dialogue Mass, we recommend: *Holy Mass: the Great Action of the Christian Community* (cards for the people, with explanatory folder for the priest), arranged by Rev. Eugene Walsh, S.S. (World Library of Sacred Music, Cincinnati, Ohio).

CHAPTER SIX

Progressive Initiation
Through Catechism

From its beginning, the modern catechetical movement has insisted that the first introduction to the Christian religion must be carried out by means of a narrative of the history of salvation. "No catechism in the early grades of grammar school" was one of the first and most fundamental principles of the movement—a principle which has not always been easy to put into practice.

But this courageous battle against the too early use of a systematic catechism has caused some people to think that the modern catechetical movement is opposed on principle to any use of a catechism, and that it only tolerates the use of a systematic catechism even in the upper grades. A few extremists who held such a view may have existed, but in general all the leading experts in modern catechetics have rejected such an exaggeration.

The fact that leaders of the modern movement hold to the great importance of systematic religious instruction according to a catechism, given in the proper way and the proper place, is clearly revealed by their strenuous efforts to improve catechisms, especially in those European countries that are the most advanced catechetically.[1] The classic example in this field is the recently published German Catechism (*Katholischer Katechismus der Bistümer Deutschlands*. Freiburg, 1955,

1. The following are among the best catechisms that have appeared in the last 13 years: *Catéchisme à l'usage des dioceses de France* (1946); *Catéchisme du diocèse de Strasbourg* (1945); *Katholischer Katechismus für das Bistum Basel* (1947); *Catechism for the dioceses of Holland* (1948); *Katolischer Katechismus der Bistümer Deutschlands* (1955). In Austria, a new catechism is in preparation; the first draft was presented to the public in the *Christlich-pädagogischen Blätter* (Vienna, 1955). In the Far East, a new catechism for the Philippines has been published: Catholic Catechism, Manila, 1956. In its special number on the Catechism Text (1950), *Lumen Vitae* gives a good survey of these various works and their results up to that year. Regarding the special subject of this chapter, see the Special Number on Teaching the Catechism (1950).

41

Herder). This catechism was commissioned by the German hierarchy, and the foremost catechetical experts in Germany worked on it from 1938 until its publication. Of course, the final responsibility for an official catechism always rests with the bishop who authorizes its publication. But we can safely say in any case that this new German catechism is the fruit of long years of hard labor and of zealous co-operation on the part of leading teachers. We do not intend here to discuss its value nor to answer the question whether it is in every way a model that we should imitate. We are merely citing this German catechism as an example of how in Germany, the homeland of the modern catechetical movement, experts are agreed on the vast importance of a good catechism.[2]

The question now is, therefore, not whether we should use a catechism or not, but rather how, in the higher grades of grammar school can we most effectively present in a systematic way, and so impart a more mature understanding of, the subject matter which the children already have grasped, in an elementary fashion, from their previous instruction in the history of redemption and in liturgy, as outlined in the preceding chapters?

What is the Particular Task of Systematic Catechesis?

Children in the primary grades are not capable of a comprehensive view of any subject, whether it be religion or anything else. Such a mature approach has no interest for them, and in the field of religion, it cannot benefit them spiritually. During these years, the child's mind is capable of assimilating only concrete details. No sensible teacher would dream of presenting to first graders a "system" of geography, mathematics or any other science. During this period, those elements of knowledge should be offered to the child which will give him, from his own standpoint and according to his own way of understanding, a view of the world he lives in. These elements of knowledge should be given in a way adapted as perfectly as possible to the living conditions and concrete needs of the child. And the view of his world which he is to gain is simply a view, not an insight and never a comprehensive conspectus. It may be that when the teaching is given by means of a continuous story, a certain but still quite imperfect conspectus of the subject will be gained. But a teacher with any knowledge of child psychology would certainly avoid burdening children of this

2. Concerning the catechetical value of the new German catechism, see Fr. Jungmann's article in *Lumen Vitae*, 1955, pp. 573-586. We must agree that this is the first catechism fully to take into consideration all the kerygmatic requirements of the modern catechetical movement.

age with a continuous history even of their own country. How can we in reason expect a child's mind to follow essentially different laws when he studies religion—which deals, after all, with very lofty subjects? Or do we expect that he will here be given some miraculous grace that makes the ordinary laws of child psychology null and void?

We find that a really astonishing amount of intellectual material will be amassed by the child during the primary grades in his years of initial spiritual awakening—when the proper kind of instruction has been given. But the need to form this jumbled world of scattered details into an ordered unity develops slowly, generally much more slowly than we adults like to admit. And even when the need is felt, the goal is not all at once a complete, all-embracing and consequently complicated order. First of all, smaller wholes are built up out of pieces of information which seem, at first glance, to belong together, and gradually these units are brought together into a more and more comprehensive and interrelated view of the world. This process closely resembles that by which a small child at home first perceives the room in which he spends most of his time as being some kind of a unit, and later he fits into one scheme the whole house, with its immediate surroundings, and still later, the whole region in which he lives. It is evident that in the instruction given in school, we have to promote this spiritual process, though we must not believe that we can benefit the child in any way by a premature systematization.

The time does come, therefore, in the higher grades of grammar school, when a certain systematization of the knowledge gathered during the previous years becomes psychologically possible and even necessary—in religion as in other fields of instruction. The greater degree of maturity now attained by the students enables them more perfectly to understand the doctrines of their faith. The teacher can now succeed in showing them more clearly the interrelationships of the various doctrines, and can present them with a certain conspectus of the whole.

Here, obviously, is the special task of systematic catechesis. It follows the order of the catechism which, of its nature, is designed to give a survey of the most important doctrines of the Christian religion. The principle of this survey is not the narration of the history of salvation— as in biblical history—but rather a logical presentation of the interrelationship of the various truths of the faith, which will show their logical unity. Its object, therefore, is to present a system of truth.

But if, from the standpoint of religious pedagogy, we are to evaluate rightly this systematic religious instruction and formulate it efficiently, we must not consider its didactic function in isolation. Its special didactic function is, as we have said, to give a synthesis of Christian doctrines and a better understanding of their interrelationship. But we must first ask: what is the significance of this function in the entire process of religious formation? What does it contribute to the realization of the final goal of all Christian instruction? In chapters two and three, we have seen that the *mystery of Christ* is actually *the central theme* of religious instruction, and that *a more and more perfect participation in the mystery of Christ* is its chief goal. This, of course, is true not only of the first years of religious instruction, but of all of them, and increasingly so, for it is a question of progressive initiation into the mystery of Christ. We may, therefore, formulate the question as follows: In what way does the systematic instruction to be given in the upper grades contribute to the children's deeper understanding of the mystery of Christ, and to their more perfect participation in it?

If the religious instruction in the primary grades has been given properly, then Christ and His mystery formed its center. The children will already have experienced religious instruction as being "instruction about Christ" and about what He taught and gave us. In the systematic instruction now to be given, the student must, then, be brought to understand much more clearly and practically how Christ truly is the center of Christian teaching and of Christian life. He must be enabled to see Christian teaching more and more clearly as the teaching of the mystery of Christ, and Christian life more and more as our participation in this mystery. The student has now come to the stage where he is capable of grasping the interrelationship of all Christian doctrines with this central mystery of Christian revelation. And so all his knowledge of his religion will develop more and more fully into a Christian view of the world in the full sense of the word. This view will be Christian not only because it was revealed to us by Christ, but even more because it is centered in Christ; that "in all things He may have the first place. For it has pleased God the Father that in Him all His fullness should dwell, and that through Him He should reconcile to Himself all things, whether on the earth or in the heavens" (Col. 1:19 f.).

If we look at it in this light, we see clearly that the systematic religious instruction to be given in the upper grades has, in the first place, to fulfill an important intellectual task. It is to contribute to a fuller intellectual penetration of Christian doctrine. But we must not conclude from this fact that this instruction should be any the less concerned with Christian life than is the instruction given in the primary grades. "Systematic" need not and should not mean theoretic and remote from life. The "system" must never alter or obscure the central idea or the inner structure of the doctrine presented, but rather elaborate it as clearly as possible. This is, obviously, the special teaching function of a system.

In systematic instruction, therefore, Christian doctrine must continue to be presented as what it essentially is: the teaching of our way to God through Christ; the teaching of the glory of the Christian life, consisting essentially in participating in the life of Christ. Thus, in the end, systematic instruction should become the servant, not of religious knowledge merely, but of Christian life; it, too, should contribute to our more perfect participation in the life of Christ. We can even go so far as to say this: systematic instruction is justified to the degree to which it helps the student to perceive Christian doctrine as a compact organic unity, and to understand more fully its central mystery and its value in his life.

How Can the Particular Task of Systematic Instruction be most Effectively Realized?

Now that we understand more clearly the special catechetical function of systematic catechism instruction, we can answer the next eminently practical question of how most effectively to carry out this task. As we have seen, this systematic instruction must give the students their first real survey of the doctrines of their faith. Let us not forget, first of all, that in the higher grades of grammar school our students are still children, only some ten to fourteen years old. At this age, interest and capability for "systems" and "summaries" exist only in a rudimentary form. If the system is really to fulfill its function, the arrangement of the catechism must be as *simple, clear, and impressive as possible.* This should be true both of the main divisions of the catechism and of their subdivisions. If a clear and impressive arrangement of the lessons is made possible by means of a proper organization of the basic catechetical formulas so called (the Creed, the Sacraments, the Our Father, the Commandments), then our task will be simplified.[3]

But this clarity is not all that is necessary. Our actual task here is, as we have seen, a much more perfect catechetical concentration than was possible in the biblical and liturgical instruction of the primary grades. The basic idea of the Christian "good news" and, consequently, of our Christian life, is to be developed and emphasized, and indi-

---

3. The relationship of systematic instructions to these basic catechetical formulas is particularly important when only a limited amount of time is available for religious teaching, as is often the case with missionary catechesis, and also with the religious instruction given to students in public schools. In these instances, we are, of course, concerned above all firmly to establish, by an understanding of these basic formulas, the necessary religious knowledge.

vidual doctrines are to be presented entirely in the light of this basic idea. And again, the catechism as a whole, and in its individual parts, must *develop the central theme of Christian revelation, the mystery of Christ, as radiantly as possible.* The very arrangement of the main sections of the catechism should reveal the centrality of this theme, and so should its individual parts.

In chapter two, we pointed out how all the important doctrines of the faith should be seen and presented entirely from the central viewpoint of Christian revelation. And since the goal of all catechetical instruction is Christian life, our systematic instruction must reveal not merely the intellectual relationship of individual doctrines to the mystery of Christ, but more especially their "Christian" value in life. In other words, by means of this teaching, the student should grow continuously in the understanding of how all the doctrines of the catechism lead to Christ, and of how they all contribute to a fuller comprehension, a deeper appreciation, and a fuller unfolding of our life in Christ.

We must admit that these necessary qualities are only imperfectly realized in the catechisms and text-books of religion produced in the era before the advent of modern kerygmatic efforts, even though these books show improvement with regard to methods. There is question here, not only of the important problem of a better arrangement of the catechism as a whole, but also of the proper presentation of the individual doctrines.[4] The realization that small alterations and a few minor changes and additions in the text of catechisms are not enough has led, in almost all catechetically advanced countries, to the *introduction of new catechisms.* We do not by any means maintain that these new catechisms are entirely satisfactorily in all cases. But the seriousness with which the most outstanding experts in modern catechetics are searching for a solution certainly indicates the vast importance of this problem.

It may be argued that, in modern catechetics, the fact is always stressed that the teacher and his *living instructions* are much more important than the lifeless textbooks or syllabus. This, of course, is true. A catechist who is well trained in the kerygmatic outlook, who truly sees the Christian message as centered in the mystery of Christ and who brings it home to his students in this way, will be able to work even with an unkerygmatic textbook. But how many of our catechists are so skillful? It is an open secret that even in countries where efforts to promote the kerygmatic approach were made very early and were reasonably successful, a good many catechists still have

4. We shall try to answer these important questions in parts two and three of this book.

to be won over and trained in this new way of teaching. And, to a great extent, this new training can only be done by means of better texts. In Germany, for example, leading catechetical circles have never tried to conceal the fact that this is the first and most important task which the new catechism and commentaries on it must fulfill.

But, obviously, so long as an adequate catechism does not exist, it is all the more important to offer help to catechists by means of other catechetical literature. And, of perhaps even greater importance is the *proper training of future catechists* in the seminaries; in the houses of formation of teaching religious, where, in many cases, courses in theology are already being provided; and also in the training courses for lay teachers, so zealously promoted by the Confraternity of Christian Doctrine. For the catechist himself must first learn to see his message entirely in the light of Christ; otherwise even the best text will not be of much use to him, unless it contains introductory remarks or good comments that will open to him the true meaning of his teaching.

We should, perhaps, point out here explicitly that this new way of teaching catechism, which strives without artificiality to present each individual lesson in the radiant light of the whole, will also influence the *catechetical method*. For the method must be entirely at the service of the message to be communicated and of the actual goal of the instruction. A truly kerygmatic instruction will naturally emphasize "deepening", a process which modern authors of catechisms usually add after the formal step of "explanation". Obviously, in carrying out this "deepening", catechetical tact is needed in the teacher, so that he does not offer too much or too little, and everything at the proper time. In the higher grades, for example, when the subject is the resurrection of Christ, we should certainly point out its relationship to our own resurrection, and also to the wonderful but now hidden life which we received at our resurrection in Baptism. In the higher grades, again, Christ's first coming at His incarnation and birth should not be taught without instruction also concerning His second coming at the end of time.

In conclusion, when we compare the three chief ways by which we are to initiate our students in grammar school step by step into the mystery of Christ, we must say that the *biblical-narrative catechesis is the basic way*, and that *systematic catechesis* is, from the point of view of religious understanding, *the most perfect way*. But since the final question is not one of religious understanding, but of life in Christ, the *liturgical way always deserves the priority*, because it gives what it teaches, and thus is both the way and the goal. Long after they have completed their religious instruction in school, the liturgy will remain the master teacher in leading our former students to Christ. And even our vision of God in heaven, which alone will give us final, complete and joyful insight into the mystery of Christ, will be more like this liturgical way than any other, for in heaven also we shall know God in prayer, and in adoration participate in God's glory.

In addition to these three ways of progressive initiation into the mystery of Christ, a fourth way is frequently mentioned, that of *life*. This means that the child, or young man or woman, is to be formed into a more and more perfect Christian by means of a truly Christian way of life in his family, his school, and in youth organizations. That religious training must not be restricted to religious instruction given in the classrooms is rightly one of the principles most strongly emphasized in the modern catechetical program. Only through a proper realization of what Christian life is, a realization which, in the course of the years, becomes more and more deeply understood and conscious, does the young person grow to the full stature of a mature Christian. The life and action which, at first, were the results mainly of good habits, must increasingly become the expression of personal conviction and of conscious adherence to Christ, as well as a holy living union with Him. There can be no possible doubt that, in the decisive religious situation of the present day, we are, more than ever before, in urgent need of such mature Christians. Can we say, then, that all our religious training is as yet consistently directed toward their formation?

Part II

The Structure of Our Message

CHAPTER ONE

Is the Question of the Right Order Really Important?

A Christ-centered proclamation of our message does not involve, of course, any undue simplification and limitation of religious instruction. St. Paul, who so strikingly emphasizes his mission to proclaim the Mystery of Christ, is the sacred writer who excels both in the profundity and the richness of his doctrine. For he felt himself obliged to teach his faithful and his catechumens, not only Christ Himself, but also all the important Christian doctrines that, as Christ's herald, he was commissioned to proclaim. And he was entirely right. In His deep love for us, God has revealed many doctrines to us. He has told us how important they are for us so that we may know Him as befits His beloved children, and journey home to Him safely and happily. It is evident, then, that we heralds have no right to be careless with these riches given to us, and to transmit to our charges only some fragments of the whole message.

But the very richness of our message gives rise to a three-fold kerygmatic problem. First, what is the central theme of the whole message, which must stand out clearly and impressively in our proclamation? This question has already been answered in the first part of this book. Second, how shall we select the doctrines to be presented according to the capacity and the special needs of those whom we are addressing? This question will be answered in the third part. And, finally, there is the question of the right ordering of the material of our message, and it is this question which now concerns us.

The multiplicity of doctrines to be proclaimed of itself raises the question: is it sufficient if we teach all the important doctrines correctly, one after the other, in any order that may occur to us, or should they be presented according to a certain well-thought-out order so that each particular doctrine may be perceived as a part of one great coherent whole? If it is true that such an organic ordering is necessary,

51

what is its importance in teaching, and what are the leading principles that we should follow in laying it out? And, particularly, what might be the most suitable ordering of the catechism?

The problem that we are dealing with here is, obviously, by no means restricted to the particular question of how best to arrange Christian doctrine in a catechism. But, this concrete question is, perhaps, at once the most striking and the most urgently needed example of the general problem. We shall, then, study this problem first of all from this particular point of view and offer a solution to it.

MODERN CATECHETICS STRESSES THE IMPORTANCE OF THE RIGHT ORDER OF PRESENTATION.

The question of how best to order the material of catechetics has been, at least in the last twenty years, one of the problems most thoroughly considered. In the first decades of this century, however, the leaders of the movement repeatedly brought out the necessity of giving religious instructions in the lower grades of elementary school by means of Bible narratives, which would follow the historical order. Our present question was thus clearly answered so far as the first years were concerned.[1] But for the systematic catechesis in the upper grades, the leaders of this era simply used the traditional arrangment found in the famous catechism of Fr. Josef Deharbe, S.J., the order of which is basically the same as that which we find today in the Baltimore Catechism: Faith, Commandments, Means of Grace (i.e., the Sacraments and Prayer).[2] These men did not deny the necessity of a clear and workable order, but they were considering the whole problem from the viewpoint of teaching methods, and, generally speaking, considered the traditional division of the catechism as something which could not be tampered with or changed in any way. Thus, for example, Msgr. William Pichler, the recognized leader of the Viennese Catechists of the time, tried to prove that the above order was the ideal one, and the best suited to the nature of the material.[3] Others considered the problem of the ordering of the catechism as sufficiently well solved for

---

1. On this aspect of our question, see above pp. 23-30.

2. Josef Deharbe, S.J., *Katechismus oder Lehrbegriff nebst einem kurzen Abriss der Religionsgeschichte von Anbeginn der Welt bis auf unsere Zeit.* (Luzern 1847). For details concerning this catechism, see W. Busch, *Der Weg des deutschen Katechismus von Deharbe bis zum Einheitskatechismus,* Freiburg, 1936. The arrangement of Deharbe goes back to Fr. Edmund Auger, S.J., the "Canisius" of France: *Catéchisme,* Lyon 1563.. On this important catechism, see F. J. Brand, *P. Edmundus Augerius, S.J.,* Cleve, 1903. And, by the same author, *Die Katechismen des Edmund Augerius, S.J.* Freiburg I.B., 1917.

3. Wilhelm Pichler, *Katechismus der katholischen Religion,* Ausgabe für Katecheten, Wien 1928, P. XXI ff.

the moment, and as being, in any case, not of such burning importance as that of the better "methods" of which they were so fond.

This attitude has changed very greatly since the end of the thirties, that is, since the rise of the kerygmatic renewal, which has directed the attention of catechists more toward the content of their message.[4] Among the questions concerning the content of religious instruction, that of the correct ordering of the subject matter was, from the very beginning, given special emphasis. The most thorough investigation of this important question was published by the author of the present book, himself a disciple of Fr. Jungmann.[5] A few years after the publication of Jungmann's *Frohbotschaft*, work was begun on a new catechism for Germany, and it was recognized from the start that the new book would have to break away from the old Deharbe divisions, of which many people had grown too fond.

Outside of Germany also, exactly the same opinion prevailed in leading catechetical circles. Indeed, the *best catechisms* appearing after the last war all show some rearrangement of the sequence of topics, a rearrangement which may not be evident to most people, but which actually is a most important change. Instead of the Deharbe sequence: Faith, Commandments, Means of Grace, the sequence: Faith, Sacraments, Christian Living (Commandments) is now preferred. This arrangement is to be found in the new catechism for the diocese of Basel, in Switzerland, in that for the diocese of Strasbourg, in France, in the new uniform catechism for all the dioceses of France (1946), and in that for the dioceses of Holland (1948).

This reordering of the main sections of the catechism clearly shows that to plan a new outline of the catechism by no means implies a dangerous revolution in religion courses, turning upside down all classifications hitherto in use and thus jeopardizing the results of previous instruction. The danger consists rather in this: that people who are actually very little concerned with the question might consider this ordering as being nothing more than a pedantic concern over trifles. Such people might easily think that it makes no difference whether a teacher presents the Sacraments or the Commandments after the doctrine on Faith, and that, in all probability, very few pupils and not

---

4. On the origin and aims of the kerygmatic renewal, see above, pp. 4-7.

5. *De apta divisione materiae catecheticae*, in *Collectanea Commissionis Synodalis*, Peking, 1940, S. 583-599; S. 729-749; 845-965. On account of the importance of this question for the catechetical situation in Europe also, Fr. Jungmann, S.J. made a German summary of the Latin work: *Die Gliederung des Katechismus in geschichtlicher Beleuchtung*, published in *Katechetische Blätter*, 1941, 89-87. See also J. Hofinger, S.J. *Die rechte Gliederung des katechetischen Lehrgutes*, in *Lumen Vitae*— 947, 719-741.

many more catechists would even notice that a different order had been used.

But the importance of a suitable ordering of subject matter is greatly stressed by modern catechetics, and not only in connection with catechisms in the proper sense of the word. Anyone who is at all acquainted with modern catechetical literature knows how much attention is given today, by the best authors writing for the faithful in general or for the higher grades of religion instruction, to the question of the best ordering of the catechetical material.

WHY DO WE NEED A FITTING ARRANGEMENT?

This question can be answered very briefly. Good teachers have always known how important it is to order their material in a way which will help the students to grasp the principal idea and the connection between the individual parts of the lessons, and not merely to retain some interesting details of it. And although some teachers, alas, do not pay sufficient attention to this important point, all students realize, from their daily experience, the didactic value of such a clear and evident ordering, not only with regard to single lessons, but to the whole content of the course. And they realize this value most especially if, in their examinations, they not only have to answer individual questions, but to show how those questions are related to one another, that is, if they are required truly to understand and to penetrate the meaning of what they have been taught.

Obviously, what is of such great importance in any teaching which aims at real understanding and formation, must be of even greater importance in the teaching of religion. Does not religious instruction, more than any other, have as its goal to form the pupil and to give him a clear, well-founded and coherent view of life?

The importance of a suitable order is obvious as soon as we consider the question in the light of our apostolic task. As God's messengers, we are sent to proclaim, not only some particular doctrines, but, above all, *the kerygma* that we have been commissioned to proclaim. And this kerygma is, as we have seen already in the first part of this book, the Mystery of Christ. What we have been given to proclaim as one wonderful whole, one divine cosmos, we must faithfully transmit as such, as a beautiful and forceful unity. It can be said, without any exaggeration, that even in teaching children in the first grade, we are more obliged to transmit the whole than any single part. Even with such small children, where there cannot be any question of any catechetical "system", we have, above all, to proclaim Christ. And we must select the individual doctrines to be brought out from the Bible narratives, from this viewpoint: what will best help these children to grasp, in their own way, God's love as revealed to us in Christ, what will help to form them to a Christlike way of life? Thus, in this very first year of instruction, we must not introduce more doctrines than will actually serve this purpose, and we must arrange our presentation of these doctrines so that it, too, will aid in achieving our true goal.

How many willing students are there in our Catholic schools, how many well-disposed faithful in our parishes, who have received any amount of religious instructions in school and in church, and yet do not really enjoy the Christian religion? They receive patiently the many kinds of religious instruction given them; they diligently "learn" religion if they are still students; they know a great deal, or at least a sufficient amount, concerning particular Christian doctrine, practices and obligations; they are ready to believe what they are taught, and to do what they are told; they are ready to do even more than they are obliged to,—but they never really grasp the beauty of the Christian religion. Christian religion, doubtless, influences their thinking and acting to some degree, yet in spite of so much religious instruction so willingly received, the Christian religion is not, in fact, the great vital force in their lives; the Christian religion does not provide them with a coherent outlook on life; it does not effectively form and unify their living; it does not make them truly happy, as the Good News should do by its very nature.

For this strange and deplorable fact, there is, of course, more than one reason. But one of the most important may, perhaps, be this: religious instruction is often too completely absorbed in teaching particular doctrines and recommending special religious practices, and too little concerned with the joyful message we are sent to proclaim. Our presentation of the various doctrines is not sufficiently inspired by the spirit and the central idea of the whole, and, in consequence, it cannot lead to this spirit and this idea.

And it is self-evident that in the proper unification of our religious instruction, the ordering of the catechetical material has a very important part. Precisely the same stones and beams which could be used in constructing a prison could also be used in building a beautiful palace; the product does not depend on the stones, but on how they are put together. And, if they are not put together at all, you will have no building, only a heap of stones. So in our catechetical apostolate. St. Paul himself said that in the work of evangelization, he was to be like a "skilled master-builder", and he expected the same skillfullness in the teachers who were to carry on the work which he had founded on the only enduring foundation, that is, Christ (see 1 Cor. 3:10-15).

Let us see for example, what a vast difference in the whole basic attitude underlying our presentation of religion is made by the apparently unimportant change in order mentioned above. If we start from the fundamental question of the purpose of human life, and present the catechetical content in the once customary sequence of Faith-Commandments-Means of Grace, then the underlying theme will certainly be the chief duties of a Christian, through the faithful performance of which we are to obtain our last end and goal. But if we begin with the fundamental statement of God's fatherly love and interest in us, of how He has called us through Jesus Christ, then we will first show what He, in His eternal love, has done, does and will do for us (Creed, Sacraments), and how we can respond to this wonderful divine love (Prayer, Commandments). Immediately the incomparable values of the Christian religion occupy the center of our catechetical field of vision, and the content of religious instruction appears as being the joyful tidings of God's love, to which we are to respond by a life of grateful reciprocal love. No trained catechist, certainly, would seriously maintain that it is unimportant whether we proclaim our message as a system of chilling obligations, or as a system of enticing values.

How Does A Good Order of Presentation Help Both Students and Teachers?

At this point, some catechists might ask whether, in any case, the Christian religion ought to be presented to the children as a "system". We have answered this question already in chapter six, part I.

But does not our insistence here on the right ordering mean that we are proposing a "system" from the very beginning? We have said already that a premature use of systematic religious instructions by means of a catechism does, in fact, contradict the mentality of young children. And precisely for this reason, the catechetical movement does not approve of the use of a catechism text for the first years in school, not even of the so-called "small" catechism. (Unfortunately, this basic demand of modern catechetics is still neglected in many places.) And, as we have said above, the ideal "arrangement" for the lower grades is undoubtedly the Bible-story method, together with constructive catechizing based on liturgical object-lessons. Even in the subsequent years of school, in which systematic instruction according to the divisions of a catechism is certainly justified, sacred doctrine should always be imparted according to a very simple and lucid "system", and in a way easily understandable by children of this age.

But the point here is this: the individual student, especially at the beginning, need not gain so clear an idea of the plan according to which he is being taught, as to be able to give an account of it. But the underlying plan will determine the whole spirit and form of his understanding of religion. The ordinary man, when he admires a magnificent building, could not describe the architectural plan according to which the parts of the building were put together, and yet the plan determines the impression of harmony and beauty which the building makes upon him. So in the first years of religious instruction, the student need not grasp the "system" as such, but the right plan of presentation will make an enormous difference in his understanding and appreciation of what he has learned.

The correct ordering of the subject matter, then, in the first place, *benefits the catechist himself,* for it enables us to see the heritage of our faith in its true aspect, so that our proclamation of it will receive the catechetical "tone" and color given it by Our Lord Himself. If the catechetical content of religion is presented, as we have said above, as being the proclamation of the eternal love of God for us and our loving response to God's love, and if the individual doctrines are presented so as clearly to flow from this central fact, then a student might not notice how this catechism was divided, or might forget its outline in latter life, but he would certainly realize that the Christian religion is the religion of love, and would find his religion class a school of Christian love. And this is what really counts.

The important point here is, then, that the catechist himself should grasp the deeper import of the main outline of the subject matter, and that, in the course of his instructions, he should arrange single lessons in accordance with the central thought of the whole. This central thought must form the ever-recurring leit-motif of the entire course of religious instruction. And when this is taken care of, it will not be difficult in due time to make the pupils also aware of the deep meaning behind the order of the main divisions of the subject-matter, so that they experience the Christian religion as a marvellous and holy unity, as the religion of intelligent and generous love.

Thus for the catechist directly, and for the student indirectly, the correct ordering of the subject-matter has both a decisive and a directive significance, even for the organization of the Bible-story narratives and liturgical training in the first grades. For the catechist, it indicates the basic course he should follow in his teaching, the predominant sequence of thought to be followed in presenting each doctrine of the faith. The catechist himself should become familiar with the intrinsic inter-relationship of the individual doctrines as this is indicated by their position in the whole outline; and he should be able to present the separate parts in their right relationship to the whole. If he does so, then his students will see and experience sacred doctrine as an organic whole, and they will continue to grow in this knowledge, even if they cannot always recite the divisions of the catechism in their given order.

We may even go a step further, and dare to maintain that it is not so important always to give each individual lesson exactly in its place in the outline. If every individual lesson is shown in its true perspective, then each part will find its place in one organic whole in the students' minds, together with the knowledge and formation already acquired. And where there is question of the ordering of sermons to be given to adults, greater freedom in the sequence of subject matter is, generally speaking, allowed and even recommended. In her liturgy, Mother Church certainly recommends reasonable freedom in the selection of themes; and, in any case, rigid systematizing is entirely foreign to the liturgy. The liturgical year, as we all agree, forms a magnificent unity, expressing in a sublime manner the fundamental truths of the Christian religion. And yet, obviously, strict systematization is out of the question in carrying out, in our preaching, the main themes of the liturgical year. What really concerns Mother Church is, clearly, not to fit all her feasts and seasons into a smooth "system" but to see to it that, in the celebration of the individual feasts, the fundamental ideas of the Christian religion and of all the Christian feasts shine out clearly and impressively.

In giving catechism instructions in school, then, it is certainly advisable to teach, lesson by lesson, according to the order given in a good text, unless occasionally there are special reasons for making an exception. This is the only way in which we can have the necessary certitude that the whole treasure of the Christian faith, with all its integral parts, is being treated. And, in this way also, the relationship of the various lessons to one another is more easily perceived. But the main point is that the individual lessons should not be taught merely by keeping to the order of the book, but that the teacher should be thoroughly animated by the spirit underlying the whole plan, and then should bring it home in each lesson.

For a good outline of the catechetical subject matter enables both teacher and student to perceive easily, at the first glance, *the spirit of the whole,* the predominant basic idea of the Christian message, and from the outset to view its main parts in the light of this leading idea. Our problem is, not merely to impart to young people more or less disconnected facts taken from Christian revelation, but to give them a true education in religion and a deeper spirituality, and, above all, to introduce them to the spirit of Christianity. And the more we are concerned with this problem, the more we shall appreciate the significance of a good ordering of the actual catechetical text. Fr. Jungmann is quite right when he writes in his *Katechetik:* "Still more important than the questions regarding the external form (i.e. question-and-answer, or explanation, "projects", illustrations, etc.) of the catechism are those pertaining to its internal character, to that selection and ordering of the content which best conforms to our catechetical task."[6]

Is it possible that, up to this time, such rudimentary questions regarding the ordering of content have been too often set aside in favor of the problems of perfecting the "method" of the catechist?

6.   J. Jungmann, S.J., *Katechetik, Aufgabe und Methode der religiosen Unterweisung,* p. 89 ff.

CHAPTER TWO

What Are the Leading Principles
To Be Followed in Rightly Ordering
The Catechetical Material?

The question will arise, sooner or later, in the United States also, whether the order of the catechism customary up till now should be rejected, and a more satisfying one put in its place. This important question obviously deserves careful attention, and, equally obviously, undue haste must be avoided in making any permanent change. For we cannot simply discard the traditional outline. We must make efforts to replace it immediately by one which, to some degree at least, will offer a permanent solution to the problem. This refers primarily to the basic structure of the catechism. The order of the individual sections within the framework of the basic plan can always be changed again without much difficulty, but the basic structure should be established correctly once and for all, so far as this is possible.

CLEAR THINKING NECESSARY

An intensive study of the various catechisms which have appeared in Europe within the past few years leaves us with the impression that a break has been considered necessary with the traditional order: Faith, Commandments, Means of Grace; but that a clear-cut and positive solution, consistently carried out, to the problem of a more satisfactory order is still lacking in most of these newer books.[1] The new national catechism for France is especially significant in this regard.[2] In the introductory lesson, the authors combine the old order with a new one, as if both came to about the same thing. And one could hardly say

1. The German catechism is a happy exception. It proposes the catechetical material as "The Good News of the Kingdom of God." But its order of presentation is not lacking in compromises, and, also, the central idea does not shine out with sufficient clarity in the formulation of the main sections: God and our Redemption, The Church and the Sacraments, Life according to God's Commandments, The Last Things.

2. *Catéchisme à l'usage des diocèses de France,* par le chanoine Quinet et le chanoine Boyer, 1946.

that the basic idea behind the new order: Faith, Sacraments, Commandments, has been consistently carried out in the lessons that follow. This inconsistency seems to result from the fact that the Sacraments are, as in the old outline, brought in as "secours", helps to salvation, and thus as sources of strength and energy, rather than as gifts of God's love given us in Christ; and, above all, that the Commandments are still treated as being divine Directions, and not mainly as our loving response to divine Love. This catechism makes no effort to define lucidly the thought underlying the new order and so to make the catechist at least aware of it and to make it easier for him to use the book properly. And from this lack results the danger that only an external transposition of parts has been achieved, which will be interpreted by the majority of catechists according to the thought of the old ordering.

Such half-measures, with the accompanying sense of insecurity, should be avoided at all costs. This was hardly possible in the pioneer work of earlier catechisms. But in those of the future, we can justifiably expect to avoid such a transitional stage. And in order to achieve this goal, we should all acquaint ourselves thoroughly with the leading principles underlying a proper ordering of the catechetical material. With these principles in mind, it will be easy to gain a clear idea and to form a correct opinion of the catechetical value of the old ordering, and to see how a more satisfactory outline should be built up and consistently carried through.

QUALITIES OF A GOOD OUTLINE

Among the characteristics of a good outline which the modern study of catechetics has seen to be necessary, are three that are of special interest to us here. A perfect outline must be: 1) clear; 2) easily understandable, 3) essential, that is, it must flow from the essence of the subject-matter and so offer a primary means of penetrating into the true nature of the matter to be taught and studied.

Clarity implies the need for only a few main topics, corresponding to one another as far as possible, which can be easily read and retained. In a scholarly treatise, it does not make very much difference whether the contents are developed by means of a small or large number of sections. But this is not true of a catechism: its main topics should be easily grasped and easily memorized. For these topics contain—or rather should contain—the quintessence of our religion in as suggestive and absorbing a way as possible. And they should also give us a short and pertinent guide for the whole program of our lives.

The famous *Small Catechism* of Bellarmine[3] (Rome, 1597), for example, offends against this need for clarity by dividing the subject matter as follows: (1) The Sign of the Cross. (2) The Creed. (3) The Our Father. (4) The Hail Mary. (5) The Commandments of God. (6) The Commandments of the Church. (7) The Sacraments. (8) The Virtues. (9) The Gifts of the Holy Spirit. (10) The Works of Mercy. (11) Sin. (12) The Last Things.

2. *Comprehensibility.* An outline that requires intensive reflection in order to grasp its meaning may be all well and good in a scholarly dissertation, but is not suitable for a catechism. Mediocre students and simple people must be able to understand and retain easily the main topics in their right order, and what is more important, they must be able to handle them easily and make use of them as a means toward leading a Christian life. The outline, then, must proceed from the nature of the subject, in such a way that the lay person does not receive the impression that it could be ordered in any other way. In the light of this necessity, the arrangement given in the catechism of Canisius, for example, is hardly satisfactory. His catechisms[4] prefer this outline: (1) Faith and the Creed. (2) Hope and Prayer. (3) Love and Commandments. (4) The Sacraments. (5) Christian Justice. True, it is quite easy to understand what is meant by each part of this outline. But how these five parts are related to one another and how they together constitute the content of the Christian religion, is less easy to perceive. And this is true also of the division used by Bellarmine. We come, therefore, to what is by far the most important factor in ordering the subject-matter aright, namely its own nature and essence.

NATURAL DIVISION

An *essential* outline divides the subject in the way that best corresponds to its nature. In this factor lies the art of making an ideal outline which will give a comprehensive view of the basic and central idea of the subject, and will present and develop it in accordance with this central point. Only in this way will the main outline provide what it is supposed to—the key to the real understanding of the matter to be presented. The essence of the subject is, therefore, of special significance, if we desire not merely to chat about it in an entertaining

3. Roberte Bellarmine, S.J., *Dottrina cristiana breve,* Rome, 1598.
4. An excellent critical edition of the different forms of Canisius' catechism has been made by Fr. Streicher, S.J., *S. Petri Canisii Catechismi Latini et Germanici.* 2 partes, Rome-Munich, 1933-1936. St. Peter Canisius did not use the same order in all catechisms. After the publication of the Roman catechism, particularly, he tried to make a compromise between its arrangement and his own.

way, but to help others easily and thoroughly to gain a correct understanding of what we have to say—as certainly should be the case in
religious instruction. For here, as we have said so often before, our
aim is not to display one or other facet of our religion, but to introduce
the pupil to the spirit of true Christianity, and to lead him into the
innermost sanctuary of the Christian religion.[5]

Seen in this way, it should be clear, without need for further discussion, that the ordering of the catechism—at least as to its major topics
—*must not be regulated by considerations of apologetics*. Outlines that
are apologetically oriented do not ask what is most essential according
to the nature of Christian doctrine, but rather what special teachings are
being attacked under the present circumstances. Such outlines place
these teachings in the foreground and so threaten the organic harmony
of the whole presentation. This defect is to be seen, for example, in the
classic catechisms of the sixteenth century. We can understand the
reasons for the arrangements made in the catechisms of Canisius,
Bellarmine and Auger, when we consider their need to take an emphatic
stand against the Protestants of their own times.[6] Canisius, for example,
added the long fifth section on Christian Justice to his catechism for
apologetic reasons. And in his so-called *Small Catechism* this topic
occupies one third of the whole book and is entirely directed against
the Protestant teaching of justification by faith alone. Yet all the
essential doctrine presented in this section is already contained in the
third main division on Love and the Commandments, and it should
have been developed there, in its organic relationship to the whole.
The frankly apologetic tenor of the divisions of Auger and, later, of
Deharbe will be discussed later on.

Obviously, any vital teaching of the faith must deal with dangerous
contemporary errors in an up-to-date and convincing way. But the
interests of apologetics should never be allowed to alter the immanent
order and structure of our Christian message. Christian teaching of
the faith must always and under all circumstances, in our schools and
in our churches, remain what it is according to its very nature, that is,
the proclamation of the glad tidings of Jesus Christ. And this fact
should be effectively presented in the outlining and ordering of the
subject matter. And, in fact, we defend our faith most effectively
when we develop and organize our presentation in this way, so as
to bring out the unique values of the Christian religion. When this

5. See Part One of this book, especially chapters 2 and 5.
6. For more complete proof of the fact that the basic attitude of these catechisms is apologetic, as is their ordering of material, see J. Hofinger, S.J., *op. cit.*,
p. 729-742.

has been done, we need only to point out, in the appropriate place—and so in organic relation to the whole—how these special Christian values are menaced by the respective contemporary errors. Apologetic questions must never penetrate into the innermost sanctuary of our teaching of the faith, or even worse, be allowed to dominate it. They should be dealt with before we begin the positive presentation of our Good News, or, better still, be treated, in their proper place in the whole.

THEOLOGICAL RATHER THAN DIDACTIC

We are now in a position clearly to perceive the necessity for another quality of a proper outline of the catechism, namely that it should be primarily theological rather than didactic. The laws of pedagogy, to be sure, show us the importance of good ordering: and they tell us that the resulting outline should be clear, easily comprehensible, and, above all, that it should be derived from the essence and vital nature of the subject matter. But what constitutes the very essence and nature of Christian teaching, the laws of pedagogy cannot tell us. This is a matter for theology alone.

It is obvious, then, what great significance for catechetics is implied in the question of what is the main object of theology, a question so frequently discussed during the last few years. The result of this discussion might, perhaps, have been greater, and certainly would have been clearer—for theology itself as well as for the teaching of religion—if the participants had begun with the central object of revelation, and, more specifically, this object as shown us in Holy Scripture.

Concerning the central object of Revelation, as it is to be perceived in the very sources of that Revelation, there can be scarcely a doubt in the mind of an impartial investigator. Not the Godhead itself, but the "God of salvation" Who has destined us in Christ to share in His glory,—this is the central object of Christian Revelation. St. Paul calls this *the* kerygma, the message (1 Cor. 1:21; 1 Cor. 2:4; 1 Cor. 15:14), which he as the herald (keryx) of Christ (1 Tim. 2:7; 2 Tim. 1:11; Acts 20:25) is sent to announce. And this message is, simply the "mystery", which contains and includes all other mysteries and is designated by St. Paul himself as the "mystery of Christ" (Col. 4:3).[7] In teaching religion, we can, obviously, have no other central object but Revelation. But one would think that true theology also, which desires to be only the handmaid of Revelation—and she should be a zealous and modest handmaid who does not try to force her own ideas on her mistress — in striving for a deeper spiritual penetration of

7. See above, p. 11.

Revelation, would have no other central object than that given us by Revelation itself.[8]

But concerning our own enquiry here, it is obvious that if we desire correct information as to the essence of our holy religion, we must seek a theological answer.[9] *What does theology tell us concerning the nature and essence of our religion* which should be made clear in the ordering of our catechetical material? It tells us that the Christian religion is, above all, a religion of Revelation, the invitation of the divine Father issued through the ages to His beloved children. This gracious invitation is much more than an appeal to mankind which a person may accept of his own volition. Our religion is essentially the history of salvation, the glad tidings not only of the magnificent goal to which God has called us, but of all that He has done and will continue to do until that blessed day when He will gather us all home in glory to our Father's house in heaven. This whole divine work of salvation, from the dawn of creation to our final beatification in the kingdom of the Father, has its focal point in Christ. He is the vital center of the history of salvation: "Christ yesterday, today, and forever" (Heb. 13:8); "for there is no other name under heaven given to man, whereby we must be saved" (Acts 4:12). He is "the way, the truth and the life. No man comes to the Father but by Him" (John 14:6). Has not the Father, with Him, given His children all things? (Rom. 8:32) For this very reason, the Christian religion is, according to its innermost nature, the *Evangelium Domini nostri Jesu Christi,* that is, the joyful message of the mystery of Christ, which "has been hidden for ages and generations, but now is manifested in His saints". And, since the time of the early Church, this message has formed the nucleus and the guiding star of every genuinely apostolic propagation of the faith.

WHAT IS REQUIRED

From this sketch of the essential elements of Christian doctrine, the following basic necessities for a good ordering of our catechetical elements are seen as self-evident.

1. Since our teaching essentially consists in the handing on to others of divine Revelation, it must express as clearly as possible the distinctive character of divine *Revelation:* the gracious invitation issued by God's love, to which our love gratefully responds by faithful obedience to His commands.

2. Since our teaching is the message, given all through the ages, of

8. See the final chapter of this book.
9. Obviously the aim of this chapter is not to offer a thorough investigation of the essence of the Christian religion. But the few thoughts given here may suffice to lay a solid theological foundation for further catechetical deductions.

what God has done, does and will do for our salvation, the main topics of the catechism should clearly portray the *historic character* of the Christian religion.

3. Since our teaching must definitely present the *history of salvation,* the ordering of the main topics must clearly present the subject matter as a *structure of values,* and not as a structure of obligations. Our outline must, therefore, be, not an enumeration of obligations or duties —which, in the present order, cannot help but seem to be primarily burdens. This outline must present the Christian religion, according to its true nature, as an unfolding of the highest values, as the proclamation of glorious messages of joy, which together, in marvellous harmony, constitute these glad tidings of the mystery of Christ.

4. Since our teaching contains the doctrines which speak of the "inexhaustible riches of Christ" (Eph. 3:8), the main topic of the catechism must clearly indicate the *Christocentric character* of our message.

Has the ordering of our catechisms up till now fulfilled these fundamental requirements? These questions will be discussed in the following chapters.

CHAPTER THREE

Is Our Catechism
Properly Outlined?

In the light of the principles we have just discussed, it will not be difficult to make an objective judgment on the catechetical value of the present outline, to note its great advantages, and also to observe and evaluate its undeniable weaknesses.

The purpose of this chapter is not to offer merely a negative criticism of the outline now generally in use. On the contrary, we particularly wish to bring out its good points. And insofar as we shall offer a criticism of this outline, we shall do so for three reasons. First, we need to consider whether the change in the ordering of the Deharbe catechism, a change which has been tried out in those countries of Europe that excel in the field of catechetics, should also be made in the United States. Secondly, a criticism of the existing arrangement offers a guide both as to what should be especially striven for and what should be particularly avoided in the eventual re-ordering of our catechism. The somewhat imperfect and transitional solutions, to be found even in catechisms published during the last few years, give one the impression that this fundamental question has not been thought out with sufficient thoroughness. This confusion should be avoided in the future. It would be better to delay any decision as to a change in the catechism for a longer time in order finally to present a thorough and permanent solution. And thirdly, even if there is never to be a revision of the order of presentation in the catechism—which is hardly likely—it is of great importance for catechists to be clearly aware of the weaknesses of the present arrangement, so that they may compensate for them as much as possible by suitable explanations.

ADVANTAGES OF THE PRESENT ARRANGEMENT

That there must be numerous advantages in the present arrangement of the catechism may be gathered from the fact of its being so widespread. If one were to collect the various catechisms by Deharbe and

67

their many adaptations, all organized on the same basic structure, we would see at once that this group constitutes the most widely circulated type of catechism ever in existence.

We should notice especially this Deharbe arrangement is far more widely used than those found in other famous catechisms such as those by Canisius and Bellarmine—and this for very good reasons. When compared with these others, Deharbe's text shows unmistakable progress. It excels the ordering of either Canisius or Bellarmine in uniformity, clarity, and consistency. Evaluated in the light of the qualities needed in a good ordering, as we saw in the last chapter, no one will deny the fact that the Deharbe arrangement possesses a high degree of both clarity and comprehensibility. From the introductory question concerning the last goal or end of man (service of God, salvation of one's soul), the three main sections follow one another with perfect clarity and comprehensibility. The proper and complete service of God, which is our life's task or assignment, consists in firm faith in Divine Revelation. And this does not mean a dead faith, limited to a mere consent of the intellect, but a living, full faith, proved by loyally following Christ, by living obediently, that is, by keeping the Commandments. In order to give this answer of complete faith, God must assist us with His grace, and we, on our part, must zealously use the "means of grace", that is, Prayer and the Sacraments.

The purpose of this arrangement, as we should clearly perceive and admit, is to order the entire heritage of the faith according to one leading idea: "the service of God—our life's task". By taking the last end of man as the starting-point, everything that follows is clearly and impressively made applicable to our own lives. This arrangement constitutes an effective "Christian Art of Life", a guide to proper Christian living. And by this arrangement, the fundamental thought of Christian revelation is repeated, insofar as Revelation is in fact, by its nature, both information and guide on our Way to God.

The procedure here is the same as that used in the *Spiritual Exercises* of St. Ignatius, in which the starting-point is also the last goal of man, and the development consistently follows this leading idea. The whole plan of the Exercises thus possess remarkable inner unity, consistency and psychological effectiveness; and it would seem as though the Deharbe catechism, following the same plan in its starting-point and sequence of three main sections, should achieve a similar result.

All these reasons abundantly justify the fact that the ordering made by Auger and Deharbe has been generally preferred above those of Canisius and Bellarmine. Moreover, Auger's ordering of the Catechism was in full accord with the religious taste of his time, which had been built up and formulated in the conflict with Protestantism, and under the influence of the religious individualism which has been increasing since the sixteenth century and has continued to be an effective force until recent times. But this latter is a very doubtful advantage.

DEFECTS OF THE PRESENT ARRANGEMENT

But notwithstanding all these qualities, the Deharbe ordering (Faith, Commandments, Means of Grace) has significant defects. In the first place, to use the question concerning the last end of man as the starting-point is not nearly so suitable, catechetically speaking, as it might appear at first sight. For the *Spiritual Exercises* to begin with this question may be entirely justifiable, since the Exercises presuppose the knowledge of religious, and even of specifically Christian truths, and their purpose is to give a practical, well-thought-out and coherent program for the reform of a Christian life. And, with Ignatius himself, this question as to man's last end is used as the directive for, and the preliminary foundation of his Exercises, but it is by no means the leading idea in their development into the "four Weeks". For the question as to man's final goal may be asked with great benefit wherever the purpose is to give greater religious orientation to people's thoughts and aspirations. But the attempt should not be made, as it is in the Deharbe catechism, to develop from this introductory question the whole of Christian doctrine. And this for two reasons:

First, any attempt to organize and present Christian teaching as the knowledge of how to realize our life's task must necessarily lead to the construction of an "obligation-structure"—a system of duties—and not as a "value-structure"—a system of what is worth desiring and working for. The fundamental thought underlying the first will always be: in order to reach our last end, we *must*, first . . . second . . . third . . . etc. And so the Christian message, the glad tidings, will appear as being a formal collection of commandments, and, therefore, of burdens—certainly a peculiar "Gospel"! It is simply unbearable that our glad tidings should end by becoming a mere listing of Christian obligations! Therefore in any genuinely Christian, and so unadulteratedly "evangelical" proclamation of doctrine, the messages of joy, the "values", must, under all circumstances, have absolute precedence. Only by being taught in this way will Christians once again come to experience that the yoke of the Lord is "sweet", that is, brings gladness to him who bears it. Only thus will they understand that to carry it is a relatively cheap price to pay for the unfathomable riches of Christ (Eph. 3:8); only thus will they count all values of the natural order "as dung, in order to gain Christ" (Phil. 3:8).

And we should take into consideration the fact that, in our times, Christianity is no longer, even in principle, generally considered to be something of value. Our instructions are not to be given only to children from good Catholic families, who may be supposed to have imbibed an appreciation of the faith from their parents. We hope to bring Christ's doctrine of salvation to millions of people of other faiths; we desire to reach those millions of Catholic young people who come from religiously indifferent families, and to win them also effectively for Christ. And therefore it is of the utmost importance that the Christian religion be presented to them as attractively as possible. For example, some years ago a missionary asked a promising and morally zealous student from a prominent Catholic middle school in China whether he would like to become a Catholic. The student answered that he saw no reason why, in addition to the already numerous rules of the school, he should burden himself with the regulations of the Catholic religion. He looked upon the Christian religion as being primarily a system of rules. But why? Obviously because in hearing instructions in the faith, so far as this young man understood the teaching, the obligations were what predominated and not the values. Do situations like this exist only in China?

Secondly, the question concerning the last end of man is not perfectly fitted to present the *specifically Christian* aspect of our teaching. Here, indeed, some other solution could be found which would express far more clearly the Christocentric character of our catechetical material. Or perhaps we might state it in this way: we are put here on earth to become children of God by means of our close union with Christ, to live as children of God, and, finally, to share in Christ's glory. But then we should not be following the sequence: Faith, Commandments, Means of Grace, which is just the point at issue. And no one would maintain that this or any similar formulation seems very suitable for teaching children, however correct it may be theologically speaking. The difficulty still remains which seems inherent in beginning with the question of our last end. This idea of our goal certainly includes a value of great power, with strong motivating force. But it is hardly possible, catechetically speaking, to develop this value properly at the beginning of religious instruction. Nobody can appreciate very much of what is implied in the Christian idea of life everlasting until he has learned something of God's love as shown us in Christ. And one can hardly find a single catechism that attempts to do so; it is simply not feasible. Thus, a value which should be developed in the course of instruction is here placed too suddenly at the beginning. Given in such a form, it seems more like a logical aid to a clear-cut classification of the material to be treated, than as the supreme motivation which is to give a lasting impulse both to learning and doing. And we should remember that this kind of logical and strict alignment toward a goal appeals more to adults and to young people of greater maturity of mind than it does to a child.

But also, entirely apart from its starting-point, the sequence: Faith, Commandments, Means of Grace, has distinct disadvantages. More than seventy years ago, another Fr. Josef Jungmann, S.J. who died in 1885, advanced two criticisms of this arrangement.[1] For one thing, the classification of the material according to Faith, Commandments, Means of Grace may easily give the impression that only the first main section, Faith, has to be "believed". In reality, of course, the whole content of what is to be taught is self-evidently a message from heaven, an object of faith, and this should be especially clear in the teaching about the Sacraments. That this should be clearly recognized is certainly of great importance both for students and for catechists. But the revealed character of the whole Christian religion hardly appears clear when the customary classification is used.

And Fr. Jungmann's second objection was that the separation of dogmatic faith (treated in the first main section) from living according to faith (treated in the two following main sections) *develops the idea of faith in a catechetically deplorable way*. It is in every way desirable that, when we speak of faith as the term is used in the ordinary language of Scripture and especially in the proclamation of doctrine as carried out by the Apostles and the Fathers of the Church, it should always be considered as a full, complete, living faith and not merely as "something held to be true". Theology had to make the distinction between a dogmatic and a living faith, especially for use in the conflict with Protestantism, to show that mere (dogmatic) faith does not justify us. But it does not in any way follow from this that, in the proclamation of Christian doctrine today, the word "faith" must always be understood and used in the narrower, later sense. Here we see that apologetic and pedantically theological considerations have regrettably penetrated into the sanctum of the teaching of Christian doctrine.

THE PRESENT DIVISION IS APOLOGETIC

In fact, the arrangement of the catechism by Auger-Deharbe is understandable as being, generally speaking, the Catholic answer to the basic errors of Protestantism. It is plainly an example of an apologetically orientated ordering of the subject matter. As Luther's catechism

1. J. Jungmann, S.J. *Theorie der geistlichen Beredsamkeit* (Theory of Spiritual Eloquence). Freiburg, 1877/8. pp. 792-796.

expressed the Protestant solution to the points at issue in the sixteenth century, by its outline: Commandments, Faith, Prayer, Sacraments, so the catechism of Auger, and the still more explicit formulation of Deharbe, proposed the Catholic solution: the basis for justification is Faith (first main section), which, however, must manifest itself in good works (second main section); but in order to keep the Commandments of God, we need His grace (third main section).

One might say, perhaps, that Auger's catechism, with its obvious opposition to Protestantism, was most suitable for this period of controversy. And, certainly, the group of catechisms by Auger-Deharbe, by their order of presentation itself, firmly established in the minds of Catholics the Catholic answer to the disputed questions of that time, and so accomplished a great deal of good by rendering Catholics generally immune to the errors then current. But when Deharbe wrote his catechism (1847), orthodox Protestantism had, in fact, ceased to be the chief opponent of Catholic doctrine. And nearly everywhere the time has long since gone by in which such a strongly pronounced stand against orthodox Protestantism could be justified to any degree from present circumstances.

And, even during the time of the struggle against Protestantism, such a concentration on contemporary errors had its grave disadvantages. We cannot deny the fact that by this onesided emphasis, an important and most regrettable transposition took place within the field of catechetical teaching. Because of this apologetic order of presentation, some important doctrines were taken out of their context in the whole unity of Christian truth, and were never restored to their true place in teaching. This is especially true of the doctrines concerning Grace, Prayer and the Sacraments.

GRACE

Grace, that is, our new divine life in Christ, is by far the highest gift that Christianity has to offer. In the order of presentation hitherto customary, divine grace by no means appears as the basic value of a Christian life, but merely as a "means" for the faithful observance of the Commandments. And so, in the section on Grace, not sanctifying, but actual (helping) grace has become the central point of catechetical interest, and at that, not as divinizing the activities of God's children *(gratia elevans)*, but as healing the weakness of fallen human nature *(gratia sanans)*. This was the focal point of the whole arrangement of the Deharbe catechism, and it is expressly mentioned in older catechisms. The Baltimore Catechism, as we know, does away with all transitions from one section to another—which is hardly an advantage.

In it, the doctrine concerning the Sacraments and Prayer follows that on the Commandments in the customary way, but it is entitled "God's Gifts". Yet if the Sacraments are to be viewed in this light, they ought to precede the Commandments. And, also, the teaching on Prayer should be detached from this main section. For the placing of the Sacraments and Prayer under one heading only makes sense if both are seen, as in Deharbe's catechism, as being "Means of Grace".

SACRAMENTS AND PRAYER

In the same way, the Sacraments do not appear as being the incomparable sources of Divine Life in which the life of the Mystical Christ is daily renewed. As a result of using the sequence: Faith, Commandments, Means of Grace, they are looked upon as means or aids to leading a good life. And so also with Prayer, which is certainly the goal and the high point of a Christian life. If it is treated as a "means of grace", then the prayer of petition for the help of grace will become the central point of our teaching; and the most fundamental function of Christian prayer, namely the prayer of praise and thanksgiving of the children of God redeemed by Christ, will recede into the background. In any catechism beginning with the question of the last goal and end of man, prayer would have to be presented in a particularly beautiful way as the real meaning and the final fulfillment of Christian living. It would have to be shown to be the worship of God offered by His redeemed children, with Christ and in Him, the adoration in spirit and in truth which the Lord Himself praises as the characteristic mark of the Messianic Age (John 4:23 f.).

And, finally, we might point out that in Deharbe's outline there is *little evidence of the historic character of the Christian religion.*

The defects noted here in the order of presentation of the Auger-Deharbe catechism were, certainly, noticed many years ago in the United States. Otherwise how can we explain the fact that the official Baltimore Catechism omits the clear-cut development of that part of the catechism which immediately proceeds from the question concerning the last end of man; that it still arranges the main sections in the old sequence, but leaves out every logical connecting link between these sections and the introductions to each; that it entitles the third main section "God's Gifts", and adds a fourth on the Sacrifice of the Mass (Baltimore Catechism No. 2). By these means, certainly, the original import of the order of presentation has been done away with to some degree, and many defects have been covered up. But did this result in a satisfactory and permanent solution? And where must the permanent solution be sought?

CHAPTER FOUR

Towards a Better Division
Of the Catechism

As we have seen in the previous chapter, the present arrangement of the catechism, in spite of its undeniable advantages, hardly fulfills the justifiable demands of modern catechetics. We must seek a better solution to the problem. But in doing so, we should use the guidance of tradition, and make use of the insights, suggestions and experience of earlier centuries.

THE ROMAN CATECHISM AND ITS ARRANGEMENT

Among catechisms already in existence, there is one in particular which, as it seems to us, opens the way for a satisfactory and positive solution of the problem, and this catechism also has the greatest claim to our consideration. For it is the so-called Roman Catechism which was published by Pope Pius V, in accordance with a decree of the Council of Trent.[1]

Among those associated with this book, St. Charles Borromeo in particular devoted himself to the completion of this excellent work with that energy and pastoral open-mindedness so characteristic of him. The book was written by the Dominicans Leonard Marine, Gilles Foscarini, and Franz Furiero, to which the name of Mucio Calini should also be added.

The Roman Catechism was not composed for children. As its title expressly states; it is intended for pastors, that is, for those in charge of souls; and its purpose is to give these pastors authoritative guidance for all the various phases of catechetical instruction. For our purpose here, it is most important to notice that the scope of its directives is by no means intended to be limited to teaching in schools. It includes

1. *Catechismus ex decreto Concilii Tridentini ad parochos Pii quinti Pont. Max. iussu editus,* Romae, 1566.

the general proclamation of the Christian faith. Now, how does this "most Catholic" of all Catholic catechisms arrange its material? In four books, it treats the four basic catechetical formulae, in the following order: the Apostles' Creed, the Sacraments, the Commandments of God, the Our Father. Could we, perhaps, make use of this sequence today?

Many years ago, the Jesuits Josef Jungmann (d. 1885) and Michael Gatterer[2] favored the order of the Roman Catechism rather than that of Deharbe. It is true that the reasons for their preference were insufficient, and wrong in part. For they maintained that the ideal arrangement should consist of a simple extrinsic enumeration of the most important catechetical formulae (Symbol, Sacraments, Commandments, Our Father), which would consciously avoid any order of presentation deduced from the nature or essence of Christian doctrine. And they further maintained that the right ordering of the individual parts of the catechism could be determined only from the authority of the ecclesiastical magisterium.

Obviously, such a peculiar interpretation contradicts not only the principles of modern pedagogy, but even those of theology itself. It is difficult to understand how anyone could hold that only the teaching material of catechetics should be denied any intrinsic ordering or arrangement. For it is the duty of those who give instruction in Christian truth to bring divine Revelation to human beings, who live and think. Revelation has been handed down to us from God, Who is the Source and Lord of all right order, not as a confused medly of unrelated doctrines, but as a sacred and organic whole to be clearly announced to mankind. It is the task of those who teach sacred doctrine to find that order of presentation for this sacred unity which is inherent in divine Revelation itself, to make others aware of it, and, if possible, to allow this order to shine out even in the basic arrangement of subject matter.

It was only during the time of the last war that any attempt was made to clarify the real purpose of the ordering of the Roman catechism, and to make it practical for use in present-day catechisms.[3] So far as we know, the Roman Catechism itself makes no attempt anywhere to justify its arrangement by any mention of having developed it from the nature or essence of Christian doctrine.[4] Nevertheless, the order of its four main topics does actually have a profound meaning,

2. In connection with this, see M. Gatterer, S.J., *Katechetik*. Innsbruck, 1931, 282 ff.
3. J. Hofinger, S.J. *op. cit.*, Pars III. De Catechismo Romano, pp. 854-859.
4. Compare, e.g. *Catechismus Romanus*, Proemium, cap. 12.

and can lead us into the innermost sanctuary of Christian teaching. Looking closely, we see that the first two main sections (The Creed and the Sacraments) might be combined under an even more basic heading, as might the last two sections (the Commandments and the Our Father). St. Thomas Aquinas himself wished to have the teaching about the Sacraments given in close connection with that on the Symbol.[5] And, surely, the Sacraments and the divine life which they communicate to us constitute the greatest of the blessings which, through the mediation of the Church, are given to us in the Communion of Saints.[6] In this light, we see that the first two sections of the Roman catechism show us what God in His eternal love has done for us, what He is doing now and what He will do until we attain our full participation in the glory of the First-born; in other words, these two sections give the history of the eternal love of God for man. And the two following main sections show the right response of redeemed mankind to this eternal love: Love for Love. Our grateful answering love manifests itself in the first place in prayer, which is the loving look of the child up to his Father, and by the keeping of His Commandments from a heart filled with love.

PERFECTING THE ARRANGEMENT OF THE ROMAN CATECHISM

In the previous section, we have shown how the order of presentation given in the Roman Catechism could be improved so that its significance would be expressed even more clearly. The doctrine on the Sacraments should, whenever possible, not be placed immediately after that on the Symbol, but according to the model given by St. Thomas, it should form an organic part of the teaching given on the third section of the Symbol itself. Symbol and Sacraments should no longer be presented even as two closely linked or even interlocking basic formulas of catechetics; they should be fused into one harmonious whole, the History of the Eternal Love of God, the chief phases of which are already fittingly indicated in the Apostle's Creed. "The Sacraments should not be taught simply as theoretic points of doctrine; they should rather be combined with the doctrine about the Church,

---

5. St. Thomas Aquinas, *De articulis fidei* (ed. Mandonnet, III, p. 1; *Expositio super Symbolo Apost.* (ed. Mandonnet, IV, p. 381). Compare also J. Hofinger, *op. cit.* p. 594 ff.

6. St. Thomas explains the word "sanctorum" in the Creed as being the genitive of *sancta,* that is, of *res sanctae,* the good things of salvation, among which the Sacraments are supreme. So also the Roman Catechism, I, 10, 22. Concerning other catechisms, see J. Hofinger, S.J. *Geschichte des Katechismus in Österreich, Innsbruck,* 1937, p. 150 ff. For the entire question, see also, J. Jungmann, S.J., *Die Gnadenlehre im Apostolischen Glaubensbekenntnis,* in *Zeitschrifft f. kath. Theol;* 50 (1926), 196-219.

its nature and growth; and we should show at the same time that they (the Sacraments) accompany the life of the Christian from his entrance into the Church until his going home to God."[7]

The ordering of the second main section of the Roman Catechism (consisting of the last two topics as given above) could be further perfected by placing the doctrine on prayer first, and then that on the Commandments. Such an arrangement would be more in line with the best psychological order. The gratitude of a redeemed child of God expresses itself above all in true, spontaneous, childlike prayer (Rom. 8:15; Gal. 4:6). Such a presentation of Christian prayer gives the priority to the prayer of praise and gratitude which should dominate the prayer-life of true children of God. And here would be the ideal place for teaching about Holy Mass, our highest act of prayer. For in the Mass, more perfectly than anywhere else, we offer to the Father in heaven our common homage of grateful love through and with and in Christ, our Head and Mediator. The observance of the Commandments follows from this. What we offer and promise by taking part in the Mass—our complete surrender to the Father—must be carried out in the daily humdrum round of a Christian life, in the answer of an active love, the faithful and loving observance of the Commandments.

Such an outline of Christian doctrine is that which is now recognized by modern catechists as being the most satisfactory and appropriate. It is approved, in particular, by Fr. Josef Jungmann, S.J., in his recently published *Katechetik,* which for the time being at least, is perhaps the leading manual of catechetical instruction, particularly with regard to its material content.[8]

And, finally, it would be of great advantage to the whole order of presentation, if the two main sections of the catechism (The Love of God, Our Response) were each preceded by a short introduction. As Fr. Jungmann says: "At the beginning of the catechism, there should be a short chapter which, like a frontispiece, or a basic chord, contains in brief what is to follow. In this, Christ should come before the eyes of our mind, He Whom God has sent into the world, Who calls us and invites us into the Kingdom of God".[9] By this means, the contents

---

7. J. Jungmann, S.J. *Katechetische Fragen im deutschen Sprachgebiet,* Lumen Vitae, 1946, 66. Compare also, J. Hofinger, S.J., *The Apostles' Creed is a Real Prayer,* Lumen Vitae, 1954, 93-208.

8. J. Jungmann, S.J., *Katechetik,* Freiburg, 1955, 2nd ed. Similarly, the directives for religious instruction in the Belgian middle schools: *Programme-Religion* (Fédération Nationale de l'Enseignment Moyen Catholique), Lierre, 1953.

9. J. Jungmann, S.J. *Katechetische Fragen,* p. 66, and *Katechetik,* 2nd ed., p. 92 ff.

of the catechism would, from the outset, be characterized clearly as being Christian Revelation, and, more directly, as being Christ's message, and thus the mind of the Christian would be from the beginning directed toward the figure of Christ.

EFFECTS

The ordering of the catechism outlined above fulfills all the requirements which, as we saw in Chapter Two, should be taken into account. This scheme is not only clear and easily comprehensible, but it actually leads us into the innermost sanctuary of Christianity. Through it the whole contents of the catechism are seen to be *entirely Christian,* that is, to be Revelation given to us through the mediation of Christ, a gracious invitation from the heavenly Father, which came to us in Christ, and to which we, likewise in Christ, gratefully respond. For just as Christ is the central focus of the History of Salvation, treated in the first main section, so is He also the focus of our loving answer, of our Christ-informed praying and working; furthermore, Christ prays and works in us.

In this arrangement, the subject matter no longer seems to form a burdensome structure of obligations, but rather stands out in its true nature as a wonderfully desirable *structure of values.* Indeed, while the entire first section treats of the immeasurable riches of the everlasting divine love, even the second section—no matter how clearly it speaks and must speak of Christian obligations—no longer makes our duty seem oppressive or restrictive. Rather it gives us the longed-for answer to the question raised by the first section: What can I do in response? The basic question is no longer the wearisome: "What must I do?", but the redeeming and elevating: "What can I do?" The content of the second main division thus is shown to be the ideal of a Christian way of life, the glorious life of God's children, the incomparable, even if sometimes austere, beauty of the laws of Christian living.

Teaching according to this arrangement of the catechism has the further advantage of *growing organically out of the biblical-historical* method of teaching which should be used during the first years of religious instruction. In both cases, the story of divine love forms the fundamental theme. In the first years of religious instruction, the catechist repeatedly directs the students' attention to God's love, as shown so wonderfully in the Bible stories which form part of the history of salvation. Then, in the following years, in systematic religion courses, the principal phases of the history of salvation are treated again from the same aspect of divine love, but this time in a more specifically dogmatic way. And this first main section of the history of salvation is shown in relation to the second main section, the response of the redeemed children of God. The content of this section also will be sufficiently familiar to the children from the biblical-narrative teaching already received. In those earlier instructions, the young Christian has already become accustomed to look at Christian living as a program of grateful filial love. Only in this early stage, the directives for Christian living were given here and there as they came up in the course of the Bible-story instruction. But in the later systematic teaching, these same directives are systematically summarized in a way adapted to the increasing intellectual maturity of the student, and are shown as, all together, constituting our response to divine Love.

This is the Apostolic Method

This order of presentation as given above has still another advantage, that is, it can rightly appeal to the *Apostolic method* of teaching. When the Apostles went out to proclaim the truths of the faith, their teaching was characterized by the fact that it was the values of the Christian religion that they developed above all to their wondering hearers. On the feast of Pentecost, "drunk" with enthusiasm, filled with the Holy Spirit, they went out to announce "the wonderful works of God" (Acts 2:11). This was their general and common theme. The bare sketches given us in the *Acts* of the catechizing of the two Princes of the Apostles all show the same structure. First the values of Christianity are unfolded, and this is done mainly by pointing out what God has done in the History of Salvation. And then the duties of a Christian are explained. Particularly characteristic is the first mission sermon of the first pope. The theme of his sermon is: Now the fullness of time has come, in Jesus Christ the Messias, who was crucified and lives again. Only when the listeners themselves ask: "What are we to do?" does he impress upon them their particular obligations (Acts 2:14–41). From such value-saturated, Apostolic, doctrinal teaching came the glowing zeal of the early Church and its astonishingly vital religious energy.[10]

Suggestions to Catechists

There are, perhaps, a large number of catechists who whole-heartedly

---

10. For further material concerning the method of teaching used by Sts. Peter and Paul, with a brief analysis of the sketches of their instructions preserved for us in Holy Scripture, see J. Hofinger, S.J., *De apta divisione materiae catecheticae*, pp. 852-854. The content and structure of St. Paul's Epistles point in the same direction; for the most part, the first section is more dogmatic, and shows the greatness of the Redemption given us in Christ and the glory of our calling, and the second section is more practical, applying all this to Christian living.

approve of the principles set forth above, and who would like to see these principles applied in catechetical instruction. For the time being, such teachers have to use a catechism which does not perfectly follow these principles. And it will certainly be quite a long time before a new catechism appears, if only for the reason that a good catechism cannot be prepared overnight. Unless such an important work is done carefully and thoroughly, a slipshod product might be the result which, soon after publication, would need to be revised. But what should teachers do during this more or less lengthy time of waiting?

Can we not, immediately, without changing the catechism itself, teach according to the order of presentation: Faith — Sacraments: Prayer (with the Sacrifice of the Mass)—Commandments? And more important than making such an external rearrangement, which should not meet with any considerable difficulties, is to make sure of the inner transformation of the teacher's own outlook which will result in the right presentation according to the two main divisions: God's Love, Our Response. Whenever we are teaching the Creed or the Sacraments, we must indicate again and again how the content strikingly manifests at every step the gift-giving love of God and how it incites us to grateful reciprocal love. And all the lessons on Prayer and the Commandments should, in the same way, be treated as welcome opportunities for reminding ourselves and our students of how we are to thank God for His love. Thus our teaching can become truly "kerygmatic", whatever the arrangement of the texts we must use for the present.

And it seems to us also of great importance that this complete Christian view of our material should be worked out as clearly and completely as possible in all future commentaries on the catechism, especially in those made for the guidance of teachers and lay catechists.

By this transformation of our own outlook on our catechetical material and, consequently, the way in which we actually present it to our hearers, and the formulation of this transformation in commentaries and teacher's aids, the right ordering and formulations of the catechism of the future will not be merely the means for beginning the needed inner transformation of the teaching of Christian doctrine, but will rather come as the crown and external manifestation of a true re-formation already accomplished.

Significance for any Form of Catechetical Apostolate

Obviously, the ideas we have just been discussing are valid not only for religious instruction in schools, but for the whole field of the catechetical apostolate, for solid instruction of adults, as well as for the Christian formation of children. In the following part of this book, we shall try to present an exposition of our Christian message according to the order of presentation that we have just recommended, and, by so doing, we shall indicate how this arrangement may also be used in giving sermons to the faithful.

Our approval of this arrangement, however, by no means indicates that we intend to propose it as the only one that may profitably be used in teaching religion. Seeking a suitable arrangement of our catechetical material, we were concerned, in the first instance, with the problem as posed by the systematic catechesis to be given in the upper grades of school, and, in particular, with the concrete manifestation of this problem, the right ordering of the catechism text for this particular kind of religious instruction. But even for this particular purpose, the main divisions that we have proposed can not be considered as the only one which may legitimately be used. The new German Catechism, for example has a different arrangement which is of great value and deserves to be studied carefully.[11]

An important point to be considered here is that of the necessary variety we must provide in religious instruction. This is especially needed in the United States. For here we have a great deal of religious instruction, not only through all the years of grade and high school, but also in Catholic colleges. Even the most perfect arrangement of subject-matter, if repeated too frequently, will not be effective. If a guide had to show the beauties of the Swiss Alps or of the sanctuaries of Rome to one and the same group of people again and again, would he always lead them by the same route, or would he provide a variety? The same should be true for us who are guides to the beauties and treasures of the Kingdom of God.

The principles to be followed here are, above all, the following:

1. Once in the upper grades of elementary school, and then again in high school and in college, all the principal doctrines of Christianity should be presented in a way adapted to the age and maturity of the students.

2. We must not present the particular doctrines each time in the same sequence nor from exactly the same viewpoint.

3. Nevertheless, each time we must show the particular doctrines, especially the fundamental ones, in their immanent connection with the real center of the whole, that is, the Mystery of Christ. Thus, for example, in teaching the Commandments to adolescents, we should, more fully than in the grades, or than later on in college, discuss the problems concerning the development and formation of personality.

11. *Katholischer Katechismus der Bistümer Deutschlands.* (Freiburg i.B. 1955, Herder).

But we should deal with these problems as being immanently connected with our final task as Christians: the formation of Christ in us, and how we are to serve God by cooperating in this task with filial love.

4. Whatever order of presentation we may use—and we must change this in order to provide needed variety—it must fulfill the requirements of any sound arrangement, which we explained above.

Part III

The Content of Our Message —
The Joyful Tidings of Jesus Christ

THIS IS THE MESSAGE WE PROCLAIM:

In His infinite goodnes,	(Eph. 2:7)
the Father in heaven has called us	(1 Petr. 5:10)
to be united with Him in life and joy,	(John 17:21)
sharing His divine riches:	(Eph. 2:7)

through Christ, His Son—	(1 Petr. 5:10)
Him He gave as a ransom for us sinners,	(1 Tim. 2:6; 1 John 4:10)
and into His likeness He desires that we be conformed,	(Rom. 8:29)

so that, born anew of water and the Holy Spirit,	(ç:ε uɥoſ)
and thus made partakers of the divine nature,	(2 Petr. 1:4)
we may be children of God.	(1 John 3:1)

And because we are God's children,	
He has sent the Spirit of His Son into our hearts:	(Gal. 4:6)

thus being the temple of God,	(1 Cor. 6:19)
we are to live the life of God's children,	(Rom. 6:4)
following the example of Christ, our first-born brother,	(Rom. 8:29)

so that we may gain the kingdom of God and His glory,	
as heirs of God,	(1 Thess. 2:12)
joint heirs with Christ.	(Rom. 8:17)

Introduction

While teaching theology to future missionaries in China, I had an opportunity to use and test the principles brought out in the previous sections of this book. After several years of such teaching, I was to give a special summer course to some of my most promising seminarians, and I allowed them to determine its general subject. "Father," they said, "in your dogma course, you have told us again and again that in our missionary preaching we must give the essentials of the Christian message. Here, now, is your opportunity to show us, in actual concrete form, just what these essentials are and how we should present them." So my students caused me to work out a compact presentation of Christian doctrine, which would incarnate the principles of kerygmatic teaching and preaching.[1]

This section of the present book, then, is simply an attempt to show how the kerygmatic approach might work out in the concrete form of some thirty instructions or lessons, designed for adults. Our aim is not to offer fully worked out sermons or lessons, but merely outlines that will indicate what are the essential points of our teaching and how all together they form one message: the "Mystery of Christ". Designed primarily for missionary use, these lessons might also be used for the instruction of converts, and for a continuous series of sermons. But our chief purpose in including them here is to show how the kerygmatic spirit actually influences the selection and arrangement of topics, the method and manner of presentation of each doctrine, and the particular fruit to be sought from its teaching.

We hope, then, that this part of the book may assist the reader in his own meditations on the truths of the faith, enabling him more clearly and fully to see each doctrine in the light of the "mystery of Christ", and that he may also find this material capable of being adapted in various ways according to his own particular needs.[2]

1. The notes prepared for my students were published some years after the course, under the title, *Nuntius Noster, seu themata principalia praedicationiss christianae.* (Tientsin, Seminarium Regionale Kinghsiense, 1946). A Chinese edition was published in 1947, and also an edition continuing both the Latin and Chinese texts. An expanded adaptation in French was published in 1955: *Notre Message, Principaux Thèmes de la Prédication Chrétienne,* Traduction adapté par J. Seffer, S.J. (Brussels, Lumen Vitae, 1955). The material given here is an expanded English adaptation of the original notes.
2. Some suggestions for adaptations may be found in the Appendix.

Preliminary Instruction

The Riches of Our Vocation — The Father Calls Us Through Christ to His Kingdom

Aim: The aim of this preliminary instruction is strictly preparatory. Like the frontispiece of a book, it should give an idea of the whole, without going into any details. It has a function similar to that of the overture of an opera: it should win interest, bring in the "leitmotiv" of the whole work, create the right attitude.

Method: The same method should be used as in the subsequent instructions. We start from some concrete presentation. Here, as in the majority of the lessons, we begin with a Bible narrative that contains and presents the doctrine we wish to set forth. In our narration of the story, we must keep in mind the doctrine which this narrative is to explain. The narration, therefore, must be given in such a way as to develop all the elements that will facilitate the subsequent or concomitant explanation. In this preliminary instruction, the narration begins with the stirring fact that God's Only-begotten Son came to teach us, bringing us a great message from His heavenly Father. Through the parable of the wedding-feast, we shall try to give the central idea of Christ's message and of how we are to respond.

Viewpoint: The special aspect under which this lesson is to be presented is that of God's love, at once stirring us and obliging us to respond. God has called us because He loves us, and wishes to enrich us with His own life and fullness; but He expects the response of our grateful love to His loving invitation. Thus we give at once the "letimotiv" of our whole message: love for Love.

DOCTRINAL SUMMARY

A. The Father Has Sent His Son to Teach Us

Christianity is by its nature the doctrine of Christ; its very name reminds us of the incomprehensible fact that God has sent His Only-begotten Son to teach us. "God, Who at sundry times and in diverse manners spoke in times past to the fathers by the prophets, last of all in these days has spoken to us by His Son, whom He appointed heir of all things, by whom also He made the world" (Heb. 1:1 ff.). It is obvious that the message which He brings us from the Father must be an extremely great and important one. If it were not of supreme importance, the Father would have sent one of His angels. But this was a message which only the Son of God could fittingly proclaim:

"No one has at any time seen God. The only begotten Son, who is in the bosom of the Father, He has revealed Him." (John 1:18). God spoke to us through His only-begotten Son because He wished to speak to us precisely as "Father". In return for His great love, He expects us to receive His completely paternal revelation with a completely loyal attitude, in faith. What, then, is His message?

B. Christ Proclaims the "Good News of the Kingdom of God"

In the three years of His public life, Christ spent all His time, with complete devotion to the task given Him by His Father, in announcing His message. At the end of His earthly life, at the Last Supper, He Himself states this fact: "I have manifested Thy name to the men whom Thou hast given Me out of the world. Now they have learned that whatever Thou hast given Me is from Thee; because the words that Thou hast given Me, I have given to them" (John 17:6-8). Christ preached many single doctrines during these years of His public life, yet His whole teaching, finally, was concerned with one central message, "The Good News of the Kingdom of God". St. Mark summarizes Our Lord's teaching in the characteristic expression: "He was heralding the joyful tidings of God's Kingdom" (Mark 1:14. This is according to the Greek text. See also Matt. 4:17–23, and 9:35). It was the same message that His disciples were to proclaim when He sent them out to preach (Luke 9:2–6). What He meant by this Good News of the Kingdom, He explained to His disciples and to all His faithful followers in many parables, one of the most meaningful of these being that of the wedding feast.

C. The Father Calls Us to the Great Wedding Feast

"The Kingdom of heaven is like a king who made a wedding feast for his son. And he sent his servants to call in those invited to the feast . . . saying: Behold, I have prepared my dinner . . . everything is ready; come to the wedding feast". But they would not come. "Then he said to his servants: Go to the crossroads, and invite to the wedding feast whomever you shall find. And his servants went out into the roads and gathered all whom they found, both good and bad; and the wedding feast was filled with guests" (See Matt. 22:2–10).

This parable shows us the kingdom both in its final consummation and in its present stage of preparation. At the end of time, He will manifest His power and love with perfect clarity and fullness. Then will He glorify His Son, and with Him those of us who have responded to His invitation. The Kingdom of God in its final stage of completion is like a wedding feast, to the degree to which any earthly realities can in any way give us some faint notion of the incomparable delights and glories which the Father, in His love, has determined on from all eternity and made ready for His beloved children. In this heavenly wedding feast, God the Father is the King, Christ is the Bridegroom; we are not guests only, since the Bride is redeemed mankind; the new creation made perfect will be the banquet-hall. God wants to give all of us a share in this final manifestation of His divine power and love. For this reason has He sent His Son, Jesus Christ. Jesus has proclaimed the kingdom of God; He has redeemed us and made us children of God.

This kingdom is now still in its preparatory period. But, through Christ, it has already come to us. God now reigns as our loving Father, giving us a share in His own divine life. Christ, the divine Bridegroom, is already in our midst. In the Eucharistic banquet, we participate already in the eternal wedding feast. But the full glory of God's kingdom is still veiled. *Now we must decide: now we must prepare ourselves.* God's call is transmitted to us through Christ and His heralds, and we must respond to it by *Christian faith.* This is much more than a merely intellectual assent to some religious truths revealed to us by God. Faith is, finally, the grateful readiness of our Christian hearts to receive God's word as fully and actually true, and to act accordingly, to follow the loving invitation of the Father. To His love, which we have done nothing to deserve, we respond by our grateful love. In His unfathomable goodness, He has called us "into fellowship with his Son, Jesus Christ our Lord" (1 Cor. 1:9). We are to answer gratefully by our union with Christ. All our glory, all our riches are in Him.*

* On this point, see the new German Catechism, lesson 3: *The Good News of the Kingdom of God.*

Section I

The Eternal Love of God
For Us

A. God the Creator

From the very beginning, we should strive with all our skill to give to our students (catechumens, congregations, etc.) a truly magnificent idea of God. The decisive importance for any religious life, and particularly for the Christian life, of a realization of the overwhelming greatness of God, can hardly be sufficiently inculcated. This is the foundation of any religion worthy of the name. For religion essentially consist in the acknowledgment of the absolute excellence of God and of our complete dependence on Him. This is the first of the two pillars of the Christian religion:—the Great God is my Father in Christ! A lack of this foundation results in a lack of vigor in our entire religious life. No one wants to try to do great things for an insignificant God. We cannot rightly understand or appreciate the basic teachings of Christianity unless we first are possessed by a great idea of what God is. Without this, the thought of the grace of adoption as His children does not move us, sin does not frighten us, the Person of Christ does not attract us, His work does not appeal to us, heavenly life does not seem desirable.

In teaching about God the Creator, three principal truths must be inculcated at every opportunity:

1. The *reality and nearness* of God. God is to be thought of, not as a distant God Whom we know to exist, but as the *real* God, near to each of us. He is not an abstract idea, a postulate of philosophy; He is the Reality of realities. He influences our living at every moment, and we should therefore have Him always present to the eyes of our mind. "In Him we live and move and have our being" (Acts 17:28).

2. The *greatness* of God (His infinite majesty, perfection, immensity). His greatness should be shown, not by abstract reasoning, but vividly and concretely, through the teaching on creation, with examples from observation and the natural sciences (astronomy, physics, biology). Although God is so great, yet He loves me, a little creature; He created me out of pure love, He cares for me, and calls me to Himself. O wonderful mystery of love!

3. *Our absolute dependence on God.* I depend upon Him far more completely than a sunbeam on the sun, more than a new-born baby on its mother. He is our absolute master and Lord: "You are my God; In Your hands is my destiny" (Psalm 30). How foolish is any attempt to flee from Him—foolish since it is absolutely impossible, and even more foolish since no one loves me so much as does He.

First Instruction

The Eternal God and His Creation

Method: Historical-explanatory. The historical fact of creation should be set forth in an orderly way and explained at the same time. It is important here not to separate the narration from the explanation any more than is absolutely necessary. Although the instruction should follow a "historical" sequence, too much emphasis should not be given to the "works" of the individual days. These should be seen as vast spaces of time, and special mention made of those works of greater importance to us.

Viewpoint: "The heavens declare the glory of God, and the firmament proclaims His handiwork!" God's greatness and goodness are shown in the work of creation. It is the first step taken by the eternal love of God in our regard. How fitting and necessary it is that we should, in return, thank Him, love Him, serve Him!

Aim: Happy and grateful acknowledgement of the absolute dominion of God. Real acknowledgement, not mere assent. Truly You are the Lord! To serve You freely is my first duty and my special privilege. "Pay to the Lord the homage of your rejoicing, appear in His presence with glad hearts" (Psalm 99).

DOCTRINAL SUMMARY

A. THE ETERNAL GOD

Our teaching should begin with the presentation of the eternal God, Who possesses all things, Who is perfectly happy from all eternity. What a difference between us mortals, who yesterday did not exist, and the infinite eternal God, the "immortal King of the ages"! (1 Tim. 1:17).

Why did God create anything? Not out of any need of His, but because, in His inexpressible love, He wanted to communicate His goodness to us, and share His riches with us. From the beginning of creation, He thought of each of us, and prepared everything for us. Let us return love for Love!

B. The Creation of the World

"Let there be light and there was light." What "creating" means should be carefully described and explained. Use comparisons with human making. A carpenter makes a table: what is the difference between what he does and the creative activity of God? Here a mere definition explains nothing. The students must be brought to experience the wonder of what God alone can do. How much the dominion of God over His creatures differs from any human mastery over what we have made or rule. Our return, then, should be grateful and absolute submission.

He extended the heavens in His mind (cf. Isaias 40:22; Jer. 10:12; 51:15; Ps. 135:5). Behold the greatness of God! The teacher should have ready many examples using modern statistics about the number and size and vast distances between the stars. This greater-than-imaginable space is the "small" workshop of our God. He Himself cannot be contained by the heavens (3 Kings 8:24). How small we are in the face of the greatness of God! How wonderful, how fitting it is to serve so great a God! God planned all the marvels of creation, He "thought them out", He cares for all. All things are His.

He prepared the earth (Isaias 45:18), for us men, His children. He made it ready for us with fatherly love, with fatherly providence.

And He saw that all things were good (Gen. 1:25). He created them well, beautifully, abundantly, wisely. We also can see that they are good, and praise the Father who made everything so well. We praise You, O God! How can we express our gratitude and praise in deeds as well as words? By the *right use* of God's creatures, in accordance with the natures He has given them and has given us.

C. The Creation of Man

Let us make man (Gen. 1:26). The most solemn moment in the work of creation. The whole earth awaits its king and priest, who will be the crown of visible creation. All things are prepared for him.

Bearing Our image and likeness (Gen. 1:21). This is the true value of man, of each man. The more like God he is, the more perfect a man he is.

God formed man's body and created his soul. The whole man is *from* God—therefore the whole man is *for* God. If we owe gratitude to our parents, how much more to God! I give You thanks for the life You have given me. Gladly will I live my life, and may my joy in living and all my vitality be a continual thanksgiving. Body and soul soul, and the whole man ruled by God and ordered to His praise and —both are good and holy to God. The body should be ruled by the glory. All is Yours, my God, and by rightly using my soul and my body, I return them to you in grateful praise.

The first action of our first parents was prayer. Nothing is as fitting to man as to pray; to acknowledge from his whole heart the goodness and dominion of God. *Worship* is the highest and noblest act of man, and, even more, the goal of human life.

NOTES ON TEACHING THIS MATERIAL

1. Our negative purpose here is to overcome religious indifferentism and negligence. God really *is:* we cannot escape Him: we should *want* to fit ourselves into His plan for our happiness. Religious indifferentism is the worst spiritual disease of our times. So many people go to God only when they think they need His help or when they "feel" religious.

2. Today every definite idea of God and our relations to Him is frequently regarded as vain superstition. In instructing adults, the teacher or missionary needs to present the clear Christian idea of God as opposed to vague religiosity, "some higher Power", etc. Again, those young people and adults who are living in a non-Christian environment, in frequent conflict with adversaries of religion, need from time to time special conferences on our reasons for affirming God's existence, with answers to the usual objections. This is especially necessary for people of intelligence.

3. In missionary work, especially with neophytes and catechumens, we ought frequently to speak of the existence of the one true God, and of the foolishness and wickedness of idolatry. This first lesson, if clearly and fittingly given, should automatically strengthen our hearers' conviction of God's existence and absolute dominion. But also those who would never dream of adoring a god of wood or stone should be warned against the practical idolatry of living only for "security", "success", money, etc. and of venerating those who possess these things as if they were gods.

4. In tepid communities, the effect of this first lesson can be increased by one on the trial and punishment of the wicked angels. Not even the highest creatures God has made can live without Him, nor withdraw themselves from His service with impunity. A rational creature is able freely to neglect God and offend Him, but only at the price of the greatest damage to its own being. The eternal God can wait, the merciful and long-suffering God generally does wait for us to turn to Him; but in His own good time, He will most certainly demand an accounting.

5. With this lesson on God and His creation, it is not the mind alone that must be captured, but heart also, and the whole man directed

to the happy and constant service of God. These truths must be presented *clearly*, for our submission to God must be founded on firm and comprehensible reasons, if it is to endure. And they must be presented *beautifully* in such a way as to bring our hearers to love this great and wonderful God.

Second Instruction

The Elevation

The natural gifts God has given man splendidly demonstrate His love for us: His supernatural gifts show that love even more splendidly.

Method: Begin with the natural gifts given to our first parents, then the preternatural, then the supernatural. Why did God give them all these gifts so copiously, so magnificently? Because He had decreed to adopt our first parents as His children. A catechetical exposition of this material, unlike the scholastic one, should avoid all subtle inquiry into the nature of supernatural being. We wish to unfold above all the beauty and greatness of the heavenly gift.

Viewpoint: The inexpressible goodness and generosity of God. How wonderfully well He treated our first parents! How great was their obligation and their opportunity to thank Him unceasingly! (This forms the psychological preparation for the next lesson.)

Aim: A sense of truly filial gratitude. This attitude manifests itself in the prayer of God's children: "Abba, Father" (Rom. 8:15). From the very beginning, let us teach Christians to pray in a filial way to the Father. This is the classic form of Christian prayer, which ought to hold the primary place in our whole Christian life. For this essentially is the truly Christian life: continual filial prayer to the Father, by words and by living and acting as His children.

DOCTRINAL SUMMARY

A. The Paradise of Our First Parents

God made man the lord of visible creation, "to rule over it" (Gen. 1:28). Man is the vice-regent, the administrator of God. The first obligation of an administrator is fidelity (1 Cor. 4:2). We have to "render an account of our stewardship" (Luke 16:2). The guiding principles of our use of creatures should be given here: we are to *use* them according to the natures God has given them, *not abuse* them. We are to *use them, but not in an unlimited way.* Creatures should lead us to God, not separate us from Him by undue concern for them. Right use means to receive everything from His hand with gratitude, and to use things in His service. How many and great gifts He has given us in creation: with what great gratitude should we respond!

And God placed him in a garden of delights (Gen. 2:15). A vivid but restrained description of life in paradise should be given, remaining close to the data given us in Scripture. A wonderful life, with the companionship of God, happy and pleasant—no pain, no disease, no fear of death. A life worthy of man—no idleness, but free, enjoyable and effective work. Internal and external peace.

But the true paradise was in man himself. The garden was only a picture and an effect of the internal paradise. All these external gifts were given to our first parents because God had adopted them as His children. This gift of adoption is the greatest gift God can give His creatures. It is the principal gift, which necessarily and in due time brings with it all other gifts. It is the gift of God's pure generosity, and of such a nature that no creature can demand it as a right. Compare it with natural gifts, possessions, physical and mental talents. Do not use often the terms "supernatural life" or "sanctifying grace", but thoroughly explain the reality itself.*

Divine adoption is essentially superior to human adoption: it gives not only a name and a right, but real participation in the divine nature. It is one of the three greatest mysteries of our religion (the Trinity, the Incarnation, our adoption), from the theological point of view, still greater and more fundamental than the mystery of the Eucharist. We shall never be able to understand how we creatures are truly able in a completely real sense to participate in the divine life and yet remain creatures.

B. OUR PARADISE

The garden of paradise has been lost to man, but the internal paradise, far more beautiful and wonderful than the external one, now exists in the hearts of Christians. We Christians, and we alone, possess the greatest gift given to our first parents—divine adoption. How rich we are! Can we help being grateful! Our adoption is the guarantee that the gifts that flowed from it in the first paradise—the preternatural gifts of integrity, immortality, impassibility—will also be given to us in due time. And not only these joys of paradise, but higher and heavenly ones. We are immensely rich now, but our riches are for the most

---

* As an example of how to explain the "supernatural order" without using the words "supernatural" or even "grace," see *On Our Way,* by Sister Maria de la Cruz.

part an internal, hidden treasure, that we cannot be naturally aware of. They must, for the time, be believed in. Lord, I believe. *I believe in my own blessedness. I believe in Your love.*

NOTES ON TEACHING THIS MATERIAL

1. Here we mention for the first time the great gift of our religion: divine life, the gift of sonship. From now on, we should take every opportunity of inspiring our hearers with the greatest possible appreciation of this supreme gift. This initial teaching on the divine life will be complemented especially by the teaching on Baptism.

2. A special instruction on Matrimony may easily and fruitfully be connected with this lesson, or given separately. Christians everywhere should be much more perfectly instructed concerning Matrimony than many of them are now. The teaching on paradise offers a good opportunity for instruction on the institution, purpose, sanctity ("What God has joined together, let no man put asunder" or violate), and properties (unity and indissolubility) of marriage. But in order that the teaching on Matrimony be complete, it should be complemented by the "mystery of Christ and the Church". See Lesson 19 on Marriage.

Third Instruction

The Fall: Original Sin

To the wonderful goodness of the Father, our first parents responded by foul and disastrous ingratitude; they destroyed their own blessedness by their sin of disobedience.

Method: Here again, this should be historical.

Viewpoint: See the detestable ingratitude of our first parents. Their sin is the prototype of all mortal sin. Here we see our own image as in a mirror.

Aim: A truly religious *awareness of the malice of sin,* a real hatred of sin, the hope of forgiveness through the Redeemer, a serious will to satisfy for our sins.

DOCTRINAL SUMMARY

Our first parents were greatly blessed by God. How would we expect them to have responded? How did they?

A. The History of the First Sin

God gave a special command to our first parents in order to test them. He wished to give them heaven, a perfect paradise, after their life in the earthly paradise, but not without a trial. They had to merit the perfect blessedness of sons of God by obedience and submission to Him. And we must do so also. The command given to our first parents was easy to obey in every way. How easily could they—and so also we—have continued to be happy. For God had given them paradise and the gift of sonship for us also.

Our first parents were tempted by the devil, who hated them and their happiness. God wants us to be happy; the devil wants us to be miserable. God loves us, He speaks the truth to us; the devil hates us and tries to deceive us. The devil contradicts what God has said. To be tempted is not to sin. But Eve played with temptation and argued with the devil.

Our first parents, deceived by the devil, sinned grievously. What did they do? *Knowingly and freely,* they transgressed a serious command of God. Although they had received such great blessings, they were not content; they wished to be "like God", to be independent, a law to themselves. They deliberatedly rebelled against their most loving Father.

This is the essence of a mortal sin (in this supernatural order): the fully deliberate rebellion of a proud and ungrateful son of God against the most loving Father. Every mortal sin of its nature entails *abominable ingratitude* (abuse of God's blessings), *overweening pride* ("like God"), and *disobedience* ("I will not serve").

B. THE DISASTER OF SIN

As soon as they sinned, our first parents *lost the paradise of the soul.* They had cast God out of their minds and hearts; He left them, and darkness came over their souls.

The all-knowing God *called them to be judged.* They wished to hide. But God sees all things. We cannot flee from God. Did they come to their senses and seek forgiveness? No, they tried to excuse themselves.

The dreadful consequence of their sin is that they lost once and forever the happiness of paradise for themselves and for their children. Comparisons can be made here with a father who squanders his family's inheritance, or the servant of a king, who wastes the treasures the king has given him for himself and his children. God wished to have us receive from our parents the treasure first given to Adam. But that treasure is gone. Such comparisons bring out fairly clearly two important points: 1) Original sin is not a wicked act performed by Adam's descendants; it is the privation of the divine treasure (divine life) which, according to God's original plan, we should possess. But personal sins are our own bad deeds. 2) Adam's *personal* sin had this disastrous effect on us because he was given divine life not only for himself, but for all his descendants. This is not the case with the divine life we receive at Baptism; we cannot hand it on to our children. From the time of Adam on, human children are no longer born as sons of God, but as children of wrath (Eph. 2:3). So the *greatest gift* of God to man is divine adoption; the *greatest calamity* is loss of this divine life, mortal sin.

C. The Only Hope for Man After Sin

God in His loving mercy promises a Savior to our first parents. In the midst of disaster, when they had rejected God, God consoles them. Thus for us, the only consolation and hope of the sinner is Christ, the Savior of the world! Given courage by this hope, our first parents came to their senses, and did earnest and prolonged penance.

NOTES ON TEACHING THIS MATERIAL

In basic instruction of beginners (first missionary catechesis, first graders in school), the rest of Old Testament history is omitted. But in adult classes where time permits (in missionary countries: in larger communities which are visited oftener, and in the central missionary station), and in the second grade in schools and beyond, more of the Old Testament is to be given. It is always to be treated as our "teacher in Christ", with special emphasis on the persons and events which clearly show us how God Himself prepared for and foretold the "mystery of Christ".

In this connection, the Old Testament *types* that foreshadow and describe the Christian order are to be given very special attention. We must first present these types in their own context and with their own immediate significance, and then show their typical meaning and function. The most important types are: Adam, Abel, Noe, Abraham and Isaac, Joseph, Moses, David; and among the events of the Bible, the Creation, the Flood, the Covenant made with Abraham, and, above all, the main events of Exodus from the liberation of God's people from slavery in Egypt to their settlement in the Promised Land, and the return from the Babylonian exile; the institutions of the priesthood and sacrifices; the presence of God with His people in the Ark (the Tabernacle, the Temple, Jerusalem). With this teaching, we should carefully explain those passages from the Old Testament that are most important for an understanding of the Liturgy.

In teaching the Old Testament, we should often point out the imperfection of its institutions, and of individuals and of the people's understanding of God and His Plan. The reason is obvious: it was the time of preparation. Christ, Who came to perfect all things, had not yet come.

B. The Doctrine of Christ the Savior

The teaching about Christ the Savior is the heart and center of our message, and to it the catechist should give his greatest care and diligence. "This is eternal life—that they may know thee, the only true God, and Jesus Christ whom thou hast sent" (John 17:3). The doctrine of Christ our Savior not only gives us the knowledge of the Son of God, but it shows us the Father Himself in an entirely new light. Here especially, we must lead our hearers from the knowledge they are gaining of Christ to a further knowledge of the Father.

What is the essence of the doctrine we are to teach and explain? Jesus Christ—the Son of God—the Savior. (Here we might bring in the ancient Christian symbol, the fish, showing that the Greek word *ichthus* contains the initials of the fundamental formula. *Iesus Christos— Theou Uois—Soter.*

a) As to the *personality of Christ:* — *Who is He?* He is at once true God and true Man: one Christ, the eternal Son of the Father, born in time of the Virgin Mary.

b) As to the *work of Christ—what does He do?* He was made the "Son of Man" to make us sons of God ". . . who was delivered up for our sins and rose again for our justification" (Rom. 4:25). He not only destroyed sin, but communicated to us in abundance the new and true divine life, opening again the gates of paradise. He instituted a new order of things: "The former things have passed away; behold they are made new!" (2 Cor. 5:17). In this new creation, there is a new man, renewed in Christ, a "new creature in Christ" (2 Cor. 5:17), and a new way of living, "so that we all may walk in newness of life" (Rom. 6:4). Christ is the new and perfect Adam, the leader and head of a renewed human race. Just as all our misery comes from our physical oneness of race with the first Adam, and from our personal imitation of his example, so all our salvation and happiness flow from our real spiritual oneness with Christ through Baptism, and from our continual and increasing daily transformation into Christ (the Christian life).

c) In our teaching, the person and the work of Christ must always be shown to be intimately connected, even though at one time we stress doctrine concerning His Person (the mystery of the Incarnation) and, at another, doctrine concerning His work (the paschal mysteries).

Method in which all these lessons should be taught: Without any haste. This teaching, like a long-lasting and fructifying rain, should water, penetrate and fructify the ground of the Christian heart. We should give the impression that we are always eager to speak about Christ, His most sacred Person, His life, Passion and Resurrection, and to remain close to Him, gazing at Him with deep love. Our hearers should become aware that it is only with difficulty that we can tear ourselves away from this subject of our teaching, and of how we cannot help returning to it at every opportunity to this, the fundamental theme of our Christian teaching and preaching.

Our teaching should use the method of concrete historical narration. By telling the life of Christ in a concrete and attractive way, we can unfold and explain the "mystery" of Christ. Thus we can avoid the abstract dogmatic exposition which simple people and children cannot follow, and avoid also *mere* historical narration which only gives the outward events of sacred history and does not rise to their inner divine meaning. It is by means of this re-telling of the life of Christ, above all, that we desire to draw the hearts of men to the love of God. So our narration should strive to be pleasant, fervent, clear, and filled with true and reverent affection for our Lord. We should avoid any unnecessary discussions about this inexpressible mystery, and rather proclaim the "mystery of Christ" with apostolic eagerness, and explain it with great reverence.

Viewpoint: "God so loved the world . . ." (John 3:16) ". . . giving us such and so great a Redeemer" (The Exultet).

Aim: to arouse deep and habitual gratitude to God the Father. To lead our hearers toward a truly "eucharistic" life. Unfailing thanksgiving for our elevation in Christ is of the very essence of the Christian life. To lead our hearers to a full and completely personal giving of themselves to God (faith, love, fidelity): "Whether we live or whether we die, we are the Lord's" (Rom. 14:8, see also 2 Cor. 5:15).

THE SECOND EVE

Our teaching concerning the Blessed Virgin, the second Eve, should be harmoniously interwoven with, and duly subordinated to, the teaching concerning Christ the Savior, the new Adam. We should present this teaching in a completely Christocentric way: all the perfection and beauty of the Mother comes from the Son, and leads us to the Son. St. Paul's principle applies here: "Have this mind in you which was also in Christ Jesus": we want to share in Christ's own estimation of His Mother, and so we speak of her with gladness and filial affection. But we should be careful to present true Marian dogma, entirely drawn from Christology, the doctrine of the new Eve who is of such great importance because of her intimate connection with the work of our salvation. Here again we should remember the principle "not too many words, but much teaching". The perfection of preaching and teaching about Our Lady does not consist in an extended and separate treatment, but in allowing our teaching concerning her mainly to flow from that about her Son. If we properly present our instructions on the Person and work of Christ, we shall at the same time instruct our hearers in the dignity and the work of the Blessed Virgin.

NOTE TO THE FOLLOWING LESSONS
CONCERNING CHRIST

It is not difficult to set out the most important doctrines that should always be taught and preached concerning Christ the Savior. But this material can be presented in many ways. The choice of individual topics should be made by the teacher according to the circumstances of time and place under which each instruction is to be given. For example, during Advent and Christmas time, Christology should be considered mainly under the aspect of the Incarnation (the Person of Christ); from Septuagesima through Eastertime, we should think more of the work of Christ.

The method should always be historical-explanatory. First the Bible narrative should be presented, for example of the birth or the death of Christ; then its religious (and dogmatic) meaning explained and applied to the lives of our hearers. *Narration, explanation, application* are the principal divisions to be made, either in the whole catechesis, or in its chief points. This method is most especially to be used when time and circumstances allow a more detailed catechesis on Christ and His Work.

Those historical catecheses on the life of Christ are to be chosen which are most suitable to the liturgical season, which are charged with dogmatic significance, and which therefore offer the best opportunity for explaining clearly and effectively the mystery of Christ. But in every kind of teaching, the *entire mystery of Christ* must be explained in the course of these instructions in its basic phases.

Here we are selecting these five topics as containing the most important phases of Christ's life and work: the Incarnation, the Nativity, the Public Life, the Passion and Death, the Resurrection and Ascension.

Fourth Instruction

The Incarnation

Method: Historical-explanatory.

Aim: A clear and illuminating answer to the question: Who is Christ? The essence of the doctrine of the Incarnation, and a religious understanding of the wonderful and supreme blessing of the Incarnation, such as to be an effective incitement to Christian love.

DOCTRINAL SUMMARY

At last came the "fullness of time" (Gal. 4:6; Eph. 1:10), so long desired by the human race from the time of the Fall. A brief and simple summary of the Old Testament should be given in its broad outlines: how men sinned increasingly; they founded various earthly kingdoms and cultures and failed to find God. Only a few "just" men and women even among God's chosen people awaited every day more eagerly the promised Messias. Now at last He comes. Here we should try to awaken our hearers to a personal desire for redemption.

A. THE ANNOUNCEMENT OF THE INCARNATION (LUKE 1:26–38)

We see a girl, most extraordinary in virtue, noble in race, herself most humble and living in a humble condition. We see the reverence of the angel. What was his message? What is happening? The will of God is being announced to the Virgin. God had chosen her as the virgin Mother of the Messias. Each sentence of the conversation should be clearly explained, and all subordinated to the aim of this lesson, without any superfluous and extended moral applications. The humble consent of the Virgin . . . her great part in this greatest work of God, the work of the Incarnation and the Redemption.

B. THE INCARNATION

We should give a reverent explanation of this inexpressible mystery. Who is this Son of the Virgin? The Son of the eternal Father, the God-Man. God from all eternity, becoming a man in time; according to His divine nature having only a Father, according to His human nature, only a Mother. He is the second Divine Person, Who at the moment of the Incarnation assumed to the divine nature which He had from all eternity, a human nature taken from the Virgin. We can here use, with care, the example of putting a garment, pointing out the deficiency of this example. The Word's union with our human nature is a much more intimate one than that between a man and his clothing.

The human nature not only belongs to the Word in some way or other, it belongs to the Word in the intimate way in which my body is truly "mine".

C. THE CONSEQUENCES OF THIS MYSTERY FOR US

These should at once be explained, clearly and attractively. *Because our Savior is God,* we can hope for everything from His Redemption. The eternal Son of the Father can lead us sinners back to the Father. *Because our Savior is Man,* He really is our Brother, He really belongs to our family; He feels with us and for us, He can "have compassion on our infirmities" (Heb. 4:15, cf also 5:2). *Because our Savior is the God-Man,* He is by His very make-up, by being what He is, the Mediator between God and men. This Savior is able to bridge, to close the abyss which sin opened up between God and men. Christ is thus the "Pontifex", (literally *Bridge-maker*), our High Priest, since He combines perfect divinity and humanity in His Own Person.

This conclusion naturally appeals to the Christian heart, and awakens great joy and thanksgiving for so great a Redeemer.

NOTE ON TEACHING THIS MATERIAL

The presentation of this material given here presupposes hearers who have already been given some elementary instruction, and therefore it at once sets out and explains the mystery of the Incarnation. In giving elementary catechesis, several lessons are needed on Christ Himself. The doctrines of the Incarnation and Redemption should be developed in the course of several classes.

Fifth Instruction

The Birth of Christ

Method: Historical-explanatory.

Aim: To complete the previous lesson, which answered the question: Who and what is our Savior? This lesson explains further *why He came,* and why He came in such a humble and hidden way. This lesson calls for our imitation.

DOCTRINAL SUMMARY

A. HOW CHRIST CAME

The first description of Christ's birth should be reverent, filled with devotion and sincere love, and free of any softness, sentimentality or exaggeration. How winning is His loveableness, how awesome His helplessness, how amazing His humility and His willingness to be humiliated, foregoing the honor due Him. Here appears the guiding principle of His life on earth: "He emptied Himself . . . taking the form of a servant . . . making Himself obedient even to death." (Phil. 2:7 ff). And already the complementary aspect of this principle shines out: "Wherefore God exalted Him" (Phil. 2:9). This is the royal road to true glory, the only road in the order of salvation. Many holy people whom Our Lord had chosen for Himself shared in this humble and hidden way of life: Mary, Joseph, the shepherds, the wise men . . . Do you wish to follow?

B. Why Christ Came in This Way

See the work of the second Adam. The first Adam, by his pride and disobedience, brought calamity upon us and separated us from the Father. The second Adam, by His humility and obedience, leads us back to the Father again. The second Adam renounced what was due Him in order to reconcile us to the Father. The first Adam had sought himself, desiring to "be like God," in such a way as to forget God; the second Adam forgot Himself in seeking the Father's glory. The purpose of His life is "Glory to God in the highest, and on earth, peace . . ." nothing for Himself.

"I announce to you glad tidings of great joy" (Luke 2:11). Joy and thanksgiving for such and so great a Savior, Who from the very beginning loved us so much. Love for love! Let us follow Him faithfully and devotedly. He does not seek anything we have, He seeks ourselves and our happiness.

Sixth Instruction

The Public Life of Christ

In the catechesis on the public life of Our Lord, we should select those incidents from the New Testament which most particularly present Our Lord as Teacher and as the divine wonder-worker (for example, the healing of the paralytic, the raising of Lazarus, the promise of the Eucharist, etc.). As an example, we give here a lesson on the promise of the Eucharist.

Method: Historical-explanatory.

Aim: To found firmly and to deepen our hearers' faith in Jesus Christ, the Son of God, and to arouse them to a personal love of Christ and devoted following of Him. Here we want to show *what faith in*

Jesus Christ means, and how important it is. Christian faith is, by its nature, our whole-hearted and positive answer to God's revelation. The revelation of the Father, communicated to us through Christ, is much more than a statement of truths; it is, basically, the Father's gracious invitation, calling us to come to Him, to share His life. The *full Christian faith* that Christ asks of us in the Father's name, is essentially more than mere intellectual *assent;* it is by its nature complete *consent,* whole-hearted readiness to accept and to follow His divine message. Faith includes, to be sure, the humble submission of our intellect to what we cannot fully understand, but faith is much more than this: it is the submission of our whole being to Christ's Gospel, with the firm will to follow Him. How beautiful is the faith expressed in St. Peter's answer, given in the Bible story of this lesson: "Lord to whom shall we go? Thou hast the words of eternal life."

DOCTRINAL SUMMARY

A. CHRIST PREPARES FOR THE PROMISE OF THE EUCHARIST

The multiplication of the loaves. The power and skill of Christ's teaching. He teaches so well because He has the most perfect understanding of what He teaches. "On God no man ever laid his eyes; the only-begotten Son, Who rests in the Father's bosom, has Himself been the interpreter." (John 1:18). Everyone ought to hear Him because He is sent to all. His goodness: "I have compassion on the crowd". His divine power which so magnificently proves the truth of His teaching. What kind of a kingdom does He bring? He refused to be made an earthly king; He is the king of truth, Who wishes to rule in our hearts and souls. His aim is not to found an earthly temporal national kingdom, but the eternal spiritual kingdom of God. He desires to bring mankind back to full and free acknowledgement of the Father's lordship, to perfect filial submission to the Father's holy will, so that the Father may reveal His love, His power and His glory in us.

The miracle on the sea: Christ is the Lord of nature. He is not subject to the laws of nature, He is their master. See how by this miracle, as well as by the multiplication of the loaves, He prepares us for faith in the Eucharist. Christ often exposes His followers to dangers and trials in this life, but He always remains present with us, comforting, strengthening, and "visiting" us just at the right time.

B. THE PROMISE OF THE EUCHARIST

Christ began by speaking about faith, which is the first and most fundamental step on our part towards participation in the Mystery of Christ. Then later He spoke of the Eucharist itself, which is, during the time of our pilgrimage on earth, the most perfect participation in His Mystery. Sincere faith is the essential condition for fruitful reception of the Sacrament. Here we should present, not a detailed exegesis of the whole discourse, but a clear exposition of the meaning of the promise. The Eucharist is a great mystery, far surpassing our intellectual powers. The only reason for believing it is Christ Himself and His divine power. Like Christ's immediate hearers on this occasion, we also have to decide whether or not we desire to follow Christ with complete faith.*

Fruits to be obtained from this Lesson. "Lord, to whom shall we go? Thou hast the words of eternal life. We also believe and we know that Thou art Christ, the Son of the living God" (John 6:69).

NOTE ON THE TEACHING OF THIS MATERIAL

Since many adversaries of the Church try to persuade us in various ways that faith in Jesus Christ, the Son of God, is superstitious belief in a foolish fable, missionaries, and also pastors and teachers should from time to time set forth and clearly explain our reasons for affirming the Messias-ship and Divinity of Christ. In such sermons or instructions, we should show briefly:

1. Whence we obtain our certain knowledge of Christ: the Gospels are trustworthy documents.

2. What the historical facts tell us about Christ, His Person and His teaching. Christ proved His testimony to Himself by unquestionable miracles.

3. How we today, after twenty centuries, can, safely and without danger of being misled, draw on the teaching of Christ the Church. See the first note on teaching the material in the first instruction (p. 92).

Seventh Instruction

The Passion and Death of Christ

Method: Historical-explanatory. The Passion and Death of Christ should be depicted reverently and with devotion, but also discreetly: and, at the same time, their meaning and import should be clearly brought out. As we present the lesson here, we suppose that there is time

---

* It might be useful to remind our readers that "faith" here means not only so-called "dogmatic" faith, as the term is mainly used in theology today, but faith in its full sense (fides adequate sumpta) as it is understood in Scripture and in the writings of the Fathers. Theologians may need to make further distinctions, and to consider faith in a special way, as it includes intellectual assent. But in our catechetical apostolate, we must never forget that we are sent to propose and to foster faith in its fullness, that is, living faith.

for no more than one instruction on this subject. When more than a single lesson can be given, one might be predominantly historical and descriptive and another more dogmatic, or several might be given on the separate main events. In some places, it is customary to preach on the Way of the Cross. Such a method of preaching on the Passion has some particular advantages: it connects doctrine with the pictured stations on the one hand, and with both oral and mental prayer on the other. But we should take great care to make sure that the exposition of Christ's passion and death does not consist merely in a description of what He suffered, with pious moral applications. We should, instead, clearly set out the *dogmatic reasons* why Christ suffered all these things: and how our own way to glory and true perfection consists in the constant and brave following of Christ: "To die and live together with Christ" (cf. Rom. 6), "I die daily" (1 Cor. 15:31). We should carefully see to it that in any explanation of the Way of the Cross (the Stations), *the fruits of Christ's passion and death* are clearly set forth. The most important station is *the final one, the fifteenth, the Resurrection.*

In preaching the Passion, let us imitate the Church, which always organically connects the Resurrection with the Passion—see the Preface of the Cross, and also the Easter Preface. We notice the same union in Our Lord's own way of speaking of His Passion. See, for example, His predictions of His sufferings and death as given in Matthew 16:11, 17:33, 20:19. Each time He adds and emphasizes: "But on the third day, He will rise again."

Viewpoint: The work of redemption is the most excellent work of the *generosity and mercy of God.* "God so loved the world that He gave His only-begotten Son that those who believe in Him may not perish, but may have life everlasting" (John 3:16). "He Who has not spared even His own Son but has delivered Him for us all, how can He fail to grant us also all things with Him?" (Rom. 8:32). "In this has the love of God been shown in our case, that God has sent His only-begotten Son into the world that we may live through Him. In this is the love, not that we have loved God, but that He has loved us, and sent His Son to be a propitiation for our sins . . ." (1 John 4:9ff). "But God commends His charity towards us, because when as yet we were sinners, Christ died for us" (Rom. 5:8). We should notice here the important point that in all of these texts, the wonderful love of God the Father is most particularly emphasized.

Principal Fruit of this Instruction: Not a loving feeling of compassion, even though such an emotion is greatly to be desired, but the resolution to surrender ourselves perfectly and fully to the love of Christ, and to show profound and habitual gratitude to Christ and the Father, and also to have the most unshakeable confidence in Them (Rom. 8:32). The Cross shows us clearly both the horror of sin and the value of human life, and the wonder of God's love. The complete fruit of this lesson should be: a horror of sin, true and sincere conversion, appreciation of the heavenly blessings which Christ purchased for us at so great a price; the complete giving of ourselves to the love and service of God (active participation in the sacrifice of Christ).

DOGMATIC SUMMARY

A more dogmatic type of instruction may be presented with good results in addition to the explanation of the Way of the Cross or other historical catecheses on the Passion of Christ. This more dogmatic instruction completes the historical ones (and may even replace them if there is time for only one lesson). It can be outlined according to these points:

A. Who Suffered for Us?

The most *innocent Son of God* Himself, our most loving Brother, "For our sakes He (the Father) made Him to be sin Who knew nothing of sin, so that in Him we might become the justice of God" (2 Cor. 5:21). Here we should touch only lightly on the idea of vicarious satisfaction, only to the degree necessary for properly considering the second point.

B. What Did He Suffer for Us?

We should select those mysteries of the Passion which clearly emphasize the greatness and the intensity of the Passion, for example Gethsemane, the scourging, Calvary. Christ sacrificed everything for us. Blood for blood, life for life, death for death, love for love, all for all (Fr. Luke Etlin, O.S.B.).

C. Why Did Christ Suffer for Us?

1) *To satisfy for our sins.* In explaining vicarious satisfaction, let us not dwell very long on its juridical aspects, but spend far more time in praising the *divine wisdom* which is most beautifully shown in the very manner of our redemption, and which so perfectly unites the demands of *divine love and divine justice.* Let us point out the superabundance of the redemption, for "where sin did abound, grace did the more abound" (Rom. 5:20). We should bring out the fact that we must be united with Christ in order that His abundant satisfaction may be fruitful for us. A merely juridical consideration of His satisfying for our sins—the idea that the insult to God's glory given by sin was abundantly compensated for by the satisfaction offered by Christ; there-

fore God should be quite content, and we ourselves are free of all obligations—such an idea is false and very harmful. Only that man who through grace is vitally united with Christ crucified, and who puts on the spirit of Christ making satisfaction for sin, will have a share in the fruits of the Cross. *We must make satisfaction together with Christ.* Only through our oneness with Christ making satisfaction for our sins, does His satisfaction become ours. "But if anyone does not have the spirit of Christ, he does not belong to Christ" (Rom. 8:9).

2) *In order to give us new life.* Christ died that we may live. He is the grain of wheat that died in order to bring forth fruit (John 12:23–25). It was because of the disobedience of the first Adam that the Father excluded us from the family of the sons of God; it is because of the obedience of the second Adam that He receives us again and invites us once more to share in the benefits of Christ. The cross of Christ is the tree of life in the midst of the new paradise, the Church. The new order, in this life, must always have the quality of reparation— of Christian penance. And, while our period of trial endures, we are not given the delightful gifts of the first paradise. But the gift we do possess, here and now, the gift of divine life, far surpasses that given in the first paradise. Just as the second Adam is far superior to the first, so also the grace of Christ far surpasses the grace of paradise *"O happy fault!"*

D. How Did Christ Suffer for Us?

He suffered with perfect freedom, with wonderful patience, with pure love of God and of us. In giving popular instructions, this point may better be combined with point B., above. Christ's freedom, patience and love will shine out of themselves from a proper description of His Passion.

E. For Whom Did He Suffer?

For all men who desire to receive His redemption. He does not force us. No one who is unwilling is redeemed. He suffered for each one of us, and with a completely individual love, even though we were still sinners . . . "who loved me and gave Himself up for me" (Gal. 2:20).

Eighth Instruction
The Resurrection and Ascension

Method: Historical-explanatory. First, describe vividly the fact of the resurrection (narration), then show the import of this triumph (explanation and application).

Viewpoint: "Therefore God also has exalted Him, and has bestowed upon Him the Name that is above every name . . . " (Phil. 2:9–11). Just as in the life of Christ, so also in the Christian life: death and sacrifice are not the final stage, but an intermediate one on the way to final triumph and joy. The Christian religion is *the religion of true life, light and beatitude.*

Aim: "We give Thee thanks for Thy great glory . . ." (*Gloria* of the Mass). The principal attitude of those who belong to our religion of light should be one of joy and gratitude for the great glory given to us in Christ, all redounding to the glory of the Father. The victory of Christ is our victory; the glory of Christ our glory; the life of Christ our life.

Even though we thus speak primarily of the *soteriological import-ance* of the Resurrection, we should clearly indicate its apologetical importance also.

DOCTRINAL SUMMARY

A. The Fact of the Resurrection

What a difference from Good Friday! Then the enemies of Christ seemed to be victorious; now Christ triumphs, and completely. Even His enemies cannot deny His triumph. Truly "He has made all things new!" We should here describe concretely the victory of Christ by a vivid narration of the Gospel facts.

B. The Importance of the Resurrection

1) "He was foreordained Son of God by an act of power . . . by resurrection from the dead" (Rom. 1:4). Three days before His enemies had mocked Him: "If you are the Son of God, come down from the cross. If He is the king of Israel, let Him come down from the cross here and now, and we will believe in Him" (see Matt. 27:40–42). But Christ went down even to the world of the dead, and then arose to life. *Truly He is the Son of God!* And all His preaching is true. Lord, I believe. By Your resurrection, You have conquered unbelief. With the once unbelieving St. Thomas, I adore You: "My Lord and my God!" (John 20:23).

2) *"God has exalted Him and given Him a name that is above every name . . ."* (Phil. 2:9). Now God the Father gives to His beloved Son that full and perfect glory which Christ Himself had renounced when He became man, emptying Himself and taking on the form of a servant. This glory of the resurrection is the fitting reward of the humiliation He freely accepted for us. Truly "we give Thee thanks for

Thy great glory". Let us rejoice in the victory and glory of our Brother and Lord! Your joy is our joy, Your glory ours!

3) ". . . Christ has risen from the dead, the first fruit of those who have fallen asleep" (1 Cor. 15:20). The resurrection of Christ is *our resurrection,* because the life of the Head is the life of the members (Rom. 6; 1 Cor. 15). This unfailing life, this glorification and "diviniza tion" of the entire man, which we contemplate with the admiration in the risen Christ—this will be ours also. And it has already begun in us. Here on earth, this heavenly life is invisible. But at the resurrection from the dead it will become fully apparent. This life belongs to us only through union with Christ, and is subject to the same law as His: it must be the fruit of our dying with Him. This is the life of God's children, which Christ confers upon us in Baptism and the other sacraments by intimate personal union, the life which He purchased by His own obedience unto death. "But if we are sons, we are heirs also: heirs indeed of God and joint heirs with Christ, provided, however, we suffer with him that we may also be glorified with him. For I reckon that the sufferings of the present time are not worthy to be compared with the glory to come that will be revealed in us" (Rom. 8:17–18).

How rich we Christians are!—Whatever our lot in this life may be, we are rich in our union with Christ. The pattern of our life is this: to die, and to rise with Him. Already here on earth, we are to live the life of Christ. "If you have risen with Christ, seek the things that are above . . . not the things that are on earth . . ." (Col. 3:1ff— the Epistle of the Paschal night, directed above all to the newly-baptized).

The Ascension of Our Lord

A special lesson on the Ascension, whenever possible, should be given during the Easter season. And if, in a regular course of lessons, there is no time for a special lesson on this subject, then in the teaching on the Resurrection we should clearly show that the Ascension is the fitting and glorious conclusion of Christ's life, the crown of His victory. The human life, which from its first moment was lived entirely for the Father, is fittingly consummated in life with the Father, at His right hand. Through the Ascension of the Head, the meaning of the life of Christ, and of our life also, is made wonderfully clear. "I came forth from the Father, and have come into the world. Again I leave the world and go to the Father" (John 16:28). "Born of God" in Baptism (John 1:13; 3:5ff), we must suffer many things, as did Christ, during our pilgrimage on earth, and we must follow Him toward our final perfect union with our most loving Father. There in heaven is our paradise, far more beautiful than the first earthly one, the paradise of the children of God which Christ reopened to us by His victory. There He already enjoys perfect happiness and glory, and there, with a kind of divine impatience, He awaits us, His brothers, His fellow-soldiers, members of His body. "Father, I will that there where I am, they also whom Thou has given Me may be with Me . . ." (John 17:24). He is preparing a place for us with loving care (John 14:3) and especially by sending the Holy Spirit to us from heaven (John 16:7).

Method: If a special lesson can be given, the method should be historical-explanatory. First the narration of the historical fact, then the explanation and application of the doctrine.

Aim: "That we also may dwell in mind among heavenly things" (from the Collect of the Feast). That even here and now "our conversation may be in heaven" (Phil. 3:20). That the contemplation in faith of eternal life may lift up our hearts: "Where your treasure is, there will your heart be also" (Luke 12:34).

The Doctrine of the Church

Our teaching on the Church, which is the *continuation and the fruit of the Redemption,* is most fittingly placed immediately after the teaching on Christ the Savior. It is better to give this teaching here, rather than after that on the Holy Spirit, because this latter presupposes the doctrine on the Church, and also perfects it. The faithful are already accustomed to this order through the historical catechesis. The Church, instituted by Christ, and born on the Cross, is vivified and strengthened by the Holy Spirit. But of course it is also true that a full understanding of the Church requires an understanding of the doctrine of the Holy Spirit. The two cannot be separated.

Christ is the Savior of all men at all times. Through His successors, He teaches, sanctifies and directs all those who live on earth after His own earthly life had ended. See the "Christian" aspect of the hierarchy: "As the Father has sent me, I also send you" (John 20:21). Christ—the Apostles—Bishops—priests. The most important point to be made here is the Christocentric foundation of the hierarchy. When anyone grasps this fundamental principle, he will have no great difficulties with the various dogmas that more accurately determine a hierarchic power. The good Christian acknowledges, honors, hears and follows Christ Himself in the hierarchy. This hierarchical aspect of the Church, which should already be familiar to the faithful from their elementary instruction, is now to be filled out in two ways.

1.   Christ came to save all men, to restore the whole human race. Those who actually follow Him constitute the *new family of God,* that is, the Church (considered under its passive aspect). This fellowship, this community, like that of a family, should, of course, be experienced before it is explained; and here we see the importance of liturgical and community life. This doctrine of our fellowship in Christ should be clearly taught even to children, and should be frequently preached to the adult laity.

We Christians do not constitute a merely external society; what unites us is not a merely juridical bond, or the fact that together we attend certain ceremonies, or that we share a common purpose to be achieved by united external action. The ultimate reason for our intimate union with one another in the Church is our supernatural union with Christ, and, in Christ, with all His members. For we "are one body in Christ, but severally members of one another" (Rom. 12:5). We are the branches forming one supernatural organism with Him Who is the true Vine (cf. John 45:1ff).

2.   Both Christ Himself (John 15:12ff) and St. Paul infer from our unity in Christ the fact that we have a clear obligation to collaborate with one another (e.g., 1 Cor. 12; Rom. 12:4ff) and to love one another in Christ. To "love one another as I have loved you" is the teaching that Christ brought out from His simile on the Vine and the branches.

In the Church, as in any well-developed organism, the functions of the individual members differ from one another, but there are no merely passive members. We Christians not only share in the fruits of the Redemption in the Church, but are actively to collaborate with Christ in the work of redeeming and sanctifying the world, that is, in bringing it back to the Father. This is the active Christian aspect of the Church.

This Christian activity is of paramount importance, particularly in mission regions and in countries, like the United States, where Catholics are a minority. Each Christian is, according to his circumstances, to be another Christ, and therefore, an effective missionary. In all places where Catholics are a minority, the danger exists of an exaggerated or pharisaical separation of Christians from non-Catholics. To the degree that it is not possessed by the apostolic spirit, Christianity is not truly Christian—for it lacks the characteristic note of "catholicity", which consists essentially in the tendency to become ever more widespread and universal. The saying applies here: "If anyone does not have the spirit of Christ, he does not belong to Christ."

These two main principles concerning the Church form the material of the following instructions, which should be presented to the people with particular clarity and care. Our purpose here is above all to indicate the order and the manner in which these central ideas may most easily be presented.

Ninth Instruction

The Church in its Active Aspect —
Our Mother, the Church

This lesson deals with the hierarchical Church; the one that follows will deal with the active participation of the laity.

Method: Historical-explanatory. Among the many New Testament incidents that are related to our present material, the narration of the sending out of the Apostles (Matt. 28:16-20) seems most appropriate.

Viewpoint: "As the Father has sent Me, so I also send you" (John 20:21). "On behalf of Christ, therefore, we are acting as ambassadors" (2 Cor. 5:20).

Aim: The cultivation of a deep religious reverence for the hierarchical Church, as for *Christ Himself*. Gratitude for the mission of the Apostles and their successors. Filial submission—faithful cooperation.

DOCTRINAL SUMMARY

A. A BRIEF SUMMARY OF CHRIST'S OWN MISSION

The work of Christ, the second Adam, was to found a new human race, a new family of God's children, and to lead men back to the Father. This work is threefold: to teach, to sanctify (that is, actually to re-unite men with God), and to direct men thus sanctified. He possesses this power for all men. How does Christ actually teach, sanctify and guide men of all peoples and times?

B. CHRIST COMMUNICATED HIS POWER TO THE APOSTLES

During the three years of His public life, Christ carefully prepared certain men, whom He had chosen from His whole group of disciples for very special reasons. Before His Ascension, He called together these Apostles (those "sent"), and communicated to them in a most solemn way, a distinctive threefold power: "All power is given to Me . . ." Thus the power of the Apostles is expressly described as being a participation in the power which belongs to Christ as the Redeemer (cf. also John 20:21). This delegated power is then more accurately defined:

"Teach—baptize (sanctify)—teach them to observe . . . (direct)". Thus the Apostles are the legates ("Apostles") of Christ (2 Cor. 5:20). The submission of faith to the message of the Church, (that is, of the Apostles) and the acceptance of the Sacraments of the Church are strictly necessary for salvation (Mark 16:16; Luke 10:16; John 20:21).

The successors of the Apostles are the bishops. Let us acknowledge and honor in our bishops their apostolic power! Here we should give a clear and brief exposition of the structure of the hierarchy. The leader of the Apostles, by Christ's own institution, is St. Peter. The successor of Peter, the Pope, the Vicar of Christ on earth is, therefore, the leader and head of the bishops and of all faithful Christians. Where the Apostles are, there is the Church; where Peter is, there is the sheepfold of Christ!

C. THE PROTECTION AND CONTINUAL PRESENCE OF CHRIST IN THE CHURCH

How can simple men exercise such great power for the salvation of mankind, without continual abuses? "Behold I am with you all days, even to the consummation of the world" (Matt. 28:20). Christ effectively brings it about that the Church faithfully and rightfully carries out the threefold task He has entrusted to her until the end of the world. Let us give our gratitude and complete fidelity to the hierarchy of the Church, not to these men as men, but to Christ in them.

NOTE ON THE TEACHING OF THIS MATERIAL

Following on this lesson, if time allows, a supplementary one on the *Commandments of the Church* may profitably be included. But when the time for instruction is very limited, as in outlying stations in mission countries, such a separate instruction on these precepts is not essential; the individual commandments may be easily set out in some other connection. The precept on attendance at Mass may be given in the lesson on the Mass, or in that on the Third Commandment of God. That on fasting and abstinence, in the lesson on the Passion, or even better, before the sermon given on the Sundays of Lent. (Also by means of such brief explanations and comments, a missionary or pastor can frequently, all during the year, arouse his flock to think with the Church according to the liturgical cycle, and to be alert to gather the special fruit of each liturgical season). The precept of the Easter communion may be included in the instruction on the Eucharist, and then again by way of a brief comment at the time of a missionary's principal visitation. The precept of contributing to the support of the Church is treated in the lesson that follows.

But it is important above all that the faithful rightly understand the *motherly care* of the Church for their welfare manifested in her precepts. Such warnings and commands ought to lead us to a greater love for our loving mother, the Church.

Tenth Instruction

The Church as the Family of God's Children

(*the Church in its more passive aspect*)

Method: Explanatory. In this lesson, rather than a narrative from the Bible, it may be best to use a comparison taken from daily life. By a description of the make-up of a family and of the cooperation needed from all its members if it is to thrive, the teaching concerning the family of God on earth will be clarified and explained.

Viewpoint: The dignity, wealth and security of this heavenly family.

Aim: Gratitude for the many great benefits we receive in God's Church, *active* gratitude. Active cooperation to achieve the goal of our spiritual family.

DOCTRINAL SUMMARY

A. The Church, the Family of the Children of God

The Church is the family of the children of God, founded by Christ; the human race restored by Christ. It is the chief fruit of His life, passion, death and resurrection. He has placed all His treasures of salvation in the Church; they are given us by the Church, as by our mother. Heavenly teaching, the divine life given us in the Sacraments, safe guidance in the way of salvation . . . how rich are we Christians, and we alone! The riches of Christ are only to be found in the Church.* Let us use these riches diligently. In a family so well provided for, let us not perish with hunger because of our own negligence. How eager we should be to bring others to share in our riches!

* By this we do not of course mean that our separated brethren outside the Church have nothing of these riches. But we alone have them in fullness. We do not know what Our Lord gives to those outside the Church who sincerely seek Him and adhere to Him; but we do know with absolute certainty that we share in the riches of the Church not because of our merit, but because of His grace, undeserved by us. We are therefore obliged to show our gratitude by winning our brethren fully for Christ. Like Christ Himself in His first coming, we too are "not sent to judge, but to save the world" (see John 12:47).

The material to be presented here might be outlined as follows: 1) *The founder of this family:* the new Adam. 2) *Its purpose:* filial service of the Father, under Christ, our Leader and Brother. Its riches: the inheritance of God's children. 3) *The members of this family:* all Catholics and only Catholics. 4) *Its main law:* the law of charity and mutual collaboration: all of us must work together for the good and the goal of the family. The Kingdom of God cannot be established and increase as it should without the collaboration of all of us. In this great work of the children of God and members of His family, lay Catholics of course have a most important, in fact an indispensable part. They are actively to collaborate in establishing the kingdom of God over the whole world, but first of all in and around themselves. But this means essentially much more than simply to try to "save one's own soul" with a more or less egotistic attitude. It means constant and generous efforts to imbue the world in which we live with the spirit of Christ: our family, our community, our culture. "The Kingdom of heaven is like leaven, which a woman (the Church) took and buried in three measures of flour, until all of it was leavened" (Matt. 13:33). Behold the task of the Church—to renew the whole world and all human activities in the spirit of Christ! How little of this great work has yet been accomplished, even now, almost two thousand years after Christ's earthly life. And why is this so? Have we teachers of religion always stressed with sufficient earnestness the obligation of everyone to collaborate toward achieving this goal? Have we always showed our students and our lay people what they might begin to do along these lines?

B. Our Bond of Union in the Church Is not a Merely Juridical One. It Is Far More Perfect, a Great Mystery

Our union in the Church far surpasses even the union of the members of an earthly family. To the Church belongs something of the real and most intimate union of the Persons of the Trinity. We should never dare to compare our union and unity in Christ with the perfect union and unity of the divine Persons, if Christ Himself had not stressed this analogy. ". . . that all may be one, even as Thou, Father, in Me and I in Thee; that they also may be one in Us, that the world may believe that Thou hast sent Me. And the glory that Thou hast given Me, I have given to them, that they may be one, even as We are one: I in them and Thou in Me; that they may be perfected in unity, and that the world may know that Thou hast sent Me, and that Thou hast loved them even as Thou hast loved Me."

This is the doctrine of the Mystical Body of Christ. "I am the vine, you are the branches" (John 15:5). Our union with Christ is life-giving. The communication of the divine life of Christ and our vivification through the Holy Spirit necessarily follows upon our being united with Christ. We share the same life, the law of living. Since this objective union is far more perfect than that between the members of a natural family, our mutual cooperation ought also to be far more perfect. Notice the consequence drawn by Christ Himself: "This is My commandment, that you love one another as I have loved you" (John 15:12).

C. The Doctrine of the Holy Spirit, Who Gives Life and Brings to Perfection

The teaching on the Holy Spirit is not completed in the eleventh instruction. Those that follow on the Sacraments and the life given us in Baptism belong also to the teaching on the Holy Spirit, since they help us to understand more clearly the divine life which the life-giving Spirit produces in Christ's members. And, finally, the instructions on the Last Things show the perfection and consummation of this life, which is also the work of the Holy Spirit Who brings us to perfection. It is important that the faithful come to understand that all these instructions are part of the teaching on the Holy Spirit, so that they will daily more fully appreciate Him as being "the gift of God" par excellence Who is given to us in Christ.

Eleventh Instruction

The Holy Spirit

Method: Historical-explanatory. The New Testament accounts of the promise of the Spirit and of His coming on Pentecost should first be told, and then the doctrine concerning Him explained from them. To use several Bible narratives in one lesson is to be carefully avoided in the lower grades (1-4) — the "unity of intuition" is thereby lost. But this method may be used for a good reason in teaching adults, especially where the Bible narratives have such a close intrinsic connection (the Promise and its fulfillment).

Viewpoint: A religious knowledge of the Holy Spirit from the effects He produces in the Church and in men's hearts.

Aim: A great appreciation and ardent *desire for this most wonderful "Gift of God"*. Thanksgiving for the Holy Spirit so abundantly communicated to us.

DOCTRINAL SUMMARY

A. THE PROMISE OF THE HOLY SPIRIT AND THE PREPARATION FOR HIS COMING

The promise of the Holy Spirit was the *greatest comfort* that Christ Himself could give His Apostles when He bade them farewell at the Last Supper (John 14:16). The Holy Spirit will come to complete Christ's own work (*Ibid.,* esp. John 16:7-15). The formation of Christians is not accomplished by external preaching alone; the best teacher will teach in vain if the Holy Spirit does not also speak in the heart of the disciple. But we can and must prepare ourselves for the coming of the Spirit. Therefore Christ strongly urged the Apostles to prepare themselves for receiving the grace of the Spirit (Luke 24:49; Acts 1:4). How were they to prepare themselves? Particularly by recollection and prayer—ardent desire for His coming.

B. THE COMING OF THE HOLY SPIRIT

Divine revelation does not tell us a great deal about the Person of the Holy Spirit; we learn about Him mainly from the effects which He produces in the Church and in the faithful individually.

1) *The Person of the Holy Spirit.* He is the third Person of the Most Holy Trinity, He proceeds from the Father and the Son as Their love for One Another—Love so perfect that it is a Person, the Third Person in the Godhead. He is true God with the Father and the Son, "Lord and Giver of life", to be adored and glorified together with the Father and Son. He spoke through the Prophets, He came down on the Church of Christ, to the Apostles and the rest of the faithful.

2. *The Effects of the Coming of the Spirit.* The effects He produces can be clearly seen from the wonderful change He wrought in the Apostles on Pentecost. This change shows clearly the effects proper to the work of the Spirit: He fills the Apostles with Christ's own life, joining them more intimately with their Head, charging them with Christ's own dispositions. In one word, He vivified them supernaturally. What He did for the Apostles, He continues to do for the whole Church and its individual members. Without the Spirit, we would be like lifeless bodies. As our soul makes our body live and act, so the Spirit gives

us supernatural life and vitality. He came down on the Apostles under the appearance of a rushing wind and tongues of fire. The Holy Spirit is the soul of the Church, who gives the individual members their vital union with Christ, and who forms them to the image of Christ, most especially by inflaming them with love for the Father.

We must make it very clear that *here and now the Holy Spirit is communicated to men in the Church,* and that this is brought about especially by the Sacraments, above all in *Baptism and Confirmation.* This is the reason why no special lesson on Confirmation is given in these basic instructions, for it is treated here, at least in its fundamentals. Confirmation consecrates us as active members of the Church, brave soldiers of Christ, fearless witnesses to Him and His Cross. This Sacrament imposes a permanent "character", and therefore its effects can be restored, if they were formerly impeded by improper dispositions, and can be more fully attained to the degree of our cooperation with the grace of the Sacrament. This is the theological foundation for the *renovation of the grace of Confirmation.* We highly recommend, therefore, that about the time of Pentecost each year, a ceremony of the renovation of Confirmation be held, analogous to the Renewal of Baptismal Promises. Such a ceremony might very well be held on the occasion of the administration of Confirmation to new candidates.

NOTE ON THE TEACHING OF THIS MATERIAL

Although the true Christian should highly esteem and ardently desire the vital influence of the Holy Spirit, nevertheless no *separate devotion to Him* is to be urged on the faithful. "He is adored together with the Father and the Son". The Spirit is revealed to us as being the supreme Gift of the Father to His children, and therefore the Church very seldom prays immediately and separately to the Spirit. She rather prays to the Father that He may pour this Spirit into our hearts (see the Prayer for the Feast of Pentecost). Genuine devotion to the Holy Spirit, therefore, consists especially in a great appreciation of, and fervent desire for His supernatural gifts, and in diligent preparation of our hearts to receive His graces more abundantly.

Twelfth Instruction

The Most Holy Trinity

Here, finally, after the teaching on the Holy Spirit, is the best place, catechetically speaking, to give the special lesson on the doctrine of the Trinity. Theology proceeds from higher to lower, from cause to effect, and so the Tract *"De Deo Trino"* precedes the inquiry into the work of man's salvation. But the catechetical instruction of Christians should follow the opposite method, following the example of divine revelation, of Christ Himself, of the primitive Church—which method is also that recommended by modern catechetics.

Method: Historical-explanatory. The doctrine of the Blessed Trinity is not meant to be something abstract, that Christians "have to believe" merely to exercise their faith; it is rather the most intimate revelation of God's own "inner life" to His beloved children—of that life which the Father has called us to share in Christ. We begin, then, with the Bible narrative of the mission of the Apostles, since here the doctrine of the Trinity and of our participation in this mystery clearly appears as fundamental to the Christian religion.

Viewpoint: a clear explanation of the importance *for us,* the children of God, of this deepest of mysteries. *This is "our" mystery.*

Aim: Not only a firm faith (rational submission of the intellect) but also, and especially, profound joy and *reverent thanksgiving for our participation in this mystery.*

DOCTRINAL SUMMARY

A. THE SOLEMN REVELATION OF THE MYSTERY

Christ bids His Apostles farewell (Matt. 28:6–20). His last command is to delegate the Apostles to continue His work, with His power and His continuous and effective protection and guidance. The Apostles are to continue His work by: 1) Preaching the Gospel, so as to "make disciples of all nations". 2) Administering the Sacraments in which His heavenly teaching about, and His heavenly promise of divine life is realized, through which this life is conferred and increased. The dogma of the Most Holy Trinity is clearly seen to be *the* basic Christian doctrine, and Baptism the basic Sacrament through which we acquire a real and intimate bond with each of the three Divine Persons, and, in an inexpressible way, truly participate in the life of the Trinity.

B. THE RELIGIOUS EXPOSITION OF THE MYSTERY

1) This is the intimate mystery of God's inner life. Here we should give a clear exposition of the meaning of the doctrine, that is, of what we believe concerning it, in reliance on divine revelation: one nature in three Persons. One "what", three "Who's". Compare this with three men, human persons. These three men have the same human nature in that they belong to the same species, but they have three different natures numerically: each has his own body, soul, mind, will, etc.,

distinct from those of the other two men. But in God exactly the same—numerically the same—power, wisdom and holiness, one and the same divine perfection belong to the Father, are communicated from all eternity by Him to the Son, and are communicated to the Holy Spirit by the Father and the Son. All three Persons are truly and properly God; not three gods, but one God, since the divine perfection is in no way multiplied.

The wonderful union of the three divine Persons. It surpasses any union conceivable between created persons. It is the divine exemplar which every created union of persons imitates from afar. A created person can never communicate his own proper existence to another, even to his most intimate friend; he can only give something of himself, of his thoughts, affection, purposes, etc. Not so in God. The Father gives the Son the perfect fullness of the absolutely unique and undivided divine perfection, Father and Son together give this perfection to the Spirit. What joy in the common possession of this one divine fullness! How different from any created sharing of possessions. Here what is shared is not external or divisible or limited. The union of the Persons among themselves is an intimate vital union. The Father, through a vital and strictly immanent action, communicates His own proper divine nature to His Son, and Both, by a vital operation, confer the same on the Holy Spirit.

This doctrine is the most profound mystery of our religion, a mystery in the strictest sense. We can explain a little of its meaning from what Revelation tells us, but we cannot understand its inner reality. We can easily see that there must be mysteries in the Infinite God that far surpass the powers of our created minds—that are *above* our reason. When God reveals such mysteries to us, we believe, not because we understand, but because He has revealed them. Comparisons and explanations help us to understand more clearly what the mystery means, but they cannot make it completely intelligible. (When using comparisons, then, we should always clearly indicate wherein lies the likeness with what we are explaining, and wherein the unlikeness).

2) *This is "our" mystery,* not only because it is supremely interesting to us, children of God, to know the intimate secrets that our Father has revealed to us out of His love for us. As children of God, we are called not only to know about this mystery, but *really to participate in it.* From the moment of Baptism, we have a special relationship with each of the divine Persons. We become members of Christ, and because of this intimate relationship to the Word, the Son, we become children of the Father and temples of the Spirit. This is why Christ ordained that Baptism be conferred in the name of the Trinity. "Through

Christ we have access in one Spirit to the Father. Therefore you are no longer strangers and foreigners, but you are fellow-citizens with the saints and members of God's household" (Eph. 2:18 ff). The life given us at Baptism is here and now a true participation in the life of the Trinity. Our future glory in heaven will be nothing other than the ultimate development and conscious enjoyment of this same life. How rich are we Christians! How wonderful the redemption by which Christ has not only wiped out our guilt, but has united us to Himself and brought us into the innermost sanctuary of God. "But when the fullness of time came, God sent His Son, born of a woman, born under the Law, that He might redeem those who were under the Law, that we might receive the adoption of sons. And because you are sons, God has sent the Spirit of His Son into our hearts, crying, 'Abba, Father.' So that he is no longer a slave, but a son; and if a son, an heir also through God" (Gal. 4:4–7).

NOTE ON TEACHING THIS MATERIAL

Through our vital union with Christ, we participate in the life of the Trinity. And therefore the Church, following Scripture and apostolic tradition, does not so much pray to the three Persons together, to the Most Holy Trinity, as she prays *to the Father, through Christ, in the Holy Spirit.* The Church has always defended the divinity of each of the three Divine Persons, and the consequent fact that Each is to be adored, as is the undivided Trinity. But by the classical form of Christian prayer, she indicates that we who are redeemed in Christ look upon the mystery of the Triune God not from without, but, as it were, from within, since we are taken up, in Christ, into the very current of the life of the Triune God. And so also our teaching of this most wonderful mystery should not dwell too lengthily on inculcating the perfect equality of the divine Persons, but should rather, following the example of the great Greek Fathers, indicate especially the dynamic aspect of this doctrine: the life of the Most Blessed Trinity, the differences and the relationships of the various Persons among themselves.

The Sacraments

As we mentioned above, the teaching on the Sacraments constitutes part of the teaching on the life-giving Spirit. For it is in the Sacraments most especially that the Holy Spirit is communicated to us; it is in the Sacraments that He Himself confers His divine life upon us, and day by day forms us more completely to the image of Christ.

Viewpoint: The Sacraments should be taught as being, above all, the great sources of the divine life, and not merely as a means to leading a good moral life. It is true, of course, that the effects of the Sacraments should show themselves in truly Christ-like living. But such living should be shown to be the fruit of our cooperation with the grace of the Sacraments, not an effect which can be expected without the necessary efforts on our own part. Christ-like living is thus an obligation incumbent upon us from our reception of the Sacraments. What they produce immediately is a new and closer union with Christ, and, consequent upon it, an increase of divine life. This growth in union with Christ, then, obliges us to a more Christ-like life; every reception of any Sacrament includes the call to a life more fully united with Christ. To enable us to respond to this call, we certainly receive abundant "helping" (actual) graces out of regard for the Sacrament we received. But we do not receive them so much at the very moment of the reception itself, as when we need these graces, for example in moments of temptation, or when we are given special opportunities to follow Christ generously. The measure of the graces, both sanctifying and "helping", that we in fact receive, depends in great part on the disposition in which we receive the Sacrament. (Example of a pitcher in which we take water from a fountain.)

The doctrine of the Sacraments again unfolds to us the "unfathomable riches of Christ" made available to us in the Church. Therefore:

The chief effects of the lessons on the Sacraments should be a deep, heart-felt and active gratitude, which does not consist in mere emotion but in the fervent use of these fountains of grace, a gratitude which shows itself in an increasingly Christ-like life. "With joy shall you draw forth waters from the fountains of the Savior. And you will say on that day: Confess the Lord and call upon His name: make known His wonders to the nations" (Isaias 12:3ff).

Within the framework of these very fundamental instructions, a special instruction on the Sacraments in general is hardly necessary.* The necessary points can easily be given in the teaching on the Church, or on the Holy Spirit, or at the beginning of the instruction on Baptism. If time allows for a separate general instruction on the Sacraments, the image of fountains may well be used to explain the essential points. Christ Himself is the Institutor and the source of these wonderful fountains by which He confers upon us the fruits of the redemption.

---

* In teaching in the lower grades of school, it would, of course, be unsound to try to teach the general effects of all the Sacraments until we have presented each individually.

"He, however, who drinks of the water that I will give him shall never thirst again, but the water that I will give him shall become in him a fountain of water, springing up into life everlasting" (John 4:13ff). Christ gives us these fountains; we ourselves must come to the water and draw it out in abundance. Of all the Sacraments, Baptism and the Eucharist are the most important.

Thirteenth Instruction

The Effect of Baptism

From the very nature of Baptism, the doctrine concerning this Sacrament is of the greatest importance for firmly establishing a Christian life. In Baptism the divine life is given us for the first time; it is then that we are "born of God" (John 1:13). Diligent care must be taken, therefore, that Christians properly esteem the grace of Baptism, the source of Christian life and activity, and that they understand the obligation incurred at Baptism to strive to lead the Christian life.

The most important moments of Christian life are: the moment of Baptism when we are first united with Christ, and the moment of death, at which our final union with Christ is determined. Throughout our whole lives, we should give thanks for that first moment, and humbly pray and prepare ourselves for the second moment, which should be the completion of the first.

Since Baptism is so important, we should eagerly seize upon every occasion to instruct our hearers thoroughly in its wonders. And we should make use of the actual administration of this Sacrament, whether to adults or children, or even when supplying the ceremonies, to give an instruction of suitable length.

Method: Explanatory. The method of exposition here should consist, not in telling a narrative, but in the vivid description and explanation of the external rites. For the Sacraments "confer what they signify", and the person who understands the rites of a Sacrament understands the Sacrament itself. Christ wished to institute the Sacraments in such a way that we might easily understand His intentions and the special grace of each Sacrament from the external signs, and for this same purpose, the Church built up the various accompanying ceremonies.

When we are explaining the rites of Baptism, we must bear in mind the fact that we are not concerned with giving a learned dissertation on liturgical science, which would tend to enumerate, describe and minutely explain the entire rite. In addition to the essential rite, only the more important additional ceremonies should be selected for explanation, ones that can be easily understood by simple people. In this instruction, we should particularly explain those rites which show us the effect of Baptism; and in the following, those which teach us the obligations assumed in Baptism.

Viewpoint: The greatness and the excellence of the grace of Baptism, and the great dignity to which it raises us.

Aim: A most profound and, at the same time, most humble gratitude: "He lifts the poor man from the dust, the needy from the dung-hill, to seat him among the princes, the princes of His people" (Psalm 112). A living consciousness of our Christian dignity.

DOCTRINAL SUMMARY

A. Entrance Into the Church

The ceremonies begin outside the church door. The catechumen is not as yet a member of the Church. In Baptism we enter the Church of Christ, "built of living and chosen stones", the invisible Temple of which the church building is the image. In Baptism we receive a right to the treasures of the Church, particularly to faith, and to the divine life. (Cf. the dialogue between the priest and the catechumen at the beginning of the ceremonies). The Church leads us at once to Christ.

B. Union With Christ

The sign of the Cross, so often imposed on the candidate. Until now we have been subjects of the devil; in Baptism we exchange masters, we make ourselves subject to Christ. *The Baptismal character:* the Sign of the Cross traced externally on the candidate's forehead is a sign of the internal impression of the sign of Christ the Savior on our souls, our innermost beings; by Baptism the soul is united and configured to Christ. Now Christ owns us, His mark is on us, as sheep are branded to show to whose flock they belong. The exorcisms indicate that Christ drives out the former owner who had stolen us from our Creator. But the devil does not relinquish his hold on us unless we ourselves wish it—so the climax of the negative aspect of Baptism is the personal renouncement of the devil's service, immediately before the actual Baptism: "I do renounce him". Thus the necessity for attrition for the remission of personal sins is absolute, even in Baptism. Through this Sacrament the process of "conversion" is completed. The Church is the society of the converted, of those who, in Christ the second Adam, are turned toward the Father.

C.   New Divine Life

The essential rite: the washing, which is also a rebirth. Water in Holy Scripture is both destructive and creative—the Flood, the Exodus, etc. So in Baptism we are cleansed from sin—the power of the devil is destroyed; sin (original and personal) is destroyed and its punishment remitted. And at the same time, we are re-born to the life of God. The soul becomes filled with light and beautiful in God's eyes. Thus Baptism is a death, and a re-birth and resurrection. We are "plunged into" Christ's death, to die to the fallen life of sin and selfishness inherited from the first Adam; by the power of Christ risen from the dead, we rise to His divine life.

Thus united with Christ, the heavenly Father receives us as sons. This *divine adoption* not only gives us the rights and the title of children of God, it really makes us partakers of the divine nature (2 Petr. 1:4), so we are not only called sons of God, but really are sons (1 John 3:1). A human father in adopting a child can only give him rights and possessions: but the heavenly Father, in an indescribable way communicates His own life to us through the Holy Spirit Whom He infuses into our hearts. (The Trinity, the Incarnation and the divine adoption are the three chief and closely interconnected mysteries of our religion.) All these blessings are given us because of our intimate union with Christ. The Church leads us to Christ, Christ leads us to the Father, Who receives us as sons because of our close union with His Son. Example of the son of a king, who finds a poor boy, loves him, takes him into his friendship, takes him home to his father and begs him to adopt him, and shares everything with him. "But if we are sons, we are heirs also: heirs indeed of God and joint heirs with Christ" (Rom. 8:17).

D.   Consecration to the Most Holy Trinity

Baptism brings us into a completely new and intimate relationship with each of the divine Persons. Notice the form of Baptism: "In the name . . . " (In Greek, the text says "into the name . . .") of the Father . . . " This signifies primarily the consecration of the candidate to the Most Blessed Trinity. This consecration essentially surpasses in reality and importance any moral consecration by which a Christian may, from devotion, consecrate himself, to the Blessed Virgin or a saint. The Baptismal consecration is constitutive: the baptized person, through his real union with Christ, is in an entirely new manner united and given over to each of the divine Persons. He becomes an adopted son of the Father, a brother of the Only-begotten Son and a member of His body, a temple of the Spirit. Thus the whole baptized person is made holy both in body and in soul. He is far more sacred than the consecrated chalice that holds the most precious blood, because his relation to God is much more intimate. Example of Leonidas who so reverently kissed his newly-baptized little son, Origen.

Those of us who were baptized as little children could not even begin to understand these gifts. Let us always strive to understand them more fully, to cooperate with them, to be thankful for them.

Fourteenth Instruction

The Obligation Contracted at Baptism

It is most important that Christians should thoroughly understand that by Baptism they have been called out of the throng of unbelievers to the great dignity of being sons of God, to an entirely new life. How sad and shameful it would be if a baptized person were to return to a pagan life! We are children of the light, the leaven for the mass of our unbaptized fellow men. We who have been privileged to be baptized and incorporated in Christ must be the light of the world (cf. the candle given at Baptism; the candles of the Easter Vigil lit from the Paschal candle), and the salt of the earth (Matt. 15:13 f; Phil. 2:15).

Method: Explanatory, as in the preceding lesson. An explanation of the anointing with Chrism (oil and perfumes: we share in the kingship and priesthood of Christ: we are to be "the good odor of Christ" drawing others to Him), the lighted candle, the white robe of present grace and future glory, can be used instead of a narrative, together with the example of the poor boy adopted by the king.

Viewpoint: Our gratitude must manifest itself by a completely new life, one befitting a child of God.

Aim: The constant effort and eagerness to become conformed to Christ, to die to sin and to live for God.

DOCTRINAL SUMMARY

A. Comparison

By Baptism we are taken up into the family of God's children. Let us then live the life of His sons. How will the poor boy of the example act if he has any gratitude or honor? How foolish and despicable he would be if he went away from his loving father and brother, if he offended them by his rude ways. Day by day he should try to become more like the ideal son of his new father. His examplar will be his new brother, the born son of the king.

B.   EXPLANATION AND APPLICATION

We have become "Christ-ened". The complete description of our new life is that it is "in Christ". This means far more than that we are called to follow Him by trying to imitate Him. In *vital union with Him* we are to die to sin, to live to God (Rom. 6:1ff).

In Christ to die to sin. We have renounced the service of Satan, with all that this implies. We are no longer children of the first Adam, disobedient and proud; we are brothers and members of the second Adam (1 Petr. 1:19; 1 Cor. 5:7ff — "Purge out the old leaven that you may be a new dough . . . for Christ, our passover has been sacrificed" —the Easter Sunday Epistle to the newly-baptized). In Baptism we are intimately associated with Christ, assimilated to Him Who was obedient unto death, even the death of the cross. "We have been united with Him in the likeness of His death. For we know that our old self has been crucified with Him, in order that the body of sin may be destroyed (with its unregulated desires received from the first Adam) and that we may serve sin no longer" (Rom. 6:5ff). "Therefore do not let sin reign in your mortal body so that you obey its lusts . . ." (Rom. 6:12–14).

Here we should, briefly and correctly, point out the sins most often indulged in today that are particularly opposed to the Christian vocation: idolatry, tepidity in the service of God, lust, avarice, deliberate hatred towards our neighbor, injustice and so on.

In Christ to live to God. In Baptism, we are intimately united to Christ, called to an intimate fellowship with Him. "For in one Spirit all of us are baptized into one body" (1 Cor. 12:3); "wherefore it is necessary that the life of Christ be manifested in our bodies" (2 Cor. 4:10). "For all of you who have been baptized into Christ, have put on Christ" (Gal. 3:27—example of "white garment" given at Baptism); we are now to be "alive to God in Christ Jesus our Lord" (Rom. 6:11).

The life of Christ is one entirely of *filial love*. The focus of His heart is His Father—cf. His first words (Heb. 10:5; Luke 2:49) and His last word (Luke 23:46). His whole life was dedicated to the service of His Father: "He who sent Me is with Me; He has not left Me alone, because I do always the things that are pleasing to Him." (John 8:29). He wishes to communicate to us this spirit of filial love through the Holy Spirit Who cries out in our hearts: "Abba, Father" (Rom. 8:15). Here we should use some vivid and concrete examples adapted to the audience, perhaps from the lives of the saints, to show the ideal practice of such a life of love. Thus we transfer the life of Christ into our own circumstances.

This spirit of filial love, by its very nature, tends toward frequent, reverent and affectionate conversation with the Father—Christian prayer. And it tends also to be joyful service, to the offering of pleasing sacrifices. True love does not ask what it *has* to do, but what it *can* do to manifest itself. "Our citizenship is in heaven" (Phil. 3:20). Our treasure is in heaven, for our supreme treasure is the Father Whom we love with our whole heart, Whom we serve with all our heart, and with Whom we desire to be united and happy for all eternity.

NOTE ON TEACHING THIS MATERIAL

1) Since a vivid awareness of the grace and the obligations of Baptism is so important, it is most strongly recommended that in every Christian community the renewal of the baptismal promises be celebrated solemnly once a year. The ideal time, of course, now established by the Church as an integral part of the liturgy, is during the great Easter Vigil. But where this is not possible under mission conditions, some other occasion during the Easter season could be chosen.

2) If the instruction on Baptism is given well, a special separate lesson on sanctifying grace will not be necessary in such a course as this giving the essential teachings within the compass of thirty lessons.

The Holy Eucharist

The teaching on the other sacraments is closely connected with that on Baptism. For they either increase and develop the divine life received in Baptism (sacraments of the living), or they restore it (the other sacraments of the dead). But in a special way is the doctrine on the Eucharist to be closely united with that on Baptism. In Baptism we receive the divine life: in the Eucharist the wonderful Food of this life. A consideration of the Food is the best way of reaching some understanding of the life It nourishes. In the Eucharist we are given a divine and heavenly food; how divine and heavenly must be the life it feeds! Thus from the very beginning the Eucharist is to be presented as the heavenly Food of the divine life given at Baptism, and not merely as the visit of the "good Jesus".

The approach to a more complete understanding of the Eucharist is through an understanding of the Eucharistic sacrifice. In the Mass, we offer the Son to the Father, we share in the Son's offering of Himself, and we offer ourselves and are offered with Him. Then in the Communion, the sacrificial banquet, the heavenly Father gives His Son to us; the principal fruit of the sacrifice is Holy Communion. Full participation in the sacrifice includes participation in the banquet. In the 'Sacrifice, we give; in Communion, we receive. Thus it follows that the best preparation for Communion is the perfect offering of ourselves with Christ in the Sacrifice. This is the intimate interchange of love between the Father and His children. In thanksgiving (eucharist) for all the blessings of His love, we offer Him ourselves through Christ, Who makes Himself and His Sacrifice our thanksgiving to the Father. Thus to take part in the Mass is our "chief duty and supreme dignity" *(Med. Dei)*. We are most alive as Christians, most fully and perfectly in act when we take part in the Mass, when by the ministry of our priest, through Christ, with Him and in Him, we offer to God the Father a pure victim, a holy victim, an unspotted victim.

Ideal instruction on the Holy Eucharist presupposes an ideal form of participation in the Holy Sacrifice, including Communion. Here again we see the importance of the liturgical renewal which has as its particular aim to make the participation of the laity more active, intelligent and fruitful.

Fifteenth Instruction

The Institution of the Holy Eucharist

Method: Historical-explanatory.
Viewpoint: The greatness of Christ's love, the greatness of His gift.
Aim: True gratitude for this great gift and love—a gratitude which will manifest itself in the fervent use of this most exalted Sacrament. This first lesson is also a preparation for the one that follows on the sacrifice of the Mass. This first is more affective, the following more instructive.

DOCTRINAL SUMMARY

A. Preparation for the Institution

Christ sent His most beloved Apostles ahead to prepare for the Last Supper (Luke 22:7ff). Our Lord's desire (Luke 22:15), and His great love (John 13:1) on the day before He suffered.

The washing of the feet: In His great love, He humiliated Himself. "He emptied Himself, taking the form of a slave" (He became a servant in washing His disciples' feet; in the institution of the Eucharist, He makes Himself our food). "Have this mind in you which was also in Christ Jesus" (Phil. 1. 2:5), especially when we approach the Holy

Eucharist. In preparing for Holy Communion, we do not so much need to elicit "acts" of faith, etc., as to strive to be filled with the Spirit of Christ, especially with the spirit of humble love toward God and our neighbor, and so approach the sacrifice and Sacrament. "I have given you an example" (John 13:15). Although we do not recommend the use of isolated acts of faith, we can never sufficiently inculcate the necessity for the attitude of faith towards this "mysterium fidei" par excellence. This is not the most fundamental mystery, but it is the most striking since it is so strikingly opposed to what the senses suggest. Here also, faith means that we take the word of our Lord as full living reality.

Christ Himself was much concerned with the perfect purity of His disciples' hearts. And only He can cleanse us sufficiently. "You are clean, but not all." Judas was untouched by love . . . a desperate condition . . . Christ let him go away.

B. The Institution Itself

What did He say? What did He do? How? Exactly what the priest now does in the Mass.

First of all, Christ produces a most amazing change. What a great miracle! In theology, we call it *transubstantiation:* explain the reality itself, not the difficult word, which we should never use in the lower grades of school or in preaching to uneducated people. We should rather give the doctrine according to the Bible narrative. What did Christ take in His hands? Evidently, ordinary bread. What did He say? Are not the words perfectly clear? Could He not do what He said so clearly? What, therefore, was the result? What did He hold in His sacred hands after His consecratory words? But we should not dwell too long on this still preparatory point. We should make it clear that transubstantiation is by no means an end in itself. Christ effected this change for a twofold purpose: to provide us with a fitting gift that we could offer to the heavenly Father (sacrifice), and to provide us with the divine food for our life as children of God (sacrament).

Sacrifice: The bread is changed into Christ's Body "that is given up" (present tense), not only on the following day on Calvary, but also here and now. The wine is changed into Christ's Blood, which "is poured out", that is, sacrificially offered here and now as "the" Blood of the New Testament (cf. the parallel text on the blood of the former Testament shed on Mt. Sinai, Exod. 24:4ff.)

Sacrament: Given as food, "eat! . . . drink!" See the species of the Eucharist: the sacraments give what they signify. What kind of food is thus prepared by the Father's love for His beloved children? What kind of a life is it that they possess, that they need a food so truly divine?

Do this in commemoration of Me. What He did must be repeated by the Apostles in memory of Him. "As often as you shall eat . . . you shall announce the death of the Lord until He come" (1 Cor. 11:26). The Last Supper was the anticipation of the sacrifice of the Cross. Every Mass is by its nature the renewal of this sacrifice.

C. THANKSGIVING

Christ Himself gave thanks with the Apostles. This thanksgiving made together inculcates in them the greatest possible union with God the Father through Christ and in Him. "I am the vine, you are the branches" — the great commandment. "Abide in Me, and I in you . . . I am the vine, you are the branches . . . As the Father has loved Me, I also have loved you. Abide in My love . . . This is My commandment, that you love one another as I have loved you . . . that all may be one, even as Thou, Father in Me and I in Thee; that they also may be one in Us . . . I in them and Thou in Me; that they may be perfected in unity . . ." (John 15 and 17).

The principal fruit of Communion: Union with Christ, transformation into Christ (use the analogy of ordinary food, but stress the differences. This food is not assimilated into us, It assimilates us to Itself). "I live now not I, but Christ lives in me" (Gal. 2:20).

Sixteenth Instruction

The Sacrifice of the Mass

Method: Explanatory. Instead of narration, use a comparison.

Viewpoint: The Mass as "the eucharist", that is, the communal thanksgiving and praise offered to the Father by those who have been redeemed. The sacrifice of the Mass as the climax and fount of Christian life.

Aim: Knowledge and a truly religious appreciation of the Mass. This instruction does not intend to explain all the separate ceremonies, but rather to explain clearly the principal meaning of sacrifice and of the Eucharistic banquet. The lack of appreciation and the lack of participation shown by many Christians do not proceed in most cases from a lack of knowledge of the various ceremonies, but from want of realization and appreciation of the central action.

DOCTRINAL SUMMARY

In the Mass, we do what Christ did at the Last Supper: we offer the sacrifice, we receive the Sacrament. Here we desire to see what sacrifice and Sacrament meant, and how they fit together.

A. THE COMPARISON

The New Year's celebration in China. At the time of the new year, it is the custom to have a family celebration, for which faithful children often come from far away, undertaking very difficult journeys, in order to show their filial respect and affection. The central act of the celebration is the solemn New Year's offering of filial devotion and thanks to the parents. They are seated in the place of honor, waiting for the children who come one by one, led by the oldest, and express their filial love and respect by an expressive deep bow, made by getting down on both knees, and then bending over so that the forehead touches the floor—the "ko-tou". This ceremony is followed by the New Year's family meal. The meaning of this ceremony is to show gratitude to the parents, to thank them, to beg pardon for all the faults committed during the past year, and to show devotion and love. And this includes at least an implicit promise to behave well during the coming year. The parents are very pleased. How do they answer? By the family meal that follows, the symbol of family unity.

B. APPLICATION TO THE SACRIFICE OF THE MASS

Through Christ we have been gathered into *the new family of the children of God,* not by any merits of our own, but only because of the marvelous generosity of the Father. How many benefits we have received from Him, and this in spite of our numberless sins, negligences and defects. Filial devotion urges us also often to thank our Father together, to beg pardon for our negligences, to show our filial devotion, and to promise prompt obedience and filial submission in the future.

In the Mass, with Christ our Brother leading us, we offer this *community thanksgiving.* The principal celebrant is always Christ Himself, the visible ordained priest acts as His representative. We can only give the Father worthy thanks through and in Christ, not by ourselves; hence we must take our part in the sacrifice offered by the ordained priest who has received the power to act in the very Person of Christ in the Mass.

In the first part of the Mass, we prepare to offer our thanksgiving as perfectly as possible, above all by recalling the benefits we have received. The greatest of these, which includes in itself all the others, is our vocation to the life of God's children through Jesus Christ, Whom the Father sent to us, His miserable and unworthy creatures, to redeem us. Through the Epistle and Gospel and the sermon, God tells us of the wonders of our redemption in Christ and invites our further cooperation. Christ Himself, at the first Mass, explained the meaning of the Passover and the Paschal lamb and applied it to the sacrifice of the New Testament. And so through the ages, Mother Church has given us the words of God Himself in Holy Scripture, explained in the sermon by the priest, to prepare us to offer our thanksgiving. Notice the special aspect under which sacred teaching is given us in the Mass: "the Gospel of our Lord Jesus Christ," that is, the good tidings about the wonderful blessings that God has given us in Christ.

Now that we are properly disposed by recalling with happiness the benefits of the Father, we approach the act of thanksgiving itself. Would that we had a fitting gift that could adequately show our gratitude and our filial devotion to our Father in heaven. All peoples offer gifts to their gods, and we call these gifts offered to God, *sacrifices*. The sacrificial gift stands for the giver, it takes the place of the giver, it expresses our complete surrender to God in obedient submission. Christ on the Cross perfectly fulfilled the deepest meaning of all sacrifices; in His sacrifice there was not a symbol, but reality; He freely offered His own life.

What, then, can we poor men offer to God? See the gifts of our lowly condition: bread and wine. We have no gift that in any way corresponds to the infinite majesty and goodness of the Father. But bread and wine, the nourishment of our physical life, represent all the gifts that He has given us, His continuing creation and providence; they also represent our lives and our work: bread is made by human labor from the seed God causes to grow, wine from the grapes. And they represent the community of the Church, all of us together: one loaf from many grains, one cup of wine from many grapes.

The bread and wine, then, stand for all that we have and are. In themselves these are in no way worthy of God's majesty. But Christ our Brother changes these merely human gifts into His own Body and Blood. Now we have a most worthy and fitting gift. Our gift is Christ Himself! As He offered Himself on the cross, so here and now, although in an unbloody manner, Christ offers Himself to the Father. *Behold our most excellent gift!* Most *excellent* because it contains the Body and Blood of the Lord. And truly *our* gift, because it includes us, Christ's members, also. Christ offers us with Himself, and we join in offering His sacrifice, through the hands of our priest. But we shall not please the Father with even this most excellent offering unless we offer it with fervent hearts, unless we truly offer ourselves in obedient love with Christ. Therefore we must strive with all our powers to offer it worthily: in the spirit of the *humility, love, and gratitude of Christ.* At Mass, above all, we should be one in heart and soul with our Leader. What are the principal affections that we should strive to elicit at the time of the sacrificial action, and especially during the Canon? The principal affection in the Sacrifice of the New Law is simply this: the gratitude of sons. Behold the "eucharist" of the redeemed, offered to the Father by our Leader, the Redeemer.

Behold the climax of our Christian life in this world! Just as the priest is most completely a priest at the moment of sacrifice, so also the laity, the holy "people" of God, are most fully themselves, most fully Christian, most fully active as Christians when together with Christ they offer themselves to the Father and manifest their perfect submission as His children.

The heavenly Father looks down on us with affection, and gladly accepts this our offering, given in and with and through Christ.

How does the Father then respond to our thanksgiving? Greatly pleased by our gratitude, He desires to show us His goodness and His approval by giving us at once a new and wonderful gift. But even the almighty Father has no gift more excellent than His only-begotten Son. He gives Him to us in *Holy Communion;* and in Him and with Him, He gives us also all the other gifts that are necessary and appropriate for us. Above all, with the gift of His Son, He pours out abundantly into our hearts the Holy Spirit, the Spirit of the love of sons. The theological principle that "the visible mission of the Son tends towards the invisible mission of the Spirit" applies also to the mission of the Son sacramentally visible under the sacred species. Christ, the most excellent gift of the Father is the pledge, the completion and the crown of all other gifts (Rom. 8:32). And therefore the principal fruit of the sacrifice for us is the eucharistic food. Anyone who abstains from sacramental communion because of negligence thereby refuses to receive the great fruit of the sacrifice. He has only himself to blame if other, less essential, blessings are also withheld from him, for "the accidental follows upon the essential."

From this consideration of Communion, we can clearly see what kind of preparation and thanksgiving is the best. The *best preparation* is not to be sought in anything undertaken during the Mass aside from the action of the Mass itself. It consists, rather, in taking part as actively and perfectly as possible in the Mass, in offering the best possible thanksgiving to the Father in pure gratitude and love, in and with Christ . . . to wish nothing else except to praise and to please the

Father with our whole hearts. The more perfect is this thanksgiving, the more abundant and excellent also will be the Father's response.

And the *best thanksgiving* after Holy Communion will be to accept from the hands of the Father with the greatest reverence, thanksgiving and love this Gift of gifts, Christ our Lord, and to strive to correspond more and more perfectly to the intentions of the Giver. This is the will of the Father, that daily we become more and more conformed to the image of His Son, in order that Christ may be the first-born among many brethren (Rom. 8:29), and that we may daily become more transformed into Christ (Gal. 2:20).

And our gratitude also contains at least an implicit promise to finish the work to which we pledged ourselves in the oblation: to live from now on, not for ourselves, but for God. "We are no more our own" since we have given ourselves fully in Christ to the Father. The Mass must be more than a ceremony in our lives. We must live out the implications of the Mass all day long.

In order that this lesson be effective, we must also explain to our hearers in a concrete, easy and appealing way, how they should take part in the Mass in order to make it truly the "thanksgiving of sons". But a full solution of this need cannot be found without considerable reorganizing of the way in which many of the faithful still assist at Mass. It is almost impossible to show them how "active" they should be in mind and heart and will, if outwardly they are merely the "idle and dumb spectators" deplored by the Popes. Let us begin, then, with an understandable and impressive form of Dialogue Mass, and preferably one in which suitable vernacular hymns are sung at appropriate times.*
The essentials are that the faithful should be able to realize by their outward actions that they come to Mass to assemble together as God's people, to pray together, to listen to God's word together, to offer them-

---

* We might recommend for this purpose: 1) The Mass cards arranged by Rev. Eugene Walsh (see p. 40), and 2) *Our Community Mass,* by Rev. Joseph Kellner, S.J. (Institute of Mission Apologetics, P.O. Box 1815, Manila, P.I., 15c per copy. Obtainable in this country from The Liturgy Program, University of Notre Dame, Notre Dame, Ind.) This booklet, in full accordance with the rubrics for Low Mass, supplies everything needed for a fruitful form of Dialogue Mass. Its special advantage is the variety of hymns, etc., that it offers, among them several Gregorian melodies. During the Offertory, it introduces the "General Prayer," a reintroduction, suitable to modern needs, of the former *Oratio Fidelium.* During the Canon, it presents the so-called Eucharistic Anthems, while suggesting other possibilities. This booklet also indicates how in the community Mass the people might use again various Psalms and the responsorial form of chant so common in the ancient Church. This responsorial chant makes the participation of the people possible and even easy, even without a choir. The booklet is warmly recommended by the great liturgical scholar, Rev. Joseph Jungmann, S.J.

selves with Christ and to be offered with Him to the Father, and together to receive Him as the Father's gift.

Seventeenth Instruction

The Institution of the Sacrament of Penance

The teaching on the sacrament of Penance is treated only briefly here, since we presume that children are prepared by special instructions to receive the Sacrament of Penance, not only before their first Confession, but repeatedly during their formative years. And the missionary also should take the opportunity, before hearing the confessions of a Christian community, to instruct them in some aspect of this Sacrament and to help them to attain true penitence. On one occasion, he might stress one commandment, on another the motives for contrition, varying in emphasis during the various liturgical seasons.

But, whatever the best method of accomplishing our purpose under various circumstances, we should above all fight against *merely mechanical confessions.* Where there is real mortal sin (subjective as well as objective), then there is deliberate rebellion against our loving Father. This cannot be erased by any merely external ceremony, but only by a renewed and sincere conversion of heart and the grace of the Sacrament. In this matter, all untimely easiness and indulgence on the part of a priest is really impious cruelty toward immortal souls who, through such an attitude, may be left in their sins and deceived about the dangers of their condition. The priest, another Christ, is the friend and the physician of sinners. But it is no kindness to cover over real wounds; they must be effectively cured. The wonderful mercy of the Father, which goes far beyond our narrow minds, is always open to every sinner, provided he truly retracts his perverse will and really returns to the Father with a contrite heart.

Moreover the doctrine of Christian penance is "good news" also, and should be preached as such. And good preaching of this doctrine should bring out clearly the close connection between the sacraments of Baptism and Penance, which the Fathers called "another and laborious Baptism".

Method: Historical-explanatory. John 20:19-23 gives the narrative.
Here the narrative is to be closely united to the explanation.

Viewpoint: This is Christ's *Easter gift:* this is the sacrament of consolation and peace.

Aim: A great appreciation of this Easter gift—active gratitude shown by true penitence.

DOCTRINAL SUMMARY

Introduction. The connection between Baptism and Penance. The calamity and the ingratitude of mortal sin committed after Baptism. Christ could most justly completely reject an unfaithful follower who has thus broken his solemn baptismal oath, a withered member who has deliberately cut itself off from the life-stream of the true Vine. But yet Christ does not abandon the sinner. He gives him another chance. Christ will restore him to life and health if the sinner himself really desires it. This is a most special and wonderful gift. And this is the reason why Christ wished to give us this gift on the day of His glorious resurrection.

A. THE APOSTLES AFTER THE RESURRECTION

They were hiding in the Upper Room, behind closed doors. They were afraid of the Jews; they were even afraid of Christ. How cowardly and ungrateful they were. Truly they were unworthy to see their risen Master. Will He not reproach them and chide them? Such is the state of the Christian sinner.

B. CHRIST IN THE MIDST OF THE APOSTLES

The doors were locked, but the glorious Christ enters. He does not come to chide, but to give peace and consolation: "Peace be to you" (cf. Luke 2:14). Christ is the great peace-maker (Is. 9:6). To make peace is His most important work as the second Adam, the Mediator between God and men. And as the Good Shepherd He wishes to exercise His office especially in this Sacrament. He shows His apostles His hands and His side: here is the basis of our trust when we have sinned. The Blood of Christ can wipe out all sins, even the worst and gravest. See the Heart of the Good Shepherd, wounded for us! "The disciples therefore were glad when they saw the Lord". Let us share their gladness.

C. CHRIST INSTITUTES THE SACRAMENT OF PENANCE

Again He repeats the greeting: "Peace". How He wishes to emphasize the fact that He is now dealing with the Sacrament of peace and consolation! "As the Father has sent Me . . ." The Father had sent Christ as the Good Shepherd to bring men back to God. In the Sacrament, we do not find a mere man, but the Good Shepherd Himself. The priest "acts in the person'" of Christ, is Christ's instrument.

This Sacrament, then, will produce its effects in us only if we see Christ, not a mere man. In confessing our sins, we must have the sincerity and simplicity that come from realizing the presence of the all-knowing Christ; the sincerity and depth of contrition that come from realizing the presence of the Good Shepherd, Who gave His own life for our souls. The priest has Christ's power. He can forgive every sin, provided that we confess sincerely and with a contrite heart. For Christ breathed on His Apostles: He communicated to them the Holy Spirit . . . "Receive the Holy Spirit . . . " In the sacrament of Penance, the priest can breathe into the soul a new life, the Holy Spirit. What a great wonder! What a great blessing! "Whose sins you shall forgive, they are forgiven them; and whose sins you shall retain, they are retained."

Christ gives them a double power, but it must be used according to the mind of Christ. For this reason, the priest must know the real condition of the sinner. The sinner, then, must humbly and clearly make known his condition of soul, and the priest should help him, if necessary, by some questions, above all to make sure that the penitent has the right disposition. If this is lacking, no priest, not even the Pope himself, has the power of forgiveness. If true contrition is wanting, if sincere conversion is lacking, then the absolution given by the priest is completely useless, and, what is more, very harmful.

Heartfelt thanks for this wonderful Easter gift. This is indeed the sacrament of Christian resurrection. *Never be afraid of this sacrament of consolation and peace.* If the Sacrament of Penance does not bring true and profound consolation and peace of soul, we shall find that in almost every case some serious deficiency is to be found, either in preparation or in general attitude. Perhaps diligence in examining one's conscience is lacking, perhaps sincere contrition, perhaps real trust in Christ the Good Shepherd. From this last come, for example, the not infrequent difficulties and scruples of "pious" people. Prescinding from cases in which there is some psychic disease, almost all such troubles arise from false security, or the desire to find security in the wrong place. Complete security of soul is to be sought only in trust in Christ; and security founded on ourselves is to be given up.

Never abuse this Sacrament. It is much better not to go than to go insincerely, or even mechanically. Man goes to confession a sinner —if he goes sincerely and trustfully, he returns a new man, brought back to life, filled with strength.

NOTE

Even though the Sacrament of Extreme Unction has a special connection with that of Penance, it is better to explain it later (see p. 144).

The essentials concerning the Sacrament of Holy Orders have already been given in the Ninth Instruction on the hierarchical Church, and the instructions on the other Sacraments all go to build up a religious understanding of the mystery of the priestly office.

Eighteenth Instruction

The Sacrament of Matrimony

The purpose of this instruction is to explain the place of this Sacrament in the whole of Christian doctrine, to bring out clearly its religious aspect. Our aim here is not to prepare young people for marriage: there are many good books on this subject.

Method: Historical-explanatory.

Viewpoint: The awareness that marriage is a *holy vocation,* a call to cooperate with God the Creator, a kind of priesthood to be exercised in the "ecclesiola", the little church of God which is the Christian family.

Aim: The re-Christianization of the modern attitude about sexual life and family life. Christian family life is endangered today by so many centrifugal forces that very special attention is necessary to make sure that the faithful understand what Christian family life can and should be. Moreover the place of the sexual element in married life, and in life in general is greatly distorted today. "Sex appeal" is dragged into every aspect of life, entertainment, business, cultural activities. The re-formation of the true Christian attitude toward sex is the most essential step toward correcting the many existing abuses, and far more effective than attacking these abuses directly.

DOCTRINAL SUMMARY

A. THE ORIGINAL HOLINESS OF MARRIAGE

(Genesis, chapters 1 and 2.) 1) *"Man and woman He created them . . ."* The two sexes are of divine institution. Man, consisting of soul and body, is an admirable work of God. God gave us our various natural appetites, the appetite for food and drink for the conservation of the individual, the sexual appetite for the conservation of the human race. Although God could have arranged for propagation to take place by some other means, He designed this means for mankind. The sex-appetite is included in God's approval of His own work: "God saw all

things which He had made, and they were very good" (Gen. 1:31).
And why? Whenever husband and wife carry out the marriage-act
and are blessed with a child, they cooperate in one holy work with
God the Creator Himself, a work which, in the natural order, is the
noblest that can be accomplished by man (Scheeben). Therefore the
action of parents by which children are generated is not something
designed by God to be in any way degrading or beast-like; it is meant
to be a holy action, the most noble human act, in which they offer
the cooperation of their whole selves and their love to God the Creator
for the creation of a new man, who, moreover, is to become a son
of God.

2) *"Increase and multiply"* (Gen. 1:28). See what a holy vocation
it is. God Himself, Who instituted marriage, gave it this holy purpose:
"Fill the earth" . . . and we can add: Fill heaven also with men who
are to take the place of the fallen angels. Man and woman are joined
in marriage for the good of their children and of the whole human
race, not primarily for their own advantage.

3) *"Let us make for him a help-mate like to himself"* (Gen. 2:18).
The second purpose of marriage is mutual help and comfort. Woman
is not inferior to man, but a help-mate equal to him. Without true
mutual love, husband and wife cannot properly fulfill their task. Marriage
is not a punishment inflicted upon mankind, but a blessing. But this
blessing can only be enjoyed if husband and wife seek one another's
good and not their own (cf. 1 Cor. 13), if they are ready for self-
denial and sacrifice.

4) *"To our own image"* (Gen. 1:27). The marriage-bond is
a kind of reflection of the union and love of the Blessed Trinity Itself,
of the internal life and fecundity of God. God does not want the human
race to consist of single individuals thrown together, but to be organically
constituted of persons intimately joined to one another in the family.

5) *"Two in one flesh* (Gen. 2:24). Marriage in paradise was
monogamous: one man and one woman, so that they might give
to one another the total, undivided and inseparable vigor of their love,
according to God's original design for marriage. This inseparable union
was to endure until the end of life, as Christ Himself affirms (Matt.
19:8).

6) *"And both of them were naked . . . and were not ashamed"*
(Gen. 2:25). In paradise, the sexual appetite was completely under
the command of right reason. Everything took place in a most holy
way according to the law of God. Sexual pleasure was the natural
accompaniment of the marriage act as designed by the good God, but
to obtain this pleasure was not the purpose of the act. The malice

of sin against the sixth commandment is that it perverts this right order; neglecting the divinely established purpose, to intend only the pleasure. But there was nothing like this in paradise: everything was holy: the source and the institution, the purpose and the idea, souls and bodies, thoughts, intentions, actions. And, in paradise, the creative act of the parents, by a special disposition of divine love, was to be the means and instrument of transmitting not only human life, but the gift of divine sonship itself, original grace. "We come of a holy lineage; it is not for us to mate blindly like the heathen that have no knowledge of God." These words of Tobias (8:5) apply even more fully to Christian husband and wife.

B. THE LOSS OF HOLINESS THROUGH SIN

1) *Original Sin.*

a) "She gave it to her husband and he ate" (*Ibid*). The woman who was meant to be a help to man, became his seducer to sin and hell.

b) "They wove fig leaves and made themselves loin-clothes" (Gen. 3:7). The sensual appetite rebels against right reason. The innocence of paradise was lost. Modesty was made necessary to fallen man to preserve the holiness of marriage.

c) "Adam said: 'the woman gave it to me'" (Gen. 3:12). The harmony and concord of marriage was disturbed, and is preserved only with difficulty.

d) "And God said to the woman . . . in suffering will you bear children, and you will be under the power of your husband" (Gen. 3:16). The disorder caused by original sin to family life is felt most by the woman, both in relation to her husband and children, and to society in general.

2) *The abundance of sins that followed this first disordering.*

a) In sacred history: the immodesty of Cham (Gen. 9); Sodom and Gomorrha (Gen. 18 and 19); the wife of Potiphar (Gen. 39); the unchaste old men who tempted Susanna (Dan. 13).

b) Profane history: quarrels, discords, diseases, murders, wars . . .

3) *The relaxation of the law.*

To prevent all men from giving in to sin and perishing in it, God Himself in the Old Testament relaxed the holy laws of marriage "on account of the hardness of your hearts" (Matt. 19:8). In certain cases, He permitted polygamy, divorce, and the dismissal of a wife followed by another marriage. The sacred character of marriage given it at the beginning was not destroyed by sin, its God-given idea and purpose remained unchanged; but the sanctity of the marriage-contract was very often neglected by men and relegated to oblivion. This wound was healed by Christ our Savior.

C. The Restitution and Elevation of Marriage Through Christ

"Where sin abounded, grace did more abound" (Rom. 5:20). What the first Adam lost, the new Adam, Christ, not only restores but increases: marriage, which more than most aspects of human life had been injured by sin, now receives more abundant blessings from Christ. For He renews the original sanctity of marriage, and adds new dignity to it in His kingdom.

1) Christ restored the primitive purity of marriage by restoring strict monogamy and indissolubility (Matt. 19:9), and restoring the purity of true chastity even to hidden thoughts (Matt. 5:28).

2) Christ restored woman to her rightful place as man's co-equal help-mate. In the Kingdom of Christ, every woman is a younger sister of the Blessed Virgin.

3) Christ blessed the conception, birth and infancy of the children of men and He consecrated the human family, by Himself being conceived, born, and growing up as a child in a family.

4) Christ honored human marriage at Cana of Galilee and worked His first miracle in favor of the bride and groom. From that time on, Christ is present at every Christian marriage, and He Himself joins the husband and wife who enter matrimony "in Christ".

5) Christ raised marriage to the wonderful dignity of a sacrament of the New Law in which the bride and groom are truly consecrated for their sacred duty of founding and directing a new "ecclesiola", a human family which shall at the same time belong to the family of God. Through this sacrament, the Kingdom of God on earth is given the greater part of its new members, heaven is filled with saints, and the parents themselves are strengthened with ever new graces against all the difficulties of life. This sacrament of "conjugal consecration" is not administered by the priest, but by the spouses themselves. They are the ministers of this Sacrament to one another. Bride and groom are the instruments of the grace of this Sacrament to one another; in this, "dispensers of the mysteries of God" (1 Cor. 4:1) as the ordained priest is in the other Sacraments. Thus throughout married life, not only the calling and the beginning, the purpose and the idea, the rights and powers, and also all the duties and works of husband and wife for each other and their children take on a kind of sacerdotal character.

6) Christ ennobled conjugal love. Since the marriage union is the

image of the union between Christ and His Church, conjugal love is to be the image of the love of Christ for the Church and the Church for Christ (Eph. 5:25–27; 30–32). In the life and love of truly Christian husband and wife, nothing is merely natural, merely carnal, merely corporal; all is made Christ-like, all things are "in Christ", joys and sorrows, worries and consolations, labors and sacrifices, so long as they are in conformity with the most holy law of Christ. The love of husband and wife for one another is to be conformed year by year to true Christian charity, unmindful of self, patient and kind, chaste, prudent, holy. And by their married lives they are to learn how to die to self and live to God and so carry out their Christian vocation.

Thus the original holiness of marriage is not only restored, but made more wonderful still. It is incomparably more exalted than pagan marriage; truly a "great mystery" in Christ and in the Church.

Nineteenth Instruction

Christian Suffering and Death, and Our Sacramental Preparation for Definitive Union with Christ

The teaching on the Sacrament of the Last Anointing is closely connected with that on the Sacrament of Penance. Just as Confirmation is the complement of Baptism, so the Extreme Unction is the complement of Penance. The Last Anointing heals the last wounds and weaknesses resulting from sins; its healing and strengthening effects overflow to the body to restore it to physical health if God wills, or to prepare the whole Christian for the final struggle of death and definitive union with Christ. This intimate connection with the Sacrament of Penance should be often brought out in preaching. But for our purpose it seems clearer to consider this Sacrament here, after the teaching on the Sacraments that build up the Christian life itself and that on the Sacrament of Marriage which assimilates to the work of the Redemption the fullness of human life and activity. For, in the same way, the Sacrament of the Last Anointing, or, to call it by its more traditional name, the Anointing of the Sick, assimilates human sickness, the failing of human life, to the pattern of Christ's death and resurrection.

This Sacrament has the twofold purpose of 1) *Restoring us from sickness to a purified Christian life,* or 2) *completing our purification for the life of heaven.* Thus it should accomplish—and in the case of the proper dispositions it actually does accomplish—all the aspects of purification which otherwise must be completed in Purgatory, to make us ready for definitive union with Christ. Therefore in the second part of this instruction, the essential points of the doctrine of purgatory are included, and also those concerning all the sacraments for the dying. Thus the first part of this instruction deals with Extreme Unction as uniting us with Christ in grave sickness; and the second part deals with this Sacrament in connection with whole preparation for final union with Christ and leads up to the doctrine on the Last Things.

Method: Explanatory. The sacramental rites are explained.

Viewpoint: To be conformed to Christ in our sufferings and death, so as to be united with Him in His glory. Our view should be fixed on Christ, not on ourselves.

Aim: A Christocentric consideration of Christian life and death. Learning to accept unavoidable sickness and suffering in union with Christ suffering, in preparation for accepting death in union with Him. Sincere and growing desire for union with Christ in heaven. Diligent preparation, daily more fervent, like the good servants and the wise virgins in Our Lord's two parables of His coming at death.

DOCTRINAL SUMMARY

Introduction: The divine life received in the Sacraments is not yet the perfect divine life of the Risen Christ. The "seed of glory" given us in Baptism must grow to its ultimate perfection. We are still awaiting our final change to the perfect glory of God's children (cf. 1 Cor. 15:51ff; 1 John 3:2). We Christians are to love our life on earth as being God's gift and as giving us the opportunity to take part in Christ's work of redemption for the sake of our fellow men; but we are eagerly to look forward to the final completion of God's plan, to the day when the Mystical Body will have reached the full stature designed for it by the Father; when Christ will return in glory and will call His elect to share, body and soul, all together in His glorious life with the Father; the day when, finally, "God will be all in all". The decisive moment of Baptism introduces us to the first stage: life in Christ on earth— a life that still can be lost, that must grow and develop. The second decisive moment of our death, if properly prepared for and undergone in union with Christ, will introduce us to the second stage, our souls sharing in Christ's life and glory, our bodies "asleep" in Christ until the day of the Resurrection. Hence all our lives on earth are a time of preparation, a time of becoming more and more conformed to Christ dying and rising again.

A. Christian Sickness and Suffering

1) Like death, of which they are the foreshadowing, sickness and suffering are effects of original sin and of all the sins of mankind (not necessarily, of course, of each individual's sins). They are, in some sense, the work of the Enemy of mankind, who wishes to disintegrate and destroy God's work. God wishes us to fight against them by all legitimate means—Christ Himself spent His public life healing bodies as well as souls. But God still permits us to suffer, thus reminding us of the coming of death, of the unsatisfactoriness of human life, of Himself as Master of all His gifts of life and health. Christ Himself endured great suffering as well as death, and by taking upon Himself these effects of sin, transformed them for His followers into the way to true and full life. In union with Him, we can not only be resigned to suffering, but make it a free-will offering of love to the Father in union with Christ's sacrifice.

2) But Christ's strength is needed in abundance if we are to bear sickness and suffering in fruitful union with Him. Hence, wherever possible, the priest is to visit the sick, to strengthen them, teach them, pray with them, give them the special blessing of the Church, and, above all, the Sacraments of Penance and the Holy Eucharist. (Preparations needed in a house for visit of sick. Catholics in hospitals should ask for a priest to visit them.)

3) When illness is so serious as to bring us in danger of death, Christ has provided a special Sacrament, *the Anointing of the Sick*, "Extreme Unction". Description of the sacramental sign. Oil soothes pain, heals wounds, strengthens for battle, consecrates things and persons for the special service of God. So this Sacrament soothes, heals and strengthens the soul, and our whole psycho-physical being, resulting, if God wills, also in the restoration of physical health and strength. The form of the Sacrament signifies the destruction of all sins committed through the instruments of the various senses, and of the wounds and weaknesses left by past sins. But even here the indispensable condition applies of aversion to sin, conversion to God. Hence it is appropriate that Sacramental Confession should precede the administration of this Sacrament; the Confiteor reminds us of this again.

This Sacrament is to restore us to a purified, more fully Christ-like life on earth, or, if this is God's will, to strengthen and purify us for the life of heaven, and these effects are attributed especially to the Holy Spirit of Love. (Cf. the three prayers after the sacramental anointing.) But as to the degree of attaining its effects, the norms noted already in the introduction to the doctrine on the Sacraments apply here also. Hence great care should be taken that Christians understand the meaning of this Sacrament, that they approach it with the best dispositions and collaborate faithfully with sacramental grace. And, obviously, the best time to prepare them is *ahead of time,* in sermons and instructions, not to begin when they are very ill.

B. After Baptism Itself, Dying Is the Most Important Action of Our Lives

In direct preparation for this final struggle, for the final assimilation to Christ in His death which will bring us to share in His risen glory, the Church has ready for us:

1) *Final Confession.* This last confession should be, above all others, Christ's Easter gift par excellence, the Sacrament of consolation and peace. But it can be this only under the same conditions as any other confession. If all our preceding confessions have been sincere, fervent, trustful, how easy this one will be; how comforting if we are accustomed in this Sacrament to see Christ Himself seeking His sheep with great love. Our trust far surpasses even the greatness of our sins. But let us make ready, here and now, by seeing Christ in the priest every time we go to confession.

2) *Extreme Unction.* God wishes us to leave this earthly life, our time of preparation, entirely ready for the wedding feast, for final union with Christ. This Sacrament, when it is received with sorrow for the sins of our whole lives, acceptance of our sufferings and death in union with Christ's sacrifice, and ardent desire for Christ, should complete the process of necessary purification. But if a man, sharing Christ's life, is still not perfectly purified at the moment of death, God will still cleanse him in another way. For nothing defiled can enter heaven (cf. Apoc. 21:27). *This is the function of Purgatory,* to complete the process of purification, of transformation into Christ. Purgation in this world will enable us to avoid the far more painful purification in the next, so that we may immediately be received by Christ into the life of heaven.

3) *Holy Viaticum:* This is *the* Sacrament of the dying. To receive it if this is in any way possible, to see that the dying receive it, is of *strict obligation,* imposed by the very nature of the Sacrament. Hence the Church dispenses with all the precautions not absolutely essential that otherwise surround our reception of the Holy Eucharist. A dying person may receive although he has already received on the same day; no fasting rules apply; he may even receive from a schismatic priest, or a Catholic priest may use a host consecrated by a schismatic priest. All Catholics who are in imminent danger of death may receive Viaticum, even when they are not seriously ill and so cannot receive the Anointing

of the Sick, Extreme Unction (e.g., soldiers going into battle; people in grave danger of shipwreck, airplane crash, are not subjects for Extreme Unction, but if possible they should receive Viaticum).

The reason for all this is the importance of this last "journey" of death, for which we need, above all, the companionship and strength of Christ, as our *Viaticum,* "with-you-on-the-way". As the special formula says: Christ will "protect us from the malignant enemy," who desires especially at this decisive moment of death to snatch us away from God. And Christ will bring us through to life everlasting, the life He won for us by His own journey through death.

Thus this last Communion should be the best of all the Communions of our lives, as it directly prepares us for the eternal heavenly Communion. But let us not forget that all our other Communions also are to prepare us for the heavenly Communion. Here again the same principle applies as with our last Confession: the best preparation for our last Communion is to receive Communion fervently all during our lives.

4) The Church also has ready for the dying the Apostolic Blessing and Plenary Indulgence for the hour of death; and the beautiful and most instructive Commendation for the Departing Soul. How many riches and helps for our last journey! But the best preparation for a Christian death is a *good Christian life,* that looks forward to death as our meeting with Christ. The tepid Christian is in great danger that God may deny him the grace of the Sacraments of the dying, or that if he is able to receive these Sacraments, he may receive them with little or no fruit. True conversion in great illness is not an everyday grace, nor one that we can count on. "Now is the acceptable time, now is the day of salvation!" (2 Cor. 6:2).

The Teaching on What Is to Come (The Last Things)

The teaching on the "last things" is the crown of Christian doctrine. Here we see the end of the story of divine love, its final purpose; here we learn what we hope for; here we see the full extent of the magnificent task of the Holy Spirit, the Perfector: *our definitive consummation in Christ.*

Like all of Christian doctrine, the teaching on what is to come is entirely Christocentric, and should therefore be presented in a Christocentric manner. Christ is not only the way by which we tend to the Father while we are on this earth. It is in Christ that we are to be intimately united to the Father for all eternity. The joys of heaven are nothing other than our participation in the inheritance of Christ.

The teaching on the last things is by no means intended to inspire fear primarily. It should rather put our glorious goal clearly and attractively before our eyes, and so teach us rightly to distinguish the values of this passing world from the eternal values of the Kingdom of God.

The doctrine of the last things is thus *full of consolation* for those who are already striving toward our heavenly homeland in the right way; while, with convincing arguments and *salutary fear,* it recalls to the path of salvation those who are living evil lives. It is presented in such a way as actually to attain these two purposes: to offer deep consolation to Christians of good will, and to strike great terror into the tepid.

We must also be on our guard against both false "angelicism" and false religious individualism. The eternal joy that the Father has planned for us is a fully human, though entirely supernatural happiness. We are not to be separated souls for all eternity; our bodies are to share also in the glory of the Risen Christ, in the "new heaven and earth". This will be a *fully social* life and joy—the undreamed-of realization of all men's best longings for a perfect society. And, more than this, the doctrine of the last things does not deal merely with our own individual damnation or salvation, but with the fulfillment of the Father's plan, with the consummation of the entire Mystical Body and somehow of the whole world, with the final and perfect triumph of Christ, with the eternal paschal celebration in which the enemies of God will finally be brought to eternal confusion, and the friends of Christ will enter fully into His triumph.

Twentieth Instruction

Death and the Particular Judgment

Method: Explanatory. We begin from the inescapable fact of death, and give the Christian explanation of this fact. In the teaching about the judgment, a comparison with human judicial processes may profitably be used.

Viewpoint: Death should be clearly proclaimed as the definitive end to the Christian's probation. The beauty, the desirability, *the "good tidings" of a Christian death:* the intimate likeness to the dying Christ. In teaching the judgment, we should speak chiefly about the criterion on which we shall be judged: whether we have attained to that Christ-likeness to which we are called.

Aim: To fortify us against the deceits of this world, to give us the perception and the "eyes" of Christ with which to look at, to weigh and judge this transitory life.

DOCTRINAL SUMMARY

A. DEATH

It is a fact that all men die. But none of us knows exactly when or how our own death will come. In the midst of life, we are in death. Even the longest life passes very swiftly. Religion teaches us the *meaning of death.* For each man, it is the definitive end of his probation. "Render an account of your stewardship" (Luke 16:2). For the good man, it is not the end of life, but the end of a long process of "Christian dying" and the entrance into true life. The work of "I die daily" (1 Cor. 15:31) is completely finished, and gives way to a perfect life without end. But for the evil man, who has not "died" to sin, who is not filled with Christ's life, death takes on the character of punishment strictly so-called; it is the beginning of punishment and eternal death; it is truly the end of a very brief life and the beginning of eternal death. Which kind of death do you want? You make the choice all during your life.

From considering death in this way, the good Christian finds the right attitude towards death: it is not to be too greatly feared, since for us it is the gate to the life we most desire. And since we can enter into that life only through this gate, death loses its horrors; it becomes bearable and even desirable (Phil. 1:21 and 23). And we do not grieve too greatly at the death of even those dear to us: "They go ahead of us."

Thus there is a great difference between pagan and Christian sadness. "But we would not have you, brethren, ignorant concerning those who are asleep, lest you should grieve, even as those who have no hope" (1 Thess. 4:13). "In Christ has shone upon us the hope of a blessed resurrection, so that those who are saddened by the inevitable condition of having to die, may be consoled by the promise of immortality to come. For thy faithful, Lord, life is changed, not taken away; and though the house given us for this earthly sojourn is destroyed, an eternal dwelling-place is prepared for us in heaven" (Preface for the Dead). We Christians participate in Christ's victory over death. "Death is swallowed up in victory. O death, where is thy victory? . . . But thanks be to God Who has given us the victory through our Lord Jesus Christ!" (1 Cor. 15:55–57). And for this reason, our grief over the death of those dear to us ought to manifest itself differently from pagan sorrow. Christian funeral and burial customs should not imitate those of "pagans", but rather show those outside the Church what our idea of Christian death really is.

B. The Particular Judgment

"It is appointed to man once to die, and after death the judgment" (Heb. 9:27). *Comparison with a human trial.*

1) *The accusation.* There is no hope of escaping this Judge or of bribing Him. All will be given perfect justice, rich and poor, educated and unlettered. But the good will find the Judge already well known to them: He is their Brother and Savior. The bad will find the Judge Him Who avenges. For them "it is a fearful thing to fall into the hands of the living God" (Heb. 10:13).

2) *Investigation, witnesses, arguments are useless.* The judge knows everything. Prosecution and defense are pointless. All our ordinary excuses ("I did not have time!") are vain. Even prayers now come too late! Now the time of mercy is over: this means that nothing can now be changed. He who dies as a friend of Christ, a member made like to his crucified Head, will find Him a friendly Judge: "Well done, thou good and faithful servant . . ." But he who dies as an enemy of Christ's cross will hear: "You wicked servant . . .".

The essential difference between this and a human trial. In the latter everything must be explained and proved to the judge; but in this judgment, the Judge Himself will tell us about our case. Would that the judgment we now make about ourselves might be found to agree with the infallible divine judgment! The criterion will be whether we have in reality attained the end that God established for us in Christ; whether we have arrived at that Christ-likeness to which we were called (Rom. 8:29). God judges only according to Christian considerations, not human ones. What would be His judgment if I stood before His throne now?

3) The sentence cannot be changed, cannot be rescinded. There is no hope of appeal or delay, no chance to plead for mercy, no further litigation.

Twenty-First Instruction

The General Judgment

Method: Historical-explanatory. In the first part of each point, the future event should be described vividly, but not fantastically. In the second part, the religious significance of these events should be explained.

Viewpoint: The final triumph of Christ. Union with Christ alone will bring us to final triumph and happiness.

Aim: Undaunted faith in the final victory of Christ, sheer joy with Christ in His triumph; the following of Christ through all things ("together with Him to die and to triumph over death").

DOCTRINAL SUMMARY

A. The Resurrection of the Dead

"The hour is coming in which all who are in the tombs shall hear the voice of the Son of God. And they who have done good shall come forth unto resurrection of life; but they who have done evil unto resurrection of judgment" (John 5:28). How great a manifestation of the Lord's power. How greatly it surpasses the miraculous raising of Lazarus from death, and even the glorious personal resurrection of Christ Himself! All shall rise, but differently. The friends of Christ with glorious bodies that share in the glory of the risen Christ; the enemies of Christ with bodies that are fitting to the state of their souls. We do not know "how" God's power will bring this about. All subtle questions about the identity of our glorious bodies with those we now have are to be carefully avoided. The general resurrection is one of the mysteries of the Christian faith.

This will be the final and perfect paschal feast: the completion of the resurrection of the whole Christ, Head and members also. The whole of human nature sinned, the whole was restored and elevated in Christ; now the whole is to be glorified. Such glorification is due to one who is a member of Christ and a temple of the Holy Spirit, who has been so often sanctified and nourished by the most Holy Eucharist. The reverence due to a Christian body, living or dead.

The superabundant restoration of the harmony of paradise. Now finally the work of restitution will be completed. The preternatural gifts of the first paradise, not yet given back to us, then will be abundantly showered on us, and much more besides. Then finally we shall see the full significance of the phrase "O happy fault" (Exsultet).

There is only one road to this perfect glory and happiness: "Provided, however, that we suffer with Him that we may also be glorified with Him" (Rom. 8:17; see also Rom. 6 and 7; 1 Cor. 15: 42–44; John 12:23–25). Let us die now to the law of sin in our members so that the life of Christ also may be manifested in us.

B. The Second Coming of Christ

A vivid description of this coming, *comparing it to Christ's first coming.* Then He "stole in", now He is manifested to all; then He came in humility, now in glory; then to invite men, now to compel them; then to struggle and suffer, now to triumph completely.

Let us now in hope share the joy of Christ triumphant, have firm confidence in His final victory, whatever may happen. Let us greatly desire this victory.

Christ is He Who *perfects the Church.* "Whence (that is, from heaven), we eagerly await a Savior, our Lord Jesus Christ, Who will refashion the body of our lowliness, conforming it to the body of His glory by exerting the power by which He is able to subject all things to Himself" (Phil. 3:20). Then He will re-form to its complete perfection the Church now suffering on earth, laboring under so many imperfections. Come, Lord, come; we await you with holy impatience! May you find us watching, faithful, and ready.

C. The General Judgment

The Judge: Christ the Man, the God-Man, our Lord and most beloved Brother. He will judge with divine majesty.

The nature of the judgment: the divine sentence concluding the whole history of salvation will be proclaimed to the whole world.

The object of the judgment: the material object is the history of salvation: the formal object is God's salvific will, realized in Christ. In distinction to the particular judgment, this will be the judgment of all, and of each individual action and person with respect to the whole.

The passive subjects: all men and angels, divided into two classes according to their attitude to Christ. Not only individual men, but human communities, families, peoples.

The active subjects: The members of Christ who carry out the office of judging together with Christ. Joyful acclamations: "You speak to us from the heart! Your judgment is our judgment!" Now we should already judge this world in Christ. But we should strive to be rather "saviors" than "judges".

Criterion of the judgment: our relationship to Christ: "Whatever . . . you have done to Me". According to our works, whether external or internal: not according to our empty wishes or unproductive words.

The results of the judgment: the magnificent revelation of God. Then at last will His justice, mercy, wisdom, and especially His divine providence be splendidly shown forth to all creation. This will be the consummation of all rightful human longings for justice. It will be the conclusive restoration or loss of our "face" before God and men. Thoughts of this judgment are an effective remedy against vain human respect (Luke 9:26). This will be the conclusive consummation:

"Come, blessed of My Father . . . depart from Me, and so be forever removed from the Father."

NOTE ON TEACHING THIS MATERIAL

The material given above should suffice for more than one instruction if time allows. Sermons on the final triumph of Christ and the eventual defeat of His enemies assist greatly in purging our souls and uniting them sincerely with Christ. If only one instruction can be given on this subject, it might be better to begin the third point with a description of the judgment itself according to Holy Scripture (especially Matt. 25:31–46). Then in the explanation there should be a further development of the material on the purpose of the judgment. The remaining material may be used summarily within the preceding description.

It is needless to say that in teaching and preaching on this topic, all discussions of the time of the Last Judgment should be avoided.

We should take particular care here to explain clearly that this triumph is the *perfect revelation of providence*. Let us use all occasions that present themselves to remind our people about divine providence. For example in instructions on creation (natural providence); on the elevation (supernatural providence); on the fall and the Incarnation (providence for the fallen human race); on the Resurrection of Christ (the most special providence concerning the Only-begotten); the law of this providence: (through the cross to glory); on the Church and the Sacraments, especially the Eucharist (the fatherly providence of God for His children adopted in Christ). A separate instruction on divine providence will then be less necessary, provided that we really use such opportunities. But if circumstances, such as the special difficulties of our time or of our people, demand a special instruction, such a lesson can be very well added after the instruction on the last judgment.

DOCTRINE ON HELL AND HEAVEN

We give the doctrine on hell first, so as to end the first part of Christian doctrine, the story of divine love, with the achievement of the goal of that love. And, also, the teaching on hell is in a way a good psychological preparation for the teaching on heaven, since it purges the heart from earthly passions ("Blessed are the clean of heart") and so removes impediments to the contemplation of the life of heaven.

On the other hand, it cannot be denied that the religious understanding of Hell presupposes an appreciation of the heavenly reward. How could one ponder the punishment of loss without pondering what the damned miss forever—heaven? From this point of view, it would be better to teach the doctrine concerning heaven first. A good solution which would include both values might be this: to teach first the doctrine on heaven, then that on hell; and, at the very end, as a conclusion and recapitulation of the whole first part of the course of instructions, to give a summary of all that God has done for us in order to have us with Him for ever in heaven.

In these instructions, hell and heaven should not be described minutely or fantastically, but rather by means of comparisons adapted to the minds of the audience. The description of hell especially should not be drawn from one's own imagination, but entirely from Holy Scripture. While teaching and preaching these things, let us strive to put on the person of Jesus Christ in a special way; the faithful require here a deep and sincere faith, which will truly believe in these punishments and rewards that so far surpass our imagination and understanding.

Twenty-Second Instruction

Hell

Method: Explanatory. A description of hell, taken from Holy Scripture, takes the place of a narrative; though to begin the lesson, some parable, as that of Dives and Lazarus (Luke 16:19ff), or even some picture may be used. The use of pictures in instructing the unlettered and the young is not objectionable, provided that the picture is really suitable for teaching, and that the catechist himself does not let the entire lesson consist in a description of the pain of sense only.

Viewpoint: Behold the judgment of the holy and just God on mortal sin. See the great folly of sin! How stupid to yearn for pleasures that are punished with such great torments. See the malice of mortal sin, which God the Just must punish thus. See the goodness of God most merciful, Who has warned us through His Son, "Who has not spared even His own Son, but has delivered Him up for us all . . ." (Rom. 8:32), in order that we, His ungrateful and rebellious children, might be spared.

Aim: Horror of sin. "Rather die than commit sin!" This instruction is intended to bring about a radical conversion in hearers who are in the state of mortal sin; to convince them not to play with fire any longer, to remove and avoid occasions of sin at once. And this instruction is also intended to preserve the good from the calamity of sin. *Gratitude for the mercy of God,* Who has done so many and so great wonders to snatch me from this disaster ". . . thanks to the Father, Who . . . has rescued us from the power of darkness and transferred us into the Kingdom of His beloved Son, in Whom we have our redemption, the remission of our sins" (Col. 1:12–14). In this way, even this instruction will be made Christocentric, and will bear full Christian fruit.

DOCTRINAL SUMMARY

A. WHAT OUR SAVIOR TEACHES ABOUT HELL

Christ, the Good Shepherd and most merciful Savior, Who did not come to condemn, but rather to seek that which was lost, quite often spoke clearly about hell, its fire and other torments. None of us has ever seen heaven; neither have we seen hell. But Christ had: as God, He created it; as Redeemer, He frees us from it; as Judge, He fixes its limits; and as the Good Shepherd, He warns us against it. Again and again the words of Christ distinguish a *double punishment:* of loss ("Cast him out", "Depart from Me"), and of sense ("into eternal fire"). Evidently the fire is not earthly fire, but one created by God especially for this purpose. Just as God will reward beyond all created imagination, so also He will justly punish (cf. Heb. 10:31). Yet this punishment of the senses is the lesser pain, even though it makes a greater impression on us here and now. The blinded sinner, who has freely rejected God and put some worthless object in His place, is especially unable to appreciate the punishment of loss. Yet this punishment must always be pointed out and explained with fitting examples. For example, a son who for some dreadful crime is expelled from his family. He would hardly feel this punishment while his passions are still aroused. But later on, he will gradually come to feel the misery of his condition, and will be tortured by a great desire for his family.

The greatness of the punishment will be increased by two circumstances nearly always mentioned by Christ: *the eternity of hell,* and *the gnawing of conscience* ("worm").

In hell there is no hope, no Savior. A comparison of this saddest of moments for the damned with the sentence given after the sin in paradise. This is the state of complete and conclusive separation from God; now there can be no more "bridge and bridge-builder" *(pons et pontifex)* to reconcile the damned with God. But we still have hope, because we have Christ the Redeemer. "My dear children, these things I write to you in order that you may not sin. But if anyone sins, we have an advocate with the Father, Jesus Christ the just; and he is a propitiation for our sins, not for ours only but also for those of the whole world" (1 John 2:1ff).

B. WHO WILL GO TO HELL?

Only those who have sinned mortally and have not sincerely repented. No one can fall into this calamity unawares and imperceptibly. Mortal sin necessarily requires *fully deliberate rebellion against God.* See the frightfulness of sin, which must be punished in such a way by the most just and holy God. Lord, from Your way of acting, I realize the malice of mortal sin, "I believe" in its dreadfulness. The amazing appropriateness of this horrible punishment. Finally, and usually after long delay, many warnings and opportunities for penance, God repays the rebellion of His creature with the punishment of hell, which the creature chose himself by his fully deliberate rejection of God through mortal sin. In every mortal sin, the sinner freely rejects God, his final and highest good, and prefers some cheap and transitory creature to Him. In His judgment on mortal sin, God only ratifies the decision of the creature, and gives him what he himself has impiously chosen. To his deliberate turning away from God corresponds God's rejection of him (the punishment of loss); to his turning toward a creature corresponds the disastrous deception on the part of the creature (the punishment of sense); to the repudiation of eternal good there corresponds eternal separation from God. By such reasonings, we do not fully solve the "mystery of hell" or the "mystery of sin"; we only intend to prepare our hearers psychologically for the ready acknowledgment of the supreme holiness and justice of God. Ultimately these are mysteries in which we must believe; we cannot understand them fully. "Thou are just, O Lord, and Thy judgment is right" (Ps. 118:137).

But we should never forget that God created hell because of His justice, and He has clearly revealed its existence to us because of His love, in order to spare us that disaster. "Today, if you hear his voice, do not harden your hearts" (Ps. 94:8). He not only warns you, He even sends His own Son, and does not spare Him, in order that you may be spared. At the very moment when we, in His name are presenting this terrifying doctrine, He in His merciful love again invites us all, both preacher and audience, to make use of His mercy and of the blood that His Son shed for us.

"But all things are from God, who has reconciled us to himself through Christ and has given to us the ministry of reconciliation. For God was truly in Christ, reconciling the world to Himself by not reckoning against men their sins and by entrusting to us the message of reconciliation.

On behalf of Christ, therefore, we are acting as ambassadors, God, as it were, appealing through us. We exhort you, for Christ's sake, be reconciled to God. For our sakes He made Him to be sin who knew nothing of sin, so that in Him we might become the justice of God" (2 Cor. 5:18–21).

Twenty-Third Instruction

Heaven

Method: Explanatory. Following Christ's own example, the doctrine of heaven is to be explained mainly by apt comparisons.

Viewpoint: Behold the full fruition of our sonship, our final sharing in the glory of and riches of Christ (co-heirs with Christ).

Aim: Unitive love. Intimate desire for perfect union with God. The doctrine of heaven should not be presented in such a way as to arouse hope alone (the love of concupiscence) but also to arouse charity and perfect it (the love of benevolence), together with the apostolic desire to help others attain this happiness.

DOCTRINAL SUMMARY

A. Now as in a Mirror, Darkly (1 Cor. 13:12)

Comparison with the beggar-boy raised up to be an adopted child of the king. On the way to his father's palace, the true son tells him about his father, about his happy life. Even though the beggar boy cannot understand more than a part of all this, since it all surpasses anything in his experience, yet he wants to hear more. He believes what he is told, he hopes for it, yet the reality will far surpass his narrow imagination, not yet accustomed to royal dimensions. So are we with regard to heavenly happiness; we must now *"believe"* our Divine Brother. Just as a man blind from birth cannot picture to himself the beauty of the sun and the starry skies, so the beauty and splendor of heaven entirely surpass our powers of understanding and imagination. "Eye has not seen, nor ear heard, nor has it entered into the heart of man, what things God has prepared for those who love Him" (1 Cor. 2:9). "No one has at any time seen God. The only-begotten Son who is in the bosom of the Father, He has revealed Him" (1 John 1:18).

B. Behold, I Make All Things New—the New Paradise

The first Adam lost paradise through sin, the second Adam restores it to us. Our paradise is heaven. The heavenly life is the completely developed Christian life. These are the *riches of the second Adam.*

The new joys of paradise after the sorrows and hardships of this world. "And God will wipe away every tear from their eyes. And death shall be no more; neither shall there be mourning nor crying, nor pain any more, for the former things have passed away" (Apoc. 21:4). No pain now, neither present, nor to be feared in the future. How great were the joys of the first paradise . . . truly a "garden of delights", but how limited and worthless in comparison to heavenly joys. A vivid description of the joys of paradise—application to the second paradise.

New peace of paradise after the struggles of this world. Then at last the harmony of paradise will be perfectly restored. No temptations or disturbances. Perfect peace with others also. Supreme social joy . . . as many joys as companions. Perfect imperturbable peace . . . impeccability. In the first paradise, "they were able not to sin"; in the second, "they cannot sin". In the first paradise, "they were able not to suffer and die," in the second, "they cannot suffer or die".

New rest of paradise (abundance). After the labors and wants of this world, full happiness, "full" joy. Then at last the human heart will be perfectly satisfied. Then we shall taste, not single drops of happiness, but perfect beatitude.

New paradisal prayer after the aridity and spiritual dullness of this world. In the first paradise, how pleasant was the familiar conversation with God. But this was only a figure of the heavenly reality. In heaven we shall at last see God face to face, not by means of an image, but in Himself, and we will love God and delight in Him. Then at last God will be "all in all" (1 Cor. 15:29). The human heart was created for love. In the eternal embrace of the Father it will at last be satisfied. The greatest delights of earthly love are as tiny droplets in comparison to the infinite ocean of heavenly delights. This new paradisal love will consist essentially in the full effusion of the Holy Spirit into our hearts, crying, "Abba, Father" (Rom. 8:15). Then finally the work of the Spirit, the Perfector, will be completed.

Just as the second Adam infinitely surpasses the first in dignity, merits and glory, so also does the second paradise surpass the transitory and provisional paradise given to the first Adam. Our weak nature could not sustain such happiness; *God must strengthen,* support and help it with a very special assistance; He gives new insight *(lumen)* and a new heart. "And He who was sitting on the throne said, Behold, I make all things new" (Apoc. 21:5). That final, most blessed renewal will transform us perfectly into the likeness of the Only-begotten Son (1 Cor. 15:47-49; Rom. 8:29ff).

Then at last the joys of Christ will completely be our joys: His victory, our victory; His glory, our glory: in a word, the inheritance of Christ will be our inheritance (Rom. 8:17). And so the way to such happiness is also easily understood.

C.   "Provided, However, That We Suffer With Him That We Also Be Glorified With Him" (Rom. 8:17)

The *only way* to participate in the glory of the risen Christ is participation in the humility of the suffering Christ. The shortest formula of Christian life: *"To die and to live with Christ!"* The more you now become like the humble Christ, the more you will become like the triumphant Christ. There is a great diversity of degrees of sharing. Let us share more and more completely in His death and His life.

We Christians do not foster any useless sorrow because of the loss of the first paradise, rather we hasten toward the Christian paradise, led by Christ, the second Adam. We desire this paradise with our whole hearts, and we sacrifice everything for it. We can lose all things in this world. On this earth we will have many afflictions. "In the world you will have affliction, but take courage, I have overcome the world" (John 16:33). "Father, I will that where I am, they also whom Thou hast given me may be with me . . ." (John 17:24).

This is the end of the history of
the eternal divine love.

Section II

The Response of Our Grateful Love

or

The Christian Life

How We Are to Answer God's Love
by Christian Living

The first part of Christian doctrine presents the history of divine love, proclaiming what God has done from eternity, is doing and will do out of love for us. The second part shows us how we may fittingly respond to this great love. It indicates clearly the viewpoint from which teaching on the Christian life is to be presented, namely as the response of our love to God's love, of our gratitude to the divine blessings.

But in making these the two main divisions of Christian doctrine, we do not intend to suggest that in actual teaching and preaching, the doctrine of the Christian life must necessarily be presented as a second part, distinctly separate from the story of salvation. For example, it would cause no difficulty if these lessons on the nature and character of the Christian life were to be given immediately after the explanation of the Sacrament of Baptism (Fourteenth Instruction), and the explanation of the various commandments distributed through the instructions on the history of divine love. In the following lessons explaining the commandments, we will give concrete suggestions as to ways of doing this. And certainly, for pedagogical reasons, it is highly desirable, at least in the case of a series of three or more instructions (as are often given, for example, when a missionary visits his outstations) to include in each series one practical instruction on the Christian life, showing how the dogmas presented in the other instructions are to be lived in a practical way.

Yet for the purpose of this book, in order to give a clear outline of our whole message, we are presenting the lessons on Christian living all together in a systematic way. For by so doing, it is easy for the

161

teacher to see the viewpoint from which each particular doctrine is to be proclaimed.

We should continually explain the Christian life under the threefold aspect of:

1) *A life lived by faith.* "My just man lives by faith" (Heb. 2:4; Rom. 1:17; Gal. 3:11; Heb. 10:38). How strongly does St. Paul emphasize this aspect of the Christian life! The Christian life is nothing other than the response of the whole man to the revelation that he receives with a sincere heart and strives to express by his whole life: Divine revelation is given to us as the word of life (John 6:64–69; 20:31); as the doctrine of the divine life given us to bring us to true life in God (John 17:3). And divine revelation certainly is, of its own essential nature, the revelation of the divine love that chooses, calls, and enriches us in Christ. Therefore the Christian life must also be considered as:

2) *The response of our love to divine love.* The Father's love has made us sons of God in Christ; our love makes us live as good sons "in Christ", because only in Christ are we sons of the Father. In other words, the gift of the Father's love is Christ, and the return-gift of our love is also Christ, that is, Christ formed in us, Christ expressed in the idiom of our own individuality, each of us living as "another Christ". Just as the Father gives us all His divine riches in this gift of His Son and pours them out on us, so also all our powers of giving to Him are to be drawn up into this same gift.

3) *The Christ-like life.* It is obvious that these three aspects of the Christian life are interdependent; each implies and demands the other two. Would that all Catholics might come daily more and more to consider and to look upon the Christian life in this way! For this purpose, an attractive and clear *separate instruction on the Christian life as such* can be of considerable assistance, and here the illustration of the beggar-boy taken into the family of a king can be used even with simple people. A suitable occasion for such an explanation might follow the teaching on the obligation contracted at Baptism (Fourteenth Instruction), or after the Fifteenth on prayer. But, for the Christian formation of our hearers, it is of the very greatest importance that such pondering on the implications of the Christian life becomes the daily bread which we continue always to give them, now in one form and now in another; and that whenever and however we speak of the Christian life, its Christocentric character may always be made apparent.

Ideal catechetical teaching on Christian living strives not so much to explain minutely and to inculcate diligently individual precepts, but rather to convey the interior meaning of the Christian life, the ever-continuing obligation of gratitude, the privilege, glory and transcendence of the Christian life. Truly we have been born, or rather re-born for great things! O that daily we may become more worthy children of God, more closely resembling our model, living more according to Christ and in Christ, more perfectly carrying out His work in the world! This is the "good tidings" of the Christian life.

And even though, when preaching the Christian life, we dwell especially on its beauty and desirability, we must also clearly teach its obligatory character. "Noblesse oblige". Benefits bring obligations, and the greatest benefits the greatest obligations. To live as a Christian is a wonderful privilege; it is also a duty.

Thus the ideal preaching and teaching of the Christian life will, on the one hand, call Christians to eager and delighted cooperation with the grace of their Christian vocation—the greatest things are to be sought by us and with the greatest fervor; and, on the other hand, it will duly humble them . . . what a great distance between this voca-tion and our daily lives! Thus at once we rejoice, and yet are sorrowful and consumed by a holy impatience generously to overcome the obstacles created by our own sinfulness, selfishness and weakness. Our Christian calling, demanding a Christ-like life from weak men, a divine life, far surpasses our natural powers. Thus we must come humbly to acknowl-edge our own insufficiency and have recourse to God with our whole hearts. Our eyes must be turned to God from Whom comes our help. "He who called you is faithful, and will do this" (1 Thess. 5:24).

The response of Christian love, then, is twofold: first the almost spontaneous response of the Christian heart is the *response of Christian prayer, direct worship;* and, second, *love shown through action, indirect worship.* Or, for practical reasons, we might state it as being, first the response of *loving prayer* and, second, of *loving observance of the com-mandments.* But we should not forget that the most fundamental precepts of the Decalogue itself deal with prayer and direct worship. And, after all, Christian living is far more than observance of the commandments, since by fully Christian living we strive to do much more than we are strictly obliged to do.

But to divide this second section according to direct worship and indirect has two special catechetical advantages: 1) It shows how the Christian message by its nature is directed to Christian worship. Christian worship in the full sense is the fruit of our catechetical apostolate; in this way, like Christ Himself, we are "heralding the joyful tidings of the Kingdom of God" (Mark 1:14). Thus the close relationship of the catechetical to the liturgical apostolate becomes clear, since liturgy is the climax of Christian worship. And 2) It brings out clearly the close connection between prayer and worship, liturgy and life.

Christian Life Made Up of Prayer and Action

True Christian living is, above all, a life of real Christian prayer. Training in the spirit of prayer is rightly considered by authorities on pastoral and catechetical theology to be the most important part of Christian education. And such training cannot be given only by means of even the most moving sermons on the excellence and necessity of prayer. Here we should learn from the Christian mother who teaches her children to pray by praying—not by theoretical discourses but by frequently repeated suggestions and motivations, by official "family prayers" and by prayer interwoven into the fabric of daily life. So we should bring prayer into every lesson and sermon, often explicitly, always implicitly, in a few words encouraging our hearers to strive to unite themselves inwardly with God, that is, to pray.

Moreover, every doctrine should be taught in such a way as to become "prayable". Every part of our message should be so presented as to nourish the Christian mind and heart for conscious communion with the heavenly Father. Often, especially in teaching children, we should go a step further and explicitly show how each doctrine might be prayed, praying it with our hearers in a spontaneous way. But to do so, of course, requires a catechist who himself knows how to pray his message. And, like the good Christian mother, we should also frequently show our hearers by concrete examples how in each and every circumstance they may lift up their hearts to their Father in heaven, beyond any prayer-formulas at all.

But good training in prayer also requires suitable prayer-formulas. Concerning such formulas, we must take care, above all, that they reflect the genuine spirit of Christian prayer, and that, at the same time, they are formulated in a way fitted to those who are to use them. It is most helpful, if not absolutely necessary, to give children formulas that are especially fitted to their needs. But it would be completely wrong to think that adaptation to the mentality of children means sentimentality or the abandonment of the great themes of genuine Christian prayer. (Good examples of how the Mystery of Christ can be prayed by first- and second-graders may be found in the *On Our Way* series, before mentioned.)

The prayer of action necessarily follows the sincere prayer of the heart. Obviously any affection that does not effectively tend toward action is not truly sincere. And therefore the second aspect of our grateful response to God's love is the keeping of the Commandments (Matt. 7:21; John 14:21. Cf. John 14:15, 15:10; 1 John 5:3). But what pleases the Father is not our works in themselves, but their prayer-like character, the disposition to spend ourselves in the Father's service, and to do everything as perfectly as we can for His sake "... for man seeth those things which appear, but the Lord beholdeth the heart" (1 Kings 16:7).

The only Christian law is charity (Matt. 22:37). "Love"—truly and wholeheartedly—"and do what you will" (St. Augustine). For then you will do far more than the commandments prescribe. Each and every commandment is only a special application of the Commandment of love, and therefore should be explained and thought of in this light. In the last analysis, they have value and power to oblige insofar as they show us how to carry out the commandment of charity.

The Christian attitude is not a pharisaical attitude toward the law: the true Christian looks primarily to the spirit, and to the ultimate reason for the law, that is, charity. The pharisaical attitude becomes immersed in a multitude of laws; it attributes absolute value to particular laws, and thus becomes a slave to the dead letter. But because the pharisee neglects its purpose, the law for him becomes not a guide to God, but often a real hindrance. The Christian religion demands a perfect, complete self-surrender, a real holocaust. The pharisee really wants to escape from making this complete offering by making many partial gifts. His religious life is ruled, finally, not by love, but by his own self-love, and so he is prepared to sacrifice everything except himself. So he does not want to give himself to God, but to trade with God for spiritual profit.

In preaching the divine law, we should strive with all our powers to keep our hearers from this pharisaical attitude, or to free them from it, if they are already infected with it. Therefore we must show above all the meaning and purpose of Christian law, and clearly point out how each commandment flows from the law of charity. In the explanation of each commandment, its "Christian" character must always be pointed out; that is, how its observance makes us Christ-like. The commandments thus help to form in us a new man, renewed in Christ in his worship of the Father, in his relationship to his brethren in Christ, to the material goods of this world, and to truth.

The explanation of each commandment should not become a sterile enumeration and description of the sins by which God can be offended. First let us explain the exact meaning of the commandment, depict the exact Christian ideal and give its connection with the Mystery of

Christ; then show that the chief sins against this commandment are deplorable degradations of this ideal, and briefly but clearly indicate their "anti-Christian" nature.

And we should also strive to make our hearers understand that day by day they should more fully achieve the Christian attitude which no longer asks: "What am I strictly obliged to do, here and now?", but rather, "What can I do to show my love, to respond to the Father's love more and more perfectly, to become and to do what He desires?" Such stress on Christian generosity, however, must obviously not lead us to neglect making clear the distinction between commands and counsels. Neither should we omit to emphasize the chief commandments, nor to minimize the liberty of the children of God.

Abundant literature on the moral life already exists and, therefore, we are indicating here only very summarily what is to be given in the moral instructions. We wish to make clear particularly the context in which the material is to be proposed, the chief points to be presented, and the aspect under which to present them. We presuppose, as we said above, that frequent instructions are being given by which our hearers are assisted to a more fruitful reception of the Sacrament of Penance. Such instructions on Confession by their nature will explain particularly—though not exclusively—the negative aspect of moral teaching, and the sins against God's law. Therefore in the following lessons we shall emphasize especially the positive aspect. But, of course, both are absolutely necessary.

In the following lessons, we will introduce almost exclusively "Christian motives". Good moral training makes use of *naturally good motives as well*. But it should indicate how these natural values, such as reputation, family, country, etc., have been sanctified and ennobled in Christ and so have been given a new meaning for Christians.

As we said above, in actual preaching and teaching, it is better not to treat the individual commandments at the end of the whole course, but rather to distribute them throughout. In each of the following instructions, therefore, we indicate a suitable place, catechetically speaking, in which each might conveniently be treated.

I

Our Filial Response by Christian Prayer
Direct Worship (The First Three Commandments)

Two instructions are presented under this heading, both dealing with Christian worship, but from different standpoints. The first is to give an understanding of Christian prayer, its nature, qualities and excellence; prayer seen as the great privilege of God's children. But direct worship is not only a privilege, it is also a duty for God's children, and the most fundamental one. In the second lesson, it is considered from this second viewpoint, giving a catechetical explanation of the first three commandments.

Twenty-Fourth Instruction

The Excellence of Christian Prayer — Christian Prayer Our Great Privilege

In this lesson, the classic form of Christian prayer—praise and thanksgiving—is chiefly inculcated. Yet any prayer is good which proceeds from the filial spirit, and Christ Himself taught us in all our needs to seek refuge in the Father with filial trust. Psychologically, then, we may begin with impetratory prayer, but we must lead to the prayer of praise and gratitude.

The material given here is far too much for one instruction. If time allows only one instruction on this subject, the nature, properties and principal affections of Christian prayer should above all be thoroughly explained.

Method: Explanatory, developed from a comparison with the conversation of a child in a family.

Viewpoint: From the beginning, Christian prayer should be presented as child-like conversation with God. And also from the very beginning, it should be shown to be the goal and culminating point of the Christian life. True Christian prayer is by its nature Christ-like prayer, and, in consequence, above all the prayer of praise and thanksgiving.

An introduction should be given concerning Christian life in general: what we have explained above as to the meaning and main aspect of the Christian life should be explained here, or, better, in a separate preliminary instruction. In either case, the connection of the life of prayer with the Christian life should be clearly shown, and the importance of this connection should be stressed.

A. THE NATURE OF CHRISTIAN PRAYER

Comparison with the conduct of a good child in a family. To what does the thought of his father's love and goodness urge a good child first of all? To express his love for the father, acknowledging his goodness and benefits with a grateful heart. This nature of Christian prayer is formulated in Gal. 4:4–6: "When the fullness of time came, God sent his Son . . . that we might receive the adoption of sons. And because you are sons, God has sent the Spirit of his Son into your hearts, crying, Abba, Father" (cf. also Rom. 8:5). Here is the intimate relationship of Christian prayer with the "Mystery of Christ". It is the loving answer of Christian hearts to this mystery of divine love; it is, finally, the work of the Holy Spirit in our hearts. He communicates to us the spirit of Christ, and in this spirit Christian prayer is fully focussed on the heavenly Father.

B. The Principal Sources of Prayer

The principal sources from which this filial conversation is nourished: *appreciation* of the Father (knowledge of His goodness), filial *trust*, filial *love*. The chief well-springs of Christian prayer are faith, hope and charity. The quality of Christian prayer essentially depends upon the extent to which it contains faith, hope and charity; in other words, the more a prayer unites us to God in faith, hope and charity, the more perfect it is. Obviously, faith, hope and charity are not to be made three distinct "acts" in our prayers. The simple "Father!" which the Holy Spirit allows us to pray contains in the most perfect way all these three virtues.

C. The Essential Properties of Christian Prayer

The essential properties of Christian prayer may be easily understood by a comparison of the conversation of a good son with his father. They follow immediately from the nature of Christian prayer: it should be son-like, sincere, simple, personal, and especially Christ-like, following the example of our Brother. The Christ-likeness of Christian prayer consists chiefly in the fact that it is offered "in union with the same Holy Spirit" who inspired the Heart of Christ to filial prayer. Real Christian prayer is offered not only according to the example of Christ, but also "through Him, with Him, and in Him", and this is true most especially when we share in Christ's sacrifice by actual participation in the Mass.

D. The Principal Affections of Christian Prayer

Again, these can be developed from the ideal of the conversation of a child with his father: gratitude, submission, admiration, and unitive love. These same affections follow from the Christ-likeness of Christian prayer. Behold the chief affections of the Most Sacred Heart of Jesus, continually praying in the highest possible way.

E. THE MOST EXCELLENT FORMULAS OF CHRISTIAN PRAYER

The *Our Father* is the classic Christian prayer. To it is due the greatest reverence, together with thoughtful, reverent, and personal use. It shows us most beautifully the spirit of the prayer of Christ. How readily and wonderfully does it illustrate the nature, sources, properties and affections of Christian prayer. We should focus special attention on the spirit of this prayer; not so much explaining each word or phrase, but rather the spirit from which the whole prayer flows and according to which the words and phrases are to be interpreted: God in the midst of our hearts. This divine "Thou", Whom we embrace with reverence and love, fills our hearts and wholly occupies them. God is all in all, and all things are in God.

The *Apostles' Creed* is the second formula of ideal prayer. It is not a dry enumeration of dogmas which we "must" believe, but a joyful proclamation and acknowledgment of the benefits of eternal divine love, an admiring enumeration of the gifts of the loving God Who gives Himself. Every article of faith is a new gift from God. O my God, I believe in Your eternal love; O may I believe ever more steadfastly! These are the fundamental doctrines, the foundations of the Christian life. The Creed is not only to be believed, it is also to be lived. This is the way that leads to life!

The *greatest act of prayer* is the Sacrifice of the Mass. What a magnificent exchange of love! This is the most wonderful tribute and thanksgiving possible to God's redeemed children. Christ is given and received! (cf. Instruction XVI).

Twenty-Fifth Instruction

Filial Worship — the Most Fundamental Duty of God's Children (The First Three Commandments)

The first three commandments of the Decalogue are the most fundamental since they treat of our ideal relationship with God Himself. Christian moral teaching is entirely God-centered, not man-centered. This truth should be clearly and forcibly shown to the Christians of our times, but in a positive way. The main aspect under which a true Christian looks upon the whole moral life is as our submission as children of God offered to the Father throughout this life. The second section of the Decalogue, dealing with social life, must also always be considered in this light.

Although the first three commandments are of such great importance, they can be sufficiently explained in one lesson in a series for adult Christians, provided that the rest of our teaching is theocentric, and that a special instruction on prayer is given. And the chief object of these three commandments, that is, filial submission to God, may be inculcated in almost every instruction, now in one way and now in another.

In what connection: After the doctrine of the Creation and Elevation, and before the doctrine of the Fall. The doctrine of our creation and elevation offers the dogmatic foundation; the doctrine of the Fall shows the dreadful consequences of rebellion against God, and thus adds effective new motives for obedience.

Method: Explanatory. Our obligations to God are easily understood from a comparison with the duties of a good son.

Viewpoint: As with all the commandments of the Decalogue, so these first three are to be kept in a new spirit. This is divine worship, offered not in the spirit of slaves, in fear and trembling, but in the spirit of sons, with profound reverence and intimate filial love. Behold "the true worshippers . . . in spirit and in truth. For the Father seeks such to worship Him" (John 4:23) and in Christ He finds them. The Christ-like worship of God.

In explaining these commandments, we must of course show what external acts are of obligation; but we must insist especially on the internal spirit of reverence and profound adoration. It is in vain to demand the performance of external duties (daily prayers, Sunday Mass, etc.) unless our hearers are first filled with the spirit of the children of God, from which these external actions and many others not prescribed will then flow spontaneously. The fact that so many Christians neglect the life of prayer is not due to external difficulties, but rather to ignorance and lack of due reverence and love for the Father.

Aim: That the messianic age may come also for us in all its perfection; that the hour may come, and may now be at hand, "when the true worshippers will *worship the Father in spirit and in truth*" (John 4:23). The God-centered life according to the example of Christ.

DOCTRINAL SUMMARY

The foregoing lessons on our creation and elevation have shown what great benefits God has lavished on us. How rich we are! And all these blessings come from the all-good and infinitely exalted God, whose special servants, yes, and sons also, we are privileged to be. May we be perfect children! Just as in a human family, so also in the family of the children of God, the children ought:

A. DAILY TO KNOW THEIR FATHER BETTER

Pagans are ignorant of Him; they adore false gods. Even we do not know our Father well enough. How blessed we are to know Him through His fatherly manifestation in Christ: "God spoke of old to our ancestors through the prophets; at the present time, the final epoch, he has spoken to us through his Son" (Heb. 1:2). What a great blessing is divine revelation, to which we should respond by prompt and grateful faith (cf. the preliminary instruction, and also the sixth). Here we should show clearly how we truly worship God by every act of faith and hope, acknowledging Him as our supreme Lord, as infinite Wisdom and Goodness. Faith and hope are the most fundamental acts of Christian worship.

Here we should speak about the religion classes that bring us to a more intimate knowledge of the Father, and about the religious education of children in the family, which should always be urged "in season . . . and out of season". But intellectual knowledge is not enough; the acknowledgment and consent of the heart is required.

B. DAILY TO LOVE THE FATHER MORE

If you truly know Him, you will also love Him. His loveableness . . . only a most ungrateful son could deny his love to such a Father. Love for the Father necessarily stimulates us to remember Him often, to recall His blessings, and frequently to converse with Him. A son who lives with his family and yet forgets all about his father, who does not answer when his father calls him, who avoids all conversation with his father, is certainly to be considered a bad and ungrateful son. What, then, is to be thought of those unhappy Christians who carelessly neglect to pray? Morning prayers, evening prayers, Sunday prayers. But a truly loving son is not content with this minimum. How happy is the life of faithful and eager love, even here on earth!

C. DAILY TO HONOR THE FATHER MORE PERFECTLY

We honor because we love. Who would be unwilling to honor such a Father: even in a human family, the father owes it to himself and to his children to require due respect, due reverence, as an essential aspect of his children's love for him.

Reverence toward God. Reverence in prayer. Reverence in the use of God's name. Internal and external reverence. The prayer of praise. The most excellent prayer of praise is the Sacrifice of the Mass, which is the community paean of joy and thanksgiving of the redeemed children of God, united to their Redeemer Who leads them in praise. Sunday Mass, Sunday rest. The purpose of this rest: that we may have time to spend with our Father, and may acknowledge His primacy in our lives over earthly goods.

II

Our Filial Answer by Christian Work
Indirect Worship (Commandments 4-10)

Pray and work! The prayer of the heart is to be complemented, and its sincerity proved, by the prayer of labor and work. Compare with the conduct of good children in a family, who also show their devotion to their father by diligent work. The true meaning and value of work needs to be explained attractively, especially in our times. We Christians do not by any means look upon work merely as some kind of penance imposed upon us because of original sin. We esteem work very highly; but we do not evaluate it, either exclusively or primarily, according to temporal values. Even though we clearly recognize and carefully cultivate, in their due place, these temporal values established by God, nevertheless it is the heavenly values in our work that we look to and desire above all. Therefore for us even work to which temporal success is denied can have great value. Just as it would be stupid to evaluate the work done by Christ in His hidden life according to its material value, so also the labors of God's children cannot be accurately estimated by material measures alone.

The ideal Christian life is not divided into two separate compartments: the prayer by which we obtain heavenly goods, and the work by which we obtain earthly goods. As in everything else, so in our life of work, we Christians do not follow Adam before the Fall, or after the Fall, but the second Adam, the Savior. The following lessons, then, show how we Christians are to worship and serve God *in* the different phases and activities of human life.

Twenty-Sixth Instruction

The Christianization of the Family
(The Fourth Commandment)

By the Fourth Commandment of the Decalogue—the first to deal with the relationships of men among themselves—God solemnly recognizes and strongly safeguards the values of family life. But the Christian ideal is not a "humanism of the family" which would limit itself to human values; it is the Christianization of family life, which fully recognizes these values in their place, but at the same time gives them a new meaning in Christ. The earthly family becomes a symbol of the heavenly family.

In what connection: After the instruction on the birth and infancy of Christ. The Holy Family is the exemplar of the Christian family.

Method: Historical-explanatory. The life of the Holy Family provides the narrative: the care of those holy parents for the boy, Jesus; the relationship of Jesus to His parents. This description should be vivid and concrete, but not fanciful.

Viewpoint: The Christian task of the faithful family.

Aim: The Christianization of the Family.

DOCTRINAL SUMMARY

Introduction: Christ wished to be born, nourished, protected and educated in a family. By so doing, He sanctified the family. The Holy Family is the exemplar of the Christian family.

A. JESUS THE EXEMPLAR OF A GOOD SON

His reverence, His love, His obedience are profound, because they are entirely founded in God. See the dignity of parents in the eyes of Christ: they take the place of the Father. From his human parents, the true Christian ascends "to the Father of our Lord Jesus Christ, from whom all fatherhood in heaven and on earth receives its name" (Eph. 3:14ff). See how the Christian religion acknowledges, strengthens and perfects parental dignity and authority.

B. THE PARENTS OF CHRIST,
THE EXEMPLARS OF CHRISTIAN PARENTS

Because parents take the place of God the Father, they ought also to imitate His love, His truly paternal care, His mercy, His generosity. The religious awareness of their own dignity, authority and responsibility should also give them reverence for their children, in whom they ought to see little brothers and sisters of Christ committed to their care. It is not a mere child of man, but a son of God, who is given to them to bring up. You are not the owners, nor the absolute masters, but the administrators of this great treasure; you are the visible Guardian Angels of this child. The principle, "children are for the parents" is true if by it we mean the heavenly Father; it is false if applied to human parents.

But since it is a child of God who is entrusted to parents to educate and train for his lofty vocation, parents owe not only material, but mental and spiritual care to a child. To spend all their thought and energy on the acquisition of material things, even to shower them on their children, is not true Christian parental love. Parents have to strive to give themselves, the best of themselves, to their children's upbringing.

The true Christian acknowledges and gives respect to divine authority, not only in his parents, but also *in every legitimate authority*. When he himself is given authority to govern others, he exercises it, not for his own advantage, but for the common good.

Again, the true Christian considers not only the family, but civil society also as being a divine institution, and he cooperates faithfully with his fellow-citizens for the common good. *Christian patriotism*. And above all, he loves the family of the children of God, the Church of Christ, with heartfelt fervor, and cooperates with his fellow-Christians and the hierarchy for its good.

Twenty-Seventh Instruction

Fraternal Love and Assistance
(The Fifth Commandment)

Christ has gathered us into the family of God's children. The principal law of this family is the law of charity, the law of love toward our Father and toward our brethren. Our love for the Father must be shown and proved by fraternal charity. Because we love the Father with our whole heart, we acknowledge, deal with, and love all His children as our brothers. This is the mark of the true disciple of Christ. "By this will all men know that you are my disciples, if you have love for one another" (John 13:35).

In what connection: There are several suitable places in which to give this lesson, but the most fitting seem to us to be after the doctrine on the Church, or on the Eucharist. The Church is the assembly of the children of God, and its fundamental law is the law of charity. Fraternal charity is a criterion of the true Church of Christ, already called by St. Ignatius of Antioch "the assembly of charity". Christian charity also extends to men outside the Church, because all men are called to the Church and invited into the family of God. Our charity should manifest God's invitation to them. Or, again, the lesson on the Eucharist offers a good opportunity for this lesson on fraternal charity. How strongly Christ inculcated charity at the Last Supper, when, with the Apostles, He gave thanks for their first communion! Every true union among brothers comes from union with Christ. Every union of branches is derived from their union with the Vine.

Method: Explanatory. This is the principal law ordering the relationships of the members of Christ among themselves. Here the example of a well-ordered family may well be used.

Aim: The spirit of fraternal charity, from which the corresponding acts will flow in due course.

DOCTRINAL SUMMARY

A. The Foundation of Fraternal Charity

The new Christian order, in which all of us are called into the one family of God's children. Christ has brought us back into an intimate unity with one another which by far surpasses the natural unity of the family (see the Tenth Instruction; 1 Cor. 12:12ff; Eph. 4:4-6; 1 Tim. 2:5). *One God and Father* of all; one Christ and Redeemer of all; one faith and hope; one common treasure, that is, the inheritance of God's children; one Spirit and Life-Giver, Who communicates to us all the Spirit of Christ. But this is the Spirit of Christ: from love of the Father, to spend Himself in the service of the children of God; not to be ministered to, but to serve and sacrifice Himself for the salvation of others (Matt. 20:28; Luke 22:26ff; John 13:12-16).

B. The Character of Fraternal Charity

It is Christ-like—"as I have loved you" (John 13:34). Christ-like in motive, that is, for the sake of the Father, Whom we love as His children. It is Christ-like in intensity, prepared for the greatest sacrifices; Christ-like in universality, extending itself to strangers and even to enemies; Christ-like in endurance, persevering until death in spite of injuries, annoyances, the basest ingratitude.

C. The Violation of Fraternal Charity

We Christians are commissioned ceaselessly to manifest and to offer to the world the charity of Christ. We ought, in every possible way, to help men and to minister to them on the way to the Father. *See the anti-Christian nature of sins against the Fifth Commandment.* We ought to be, in Christ, "saviors" of the world, servants of our brethren and authors of happiness for them. What, then, if we purposefully or neglectfully hinder or trouble their happiness, if we injure them in any way in soul or body? "Why not rather suffer wrong? . . . But you yourselves do wrong and defraud, and that to the brethren" (1 Cor. 6:7). The special obligation of the fifth commandment in the Christian order:

it is concerned with saving and making pleasant, not the life on earth of slaves, but of sons of God. Since it is our special Christian vocation "in Christ" to be "saviors" of our brethren, to overcome sin in ourselves and in others, to promote the Kingdom of God, and thus to "cast out the prince of this world" (John 12:31), the anti-Christian malice of scandal and of deliberately leading away from Christ is obvious. Through scandal and seducing to evil, one becomes in a special way a collaborator of Satan, the Enemy of Christ.

Since these sins are in such direct opposition to the Christian vocation, we can understand the astonishing severity of Christ in indicating and censuring these sins. "It is impossible that scandals should not come; but woe to him through whom they come! It were better for him if a millstone were hung about his neck and he were thrown into the sea, than that he should cause one of these little ones to sin" (Luke 17:1–2). The Fifth Commandment is the first example that Christ uses in the Sermon on the Mount to illustrate the essential difference between the old law and the new (Matt. 5:21–26). Christ demands much, but He clearly shows why. He brands the opposing way of acting as simply pagan (Matt. 5:38–48). When Christ speaks of mortal sin or of hell, His typical example is almost always a violation of fraternal charity (Luke 16:19–31; Matt. 18:7, 23–35; 25:41–66).

D. THE BOND AND NOURISHMENT OF CHARITY

The Eucharist . . . *"Communion"*. "Because the bread is one, we, though many, are one body, all of us who partake of the same bread" (1 Cor. 10:27).

Twenty-Eighth Instruction

The Sanctity of the Body Consecrated in Baptism
(The Sixth and Ninth Commandments)

A disastrous consequence of Adam's sin was the rebellion of the flesh against the spirit. This was a just punishment for such a detestable rebellion of an adopted son against his loving Father! The "law of sin", by which the human race has been grievously oppressed ever since the Fall, is especially manifested in our being dominated by carnal desires. The new Adam, the Savior, has delivered us from the law of sin, overcoming its tyranny and leading us back to liberty of spirit. Through Christ, our whole human nature can once again be subjected to God and made holy. "Therefore do not let sin reign in your mortal body so that you obey its lusts . . . for sin shall not have dominion over you, since you are not under the law, but under grace" (Rom. 6:12-14).

In what connection? Many suitable places might be found for this lesson: for example, after the instruction on Baptism by which the whole man is made holy, or after that on the resurrection of the dead, which brings out the share of the body in Christ's glory. But for practical reasons, it is not so advisable to give this lesson in either of these two connections, since the lesson on Baptism should preferably be followed by that on the Christian life in general, and that on the Last Judgment by the explanation of the Eighth Commandment (Instruction XXX). It seems best, therefore, to connect this lesson with that on Marriage. Explaining the Sixth Commandment in this connection will make it easy to show how great is the good—the physical and moral purity of family life—which God wishes to protect by this Commandment. And in this connection also the biological and sociological importance of the Sixth Commandment will be clearly apparent. Or, this lesson might be connected with that on the Easter victory of Christ, in which case its "Christian" character becomes particularly apparent, and it must be presented in an entirely positive way. Since the positive and negative aspects complement one another, the best procedure is to insert this lesson sometimes after that on Matrimony and sometimes after that on the Resurrection.

Method: Historical-explanatory. Proceeding from the disastrous fall of Adam, and from Christ's Easter victory.

Viewpoint: Chastity is required of Christians. To be chaste is an effect of, and a participation in, Christ's victory.

Aim: That the peace of Christ may reign in our bodies also; that we may "present our bodies as a sacrifice, living, holy, pleasing to God —your spiritual service" (Rom. 12:1).

DOCTRINAL SUMMARY

A. THE FALL OF ADAM THE SINNER, THE VICTORY OF THE SECOND ADAM, THE SAVIOR

See the introduction to this lesson.

B. THE SPIRITUAL MAN RENEWED IN CHRIST

(1 Cor. 15:47-49). An attractive and positive portrayal of the Christian law as the rule of the spirit over the flesh. Our natural powers, given us by God, are not evil, nor is the pleasure which accompanies their due exercise. Rather that man is evil who inverts the right order of values, who allows himself to think of created good

things as his final end, and who allows or encourages the rebellion of his lower powers against the law of God. The spiritual man is the fully human man, perfectly subject to God, striving to subject all his desires, all his impulses to the divine will. In carnal man, the rebellion of Adam continues. Each of us must follow either Adam the rebellious, or the second Adam, the Obedient. No one can serve two masters. Even our bodies have become Christ's members at Baptism. Now they do not belong to us, but to Christ (1 Cor. 6:15-20).

C. THE VICTORY OF THE CROSS

"And they who belong to Christ have crucified their flesh with all its passions and desires. If we live by the Spirit, let us also walk by the Spirit" (Gal. 5:24). The perfect dominion of God can be restored and preserved on this earth only by means of sacrifice. We ourselves must, through continual mortification, preserve what God has provided through the cross. The spiritual man dies daily during his earthly life in order to rise again with Christ. Behold our reward: participation, body and soul, in the glory of Christ!

Twenty-Ninth Instruction

The Right Attitude of the Christian to Material Goods — The Seventh and Tenth Commandments

Sins against the Seventh Commandment spring from the inordinate desire for material goods. Avarice is the inexhaustible source of such sins. Dry up the source, and the sins will cease.

In what connection? The lesson on death and the particular judgment offers a most fitting opportunity. Man must leave his riches behind. He is not the lord, only the administrator, of material things. "Render an account" (Luke 16:2).

Method: Explanatory. Proceeding from a description and analysis of the state of a dying man about to face judgment.

Viewpoint: "Blessed are the *poor in spirit,* for theirs is the kingdom of heaven!" Lift up your hearts, to heaven where are true joys, where true riches will be yours forever!

Aim: A Christian evaluation of material goods, and a Christian use of these goods.

DOCTRINAL SUMMARY

We are not the owners, but only the administrators of the goods of this world. Would that we were always faithful stewards, always administering the goods entrusted to us according to the Lord's will! We Christians are not *slave-administrators;* we are to administer our Father's goods as His children. Our conduct therefore should be regulated by our filial devotion to the Father who has so kindly conferred these goods upon us. The meaning and purpose of material goods: fittingly to sustain our life, so that we and those committed to our care may serve God with relative ease and freedom. Material goods in excess of our needs are the means by which we can relieve the needs of others. As a matter of fact, our filial service and submission on earth consist in large part in our right use of material goods. Moreover material things have a *special dignity* for Christians: they provide the nourishment, shelter, clothing, etc., for children of God; and through them the Father manifests His paternal providence for us in many and various ways. These material things also should continuously speak to us Christians about the Father (James 1:17). Behold the keys of heaven, if you use them well (Luke 16:9). Our hearts should be filled with childlike gratitude for these good things entrusted to us (1 Cor. 10:31; Eph. 5:20; 1 Tim. 4:3).

B. THESE GOODS ARE NOT LASTING

But we are *born for greater things,* and so material possessions do not merit too great affection from the Christian heart. What a desertion of Christ's service it would be for a Christian to seek avidly after such things, to try to snatch them away from others, to make his whole life consist in enjoying them. Here we should show how the principal sins against the Seventh Commandment—theft, fraudulent business deals, etc.—flow from an anti-Christian evaluation of material goods. The necessity of restitution must be made clear. Whoever refuses to make restitution when it is morally possible clearly shows that he retains an inordinate love for the unjustly acquired goods. The disciple of Christ avoids not only actual theft, but also every unjust desire for possessions and power.

Social envy! The Tenth Commandment. The true Christian sincerely strives to arrive at perfect peace, so profound as to be disturbed by no material cares. Christ-like solicitude for the kingdom of God excludes anxiety for temporal goods. "No man can serve two masters" (Matt. 6:24). "Be not solicitous" (Matt. 6:25–34; 1 Cor. 7:30–32; Phil. 4–6). "Our citizenship is in heaven" (Phil. 3:20). "Seek the things that are above, where Christ is seated at the right hand of God. Mind the things that are above, not the things that are on earth" (Col. 3:14, used in the Mass of the Easter Vigil—the Church's reminder to the neophytes of what their new life should be).

Thirtieth Instruction

Love of Truth and the Proper Esteem of Good Reputation
(The Eighth Commandment)

In what connection? This lesson may most profitably be inserted after that on the Last Judgment. At the general judgment, Christ, the Lover and Defender of truth, will reveal to us the full truth of all history, expose all lies, and, in the presence of all society, both human and angelic, give to all men the "face", the reputation, which each truly deserves.

Method: Historical-explanatory. The story of the judgment supplies the narrative.

Viewpoint: See the Christian value of truthfulness and a good name.

Aim: Christ-like love of truth, and proper esteem of good reputation.

DOCTRINAL SUMMARY

A. Christ the Judge, Who Loves Truth
and Restores Good Reputation

Christ, Truth itself (John 14:6) is always the greatest lover of truth: "the Truth and the Life" are the chief blessings that He brought us from heaven (John 1:14–17). The misfortunes of the human race began when our first parents believed more in the devil, the "father of lies" (John 8:44), than in the all-truthful God. When they wished to be "as gods", they lost both truth and life. The second Adam came into the world for the very purpose of conquering the prince of lies and of raising up the kingdom of truth. "This is why I was born, and why I have come into the world, to bear witness to the truth. Everyone who is of the truth hears my voice" (John 18:37). In Christ's own character, His absolute veracity shines out even more splendidly than any other virtue. He is the Light of the world (John 8:12), that excludes all darkness. From this follows His almost vehement aversion to the pretence and lies of the Pharisees. This is the reason why in Christ's mouth the word "hypocrite" is the gravest censure, even a curse. Christ demanded of his disciples the strictest simplicity (like children and doves) and truthfulness. "But let your speech be, 'Yes, yes; no, no' and whatever is beyond these comes from the Evil One" (Matt. 5:37).

At the universal judgment, the King of truth will make known the complete and *conclusive victory of truth*. Then will all lies be exposed, condemned, treated with contempt by all, and severely punished. Then there will be no vain jests and delays and excuses, only a great and unbearable embarrassment and confusion, especially on the part of false disciples of Christ, lying disciples of Truth, "Pharisee-Christians". "He will make them share the lot of hypocrites. There will be weeping and gnashing of teeth" (Matt. 25:51).

Then will appear the true "face" of every man. The good name of those who deserve it will be finally and definitively restored to them, in the presence of the whole human race and the choirs of angels. God will most clearly reveal His judgment of each man, and His reasons for so judging. Then all pretense will be at an end, all foolish esteem for transitory values will cease, together with all self-deception and all misestimation by others. God's standards of reputation will prevail, standards that judge a man according to his intrinsic worth, his Christ-likeness; not the standards of men which evaluate a man by his wealth, his exterior appearance, his knowledge, success or charm. Then "many who are first now will be last, and many who are last now will be first" (Matt. 19–30). Then "He will put down the mighty from their thrones, and will exalt the humble" (Luke 1:52). How will you be judged? What kind of "face" will be yours?

B. Christ-like Love of Truth

We Christians are the disciples of truth; in Baptism, we received the Spirit of Christ, in Holy Scripture so often called "the Spirit of Truth" (John 14:17; 15:26; 1 John 4:6). Therefore we ought to seek and to love truth in all things, not only in words, but also in our actions. We should not wish to appear better than we actually are before God and men—no, not even before ourselves. *Sincerity in prayer, simplicity in conversation, truthfulness in action.* As genuine disciples of Christ, we should give testimony to the truth, especially to the truth about God. That is our vocation. But men will not accept our witness unless they find us truthful and faithful in all our words and actions. Since truth is for us a good of great value, the true disciple of Christ does not refuse to make great sacrifices in order to defend and hold fast to the truth. He courageously avoids every kind of lie.

C. Christ-like Esteem of Good Name

We are strong only insofar as we are strong in the eyes of God. We have only as much "face" as God gives us. The esteem of men does not add to our intrinsic value. Yet the good opinion of men is of *great importance in our social life,* and especially for the sake of the friendly

dealings with others becoming to children of God. Because a good reputation is of such great importance for human life, God, by means of the
Eighth Commandment, protects this great good against any kind of
unjust injury or damage from lack of charity.

Sins against the good reputation of others (calumny, detraction, unkind
words, etc.) easily become mortal sins, at least objectively, because they
often cause very serious damage to others. These sins proceed more
directly from real hatred of our brethren than do, for example, sins
against the Seventh Commandment, and therefore they violate charity
even more gravely. Those who disturb Christian peace are to be
reckoned among the worst of evil-doers. They go directly contrary to
the Christian vocation. They are not apostles of the "Prince of Peace",
but apostles of the devil. (The word "devil" comes from the Greek
word *"diabolos"*, and originally meant "calumniator, disturber of peace".)
How scandalous it is that Christ is so often calumniated in His members
by the carelessness, and, alas often the deliberate malice of other
Christians!

Because a good reputation is of such great importance in social life,
the Christian has not only a right but also a real obligation to use just
means in order to gain such a reputation for himself. For us Christians,
a good name has a special value. "For we are the fragrance of Christ
for God, alike as regards those who are saved and those who are lost; to
these an odor that leads to death, but to those an odor that leads to
life" (2 Cor. 2:15ff). Pagans must be led back to the Father through
our truly Christian example. "Even so let your light shine before men,
in order that they may see your good works and give glory to your
Father in heaven" (Matt. 5:16). But these works are not performed
for the praise of men (Matt. 6:1). Here lies the difficult art of Christian
living, which is rightly carried out for the whole-hearted love of God
alone. This true love of God will bring it about that we sincerely seek
the service of God, and not ourselves, in gaining and guarding our
good name; it will effectively guard us against using less honest means
to gain or preserve it, against over-esteeming this transitory good. And,
finally, the sincere love of God will enable the true disciple of Christ to
follow his Master, when this is necessary, even to the ignominy of the
cross. He will be able to be joyful even in the midst of persecutions and
reproaches (Matt. 5:10–12). For he has the mind which was also in
Christ Jesus (cf. Phil. 2:5–11), knowing that such a special and intimate likening to Christ crucified will, after a brief time, be followed
by an equally special and intimate likening to Christ soon to come
in His glory.

Conclusion

Longing for Perfect Worship

Now, during the time of our pilgrimage (2 Cor. 5:2–10), our filial worship of prayer and action, even at the best, can only remain a generous but essentially imperfect attempt. The Spirit of Christ given to us at Baptism continuously stimulates us to worship the heavenly Father by prayer and action. He impels us to deep gratitude and ardent love, to strive to do much more than we are strictly obliged to do. But whatever we may do to manifest our filial submission and devotion, our actual response remains far behind the Father's love. We can never respond as He deserves. In sincere Christian humility, we shall at least admit: "We are unprofitable servants" (Luke 17:10) and weak sons, far too unlike our incomparable Father. This is the proper reason for the special sorrow of Christians in this world: the inadequacy of our response.

But we know that the Lord is to come and bring to perfection these poor beginnings of our love. He will lead us home to the Father, where forever, through Christ, with Him, and in Him, we shall praise the mercies of God's eternal love, in perfect everlasting filial worship. "And when all things are made subject to Him, then the Son Himself will also be made subject to Him who subjected all things to Him, that God may be all in all" (1 Cor. 15:28).

Amen! Come, Lord Jesus! (Apoc. 22:20).

Part IV

The Heralds of Christ–
Their Personality and Formation

CHAPTER ONE

"Kerygmatic Spirituality" for the Heralds of Christ

Our intention here is not to promote the use of the word "kerygmatic", still less to propose a new method for cultivating the spiritual life; we already have more names and more methods than we need. But many of us are aware of the need for a deeper understanding of our apostolic vocation and for a more harmonious union of our spiritual life with our vocation as apostles. What, then, are the qualities of a true herald of Christ, the characteristics of truly kerygmatic spirituality?

A. A HUMBLE AND JOYFUL CONSCIOUSNESS OF OUR SUBLIME VOCATION

Anyone who has been appointed and sent to teach religion by ecclesiastical superiors is, in the last analysis, appointed and sent out by Christ Himself; he is, then, Our Lord's herald. He can say with St. Paul, "On behalf of Christ, therefore, we are acting as ambassadors; God, as it were, appealing through us" (2 Cor. 5:20). From the aspect of authority, obviously there are great differences in rank among Christ's heralds: no Sister would dream of attributing to her teaching the authority of a Bishop. Nevertheless, in opposing the Protestant heresy which does not recognize any hierarchy of authority, we may run the risk of minimizing the dignity of the non-priestly herald, the Religious or lay-teacher.

For how effective in fact for millions of Catholics would the teaching authority of the Pope and the Bishops actually be without the work of these zealous catechists? In the United States particularly where Sisters, and, through the Confraternity of Christian Doctrine, lay teachers also, have such an important share in the catechetical apostolate, innumerable young Catholics would never hear Christ's message, or hear it at all adequately, if it were not explained to them by these heralds.

187

A vital consciousness of their sublime vocation is, then, an essential element in the formation of all heralds of Christ, if they are to be truly enthusiastic about their mission. They must realize that it is to be accepted as a precious and undeserved gift, a sacred responsibility. And, in fact, such humble and whole-hearted acceptance of the task that God has given to them is an unfailing source of true joy for the teacher in the midst of all the difficulties, limitations and disappointments of his work. Christ has sent him; Christ is with him; Christ is vitally interested in the work he is doing in His name. Such a holy awareness keeps Christ's herald devoted to his task, diligent without undue anxiety, cheerful without frivolity. With it, he will continue to have the spirit necessary to prepare his lessons carefully and to teach them effectively.

Let us, whose duty it is to form future catechists, therefore, strive above all to impart to them an appreciation of the excellence of their vocation. Let us lead them to meditate on the commission which they are offering themselves to carry out, so that they may understand it and find joy in it—all in the light of Christ. Only so will they gain an adequate idea of their apostolic calling. For there exists a real danger that, in the process of formation, we may put too much emphasis on particular practices, devotions, rules, recommendations, and too little on the even more important foundation—the spiritual life of the future herald. A watchmaker must put together many little wheels and screws and springs and bearings. But what would we think of him if he put all these parts together and attended carefully to keeping them all clean—but never wound the watch. So these various rules and recommendations are necessary, but it is from the contemplation of his great vocation that the catechist must receive his inspiration.

B. Close Personal Contact With Christ

No herald will continue to carry out his task effectively unless he is closely and personally attached to the master who sent him out. Such attachment will make him careful, diligent, constant, daring. But without close personal attachment to Our Lord, the teacher will lose his zeal and his own real interest in his catechetical apostolate. He will find himself in great danger of growing more and more tired and disappointed; his teaching will no longer be a proclamation, but a tiresome "lecture". Only personal love for Christ will keep him, year after year, eloquent and inventive, zealous and practical, unwearying, and obliging, patient and winning.

Yet we have still deeper reasons for close personal contact with Our Lord. Our King is not far away from His heralds; He is always with us. While we are proclaiming His message, we are instruments in His hands; He works through us and in the souls of our hearers. Thus only by close and continuous collaboration with Him can we reach our goal. Do we really believe this truth? If we do, we realize what kind of spirituality we need as heralds of Christ who can accomplish nothing unless we are united with our Master. Obviously, therefore, in the spirituality of a catechist, the cultivation of an intimate union with Christ by faith and charity is absolutely fundamental.

And such a close personal union with Our Lord will result in our becoming like to Him. To proclaim His message effectively, we must be like Him, and it is with His spirit that we must proclaim His message. Just as the absolute consonance of His personality with His message shone out in His own teaching, so our personality and our way of life must be consonant with the message that we proclaim. Our hearers do not have the privilege of seeing and hearing Our Lord Himself, of being influenced by His winning personality. We can see in the Gospels how greatly His own personality aided His hearers to understand and to appreciate His teaching. One of the most glorious but also difficult aspects of our task, then, is that we must strive to overcome this disadvantage as completely as possible by letting Christ shine through our own Christ-like personalities. We should be able to say to our hearers what St. Paul could say: "Be imitators of me, as I am of Christ" (1 Cor. 11:1; 1 Cor. 4:16; Phil. 3:17; 1 Thess. 1:6).

Of course, no one would deceive himself into entertaining the idea that he had fully realized this high ideal; we can only continue to approach it, we can never completely attain it. But we must never give up; we must always do all that we can. From the very beginning of our formation, we must keep this ideal in view and tirelessly pursue it. Our Lord said: "When you have done everything that was commanded you, say, 'We are unprofitable servants; we have done what it was our duty to do'" (Luke 17:10).

C. Diligent Cultivation of the Specifically "Kerygmatic" Virtues

As teachers of religion, we are not so much heralds *of* Christ, as heralds *with* and *in* Christ. We are the living instruments of the one great Messenger sent to mankind by the Father. Christ is always the chief Herald; we are His collaborators, through whom He continues His work. Thus we share in Christ's own mission: "As the Father has sent me, I also send you" (John 20:22). To fulfill this mission properly, to become fitting instruments of the divine Messenger, we must cultivate the special virtues of a herald, virtues that shone forth so splendidly in Him. We might say that the chief of these are fidelity, unselfishness, winningness.

1) *Fidelity* is clearly the most important and the most characteristic virtue of a herald. As he is sent to proclaim a message to others, his fidelity causes him to proclaim his message exactly, carefully, diligently. How often the Gospels stress the absolute fidelity of our Lord to His heavenly Father. They show Him completely absorbed in the commission that the Father had entrusted to Him. How strongly our Lord Himself claims that faithfulness to the message entrusted to Him is the chief characteristic of His teaching: "The things that I heard from Him (the Father), these I speak in the world . . . of Myself I do nothing: but even as the Father has taught Me, I speak these things . . . He has not left Me alone, because I do always the things that are pleasing to Him" (John 8:26–30). At the end of His public teaching, He states again the unswerving fidelity that was the guiding principle of all His teaching: "He who believes in Me, believes not in Me, but in Him who sent Me . . . For I have not spoken on My own authority, but He who sent Me, the Father, has given Me commandment what I should say and what I should declare. And I know that His commandment is everlasting life. The things, therefore, that I speak, I speak as the Father has bidden Me" (John 12:44–50). The fidelity that our Lord speaks of here is not the nervous faithfulness of a frightened servant, but the generous, joyful fidelity of a loving son.

Our fidelity as Christ's messengers, then, requires that our teaching convey the divine message as fully as possible. We are not the masters of our message; we are not permitted to select the material according to our own tastes and personal devotion; we are not permitted to adulterate the word of God with our own ideas. And so it is absolutely essential that we convey God's message in its own wonderful internal unity; that we bring out its real essentials, and that we focus our hearers' attention on the doctrines that form its very core.

Such fidelity to our message obviously requires a thorough and specialized study of it; and this is the purpose of so-called "kerygmatic theology". This is not a new and separate branch of theology to be studied in addition to dogma, morals, etc. It is rather a special approach to the study of all theology, with the purpose of gaining a deeper and fuller understanding of revealed truth as the message we are sent to proclaim. It stresses, therefore, the doctrines that form the substance of Christian revelation and Christian preaching, indicating their interconnection and internal union in the central theme of Christianity, the mystery of Christ. And, further, this kerygmatic approach gives us the special aspect under which particular doctrines should be presented in order to gain a fittingly religious appreciation of them, and their full fruit in Christian living.[1]

Leading catechetical experts, therefore, declare that the more completely "kerygmatic" formation of teachers of religion is one of the most pressing needs today of the catechetical apostolate. And hence they urge a fuller use of the kerygmatic approach in the formation of future heralds of Christ in every seminary and convent, and urge that this approach be begun as early in the training as possible.

But even more important is the personal effort of every future herald to gain a truly religious understanding of his message by means of his own prayer and meditation. Hence, from the very beginning of his training, the future herald should be encouraged and assisted to meditate on the message he is to proclaim. One of the greatest advantages of the kerygmatic approach is precisely that it makes Christian doctrine "prayable", and thereby inspires enthusiasm for the divine message. Heralds who make this divine message the central subject of their prayer and meditation will speak from the abundance of their hearts.

If we heralds are thus faithful to our message, faithful in this full sense of the word, then unselfishness and winningness will follow of themselves.

2) *Unselfishness* is only the negative aspect of fidelity. The perfect accomplishment of the commission entrusted to us requires that we have no time or interest left over for ourselves. For in proportion to the degree to which we seek ourselves and our own glory or comfort, we inevitably become less capable in the service of God. But although this principle is clear to everyone, it is extremely difficult to practise. While our vocation does not call for artificial mortifications, it demands much more than these; it requires that we keep ourselves continuously silent, and, as it were, dead, with regard to our own interests, in order to be completely free and alive for our Lord. St. Paul's "I die daily" (1 Cor. 15:31) gives us the right perspective in which to pursue this high ideal. As heralds of Christ, we are most especially to become divested of self, so that we truly are not acting in our own name, but in the name of Christ. More than other Christians, we ought to become able to say with St. Paul, such a great herald of Christ: "It is now no longer I that live, but Christ lives in me" (Gal. 2:20).

3) *Winningness.* If Christ is thus living in us, we shall win others as did Our Lord Himself. In Him "the goodness and kindness of God our Savior appeared" (Tit. 3:4) and won men's hearts. Our Lord's attractiveness did not consist only in natural charm, but was the outward manifestation of His attitude to mankind as their Savior.

1. See the last chapter of this book.

And this is also the only adequate attitude for the herald of Christ. We have His message to proclaim, not to stones or trees, but to living men of flesh and blood, to win them for God, to cause them to live a Christian life dedicated to God. Their response to our message is to be a new life, life in Christ. Thus as His heralds, we must strive so to proclaim His message to the people of our own time that they may find it to be what it truly is, "spirit and life" (John 6:65).

So the herald of Christ should take care to allow the "goodness and kindness" of God to appear through him. But, let it be carefully noted, he should never try to win his hearer's hearts for himself, but for the Lord; he should strive to attract them, not to himself, but to Christ. In the same way, pleasing methods should be used, not to amuse our students, but to assist them to a deeper and fuller religious understanding of our message—to Christian living. And it is the consciousness of our sublime vocation that will make us eager to acquire truly Christ-like attractiveness, and to use attractive methods in our teaching, "for the love of Christ impels us" (2 Cor. 5:14).

CHAPTER TWO

The Catechetical Apostolate
of Lay Teachers

This book would be quite incomplete if there were no special chapter on the catechetical apostolate of the laity. In the United States in particular, more than in any other country of the world, through the Confraternity of Christian Doctrine, unsalaried lay teachers take a special and most important part in the Church's teaching work. "The Confraternity of Christian Doctrine is the Church's official parish society for the religious instruction of all those not in Catholic schools (Canon 711:2) . . . Through the CCD, the laity, under the spiritual guidance of the parish clergy, work to 'restore all things in Christ', by bringing to all men the doctrines of Christ."[1]

The CCD apostolate in the United States takes many forms—in general, to collaborate with the hierarchy in promoting religious formation, both doctrinal and spiritual, which begins in early infancy and continues all through life. The Parent-Educator Program shows parents how fully to exercise the most important and indispensible general form of the lay catechetical apostolate, the religious teaching and formation of their own children. Within the framework of the diocesan catechetical office, CCD members cooperate in courses for the religious formation of children and of young people, and in activities for the religious education of adults (programs during the school year, Vacation Schools, Discussion Clubs). The CCD also implements Lay Training Courses on all levels for the purpose not only of training these teachers, but also for study of the content of the Christian message, of catechetic methods, and of psychology and sociology in relation to the catechetical apostolate. And, finally, the CCD Apostolate of Good Will strives to develop in all Catholics increased love and understanding of their non-

1. This quotation and the summary following in this paragraph of the work of the CCD is taken from *"Information about the Confraternity of Christian Doctrine,"* published by the National Center.

Catholic neighbors, to promote truly tactful and enlightened zeal for their conversion.

The Confraternity of Christian Doctrine is primarily a parish society. But it is the special work of the Diocesan Office of the CCD to train, supervise and guide catechists. This Office draws up the programs for the training of teachers, lays down the conditions for the reception of applicants and the training qualifications for their official appointment as CCD teachers. This Office also has the right and the responsibility to supervise the training of teachers and their actual teaching. The syllabus and textbooks, the method and content of all Confraternity classes in the diocese are to be determined by this Office. The Diocesan director again, is to provide all the help needed by teachers in the course of their work and to offer them opportunities for further spiritual and professional guidance. The function of the National Center of the CCD is of an advisory nature, but it has a vital role in the whole organization. Its chief functions are mainly 1) to provide the best available training for CCD Leaders; 2) to inform the Diocesan Offices of the progress of the various forms of the CCD apostolate in the United States and in other countries; 3) to prepare and make available teacher-training manuals and all the other material needed in the various forms of the CCD apostolate.

Such a summary description of the work and the organization of the CCD cannot give any idea of the abundance of catechetical material on various levels published under its auspices, of its detailed program for the selection, training and authorization of lay teachers, or of the number of children, young people and adults actually reached. Suffice it to say in particular that, without the cooperation of CCD lay teachers, the problem of giving an adequate religious formation to the millions of Catholic children attending public schools would be completely unsolvable, as would that of the continuing religious formation of minimally instructed adult Catholics. No wonder, then, that the Apostolate Delegate, His Eminence, the Most Rev. Amleto Cicognani, has issued to all faithful Catholics the call: "Devotedly, therefore, and to the utmost of your ability, cooperate with the Confraternity of Christian Doctrine."

The CCD itself is well aware of the many and difficult problems attending all the phases of its many-sided apostolate, and is continually studying them and finding new and improved solutions. But it might fall within the scope of this book to point out the special value of the lay catechist, his special needs and difficulties, and also to bring out some special aspects of the training and the help that he needs. By so doing, we may, perhaps, suggest to our priest and religious

readers some further means of interesting zealous members of the laity
in this official lay catechetical apostolate, and of inspiring and assisting
those already engaged in it.

THE SPECIAL VALUE OF THE CATECHETICAL APOSTOLATE OF THE LAITY

In their daily life in the world, lay catechists personally experience
the irreplaceable value of religion for such a life. From their own
experience, they know how religion could and should penetrate, transform and ennoble the "ordinary" life of people in the world. Thus
Our Lord and His Church expect from laymen authorized to proclaim
His message a special *vital quality* in their religious teaching, giving
their students a formation that is close to life and fully directed to
living, and which is, in consequence, especially capable of standing the
test of life.

Again, the religious formation given by a lay teacher should have
a special quality of *naturalness*. It should, that is, really be adapted
to the concrete conditions, needs and potentialities of the students,
leading them toward Christian living informed by a spirit quite different
from the secular spirit of our times, and also quite different from that
of any Christian "ghetto".

Needless to say, such vitality and naturalness are of special importance
in teaching children who do not attend Catholic schools. To a large
extent, they come from Catholic families with little Catholic life, and
so these children have a special need for a truly vital religious formation,
which is at the same time truly "actual" in terms of their own needs.
Such children are under the constant influence of the secularized
education given in the public schools. Even if they are in no way
directly influenced against religion, the very lack of any kind of religious
teaching gives the impression that religion is of no great importance
in human life. Their brief "released-time" or Sunday lessons in religion,
then, have at once to convince them of the supreme role of religion
in their lives and to give them religious instruction. Who could be
expected to carry out this most difficult twofold task more effectively
for such an audience—a Religious whom these children cannot help
considering as coming from "another world", or a fervent layman
or woman, who by the very fact of his religious vitality, of his eagerness
to teach the truths of the faith, shows the compatibility of religion
with "real life", and the importance of religion in life? In the first years
of the grade school, it may not make much difference, but there can
hardly be a doubt that for innumerable boys and girls in the upper

grades and in high schools, an intelligent, tactful and zealous lay teacher can far more easily demonstrate the value of religion in daily living than can an equally gifted priest or sister.

Our Lord expects that His lay heralds will in a special way *form apostles,* above all, lay apostles, among their students. The fact that their teacher is a layman or woman, who in most cases is using for this teaching whatever time he or she can spare from the work of earning daily bread, of itself gives the students a practical idea of the lay apostolate.[2] This will be the more true, the more the teacher gives his message with genuine Christian vitality, the more he shows his students again and again the important role of the lay apostle in the life of the Church today, and the more he knows how to begin to train his students as early as possible to take part in that apostolate.

He will, of course, continuously indicate and stress the special role of the ordained priesthood in Christ's Church, and point out to his students the different values of the priestly, religious and lay life, giving each its own rank and special splendor in the harmony of the different members of the Mystical Body. And he will also bring out continually the *absolute necessity for genuinely Catholic subordination* to, and harmonious collaboration with the priestly leader in the lay catechetical apostolate. Here again, a qualified lay teacher has special advantages in influencing boys and girls of junior high school and high school age. And in all teaching, the layman can more gracefully and therefore more effectively emphasize the priest's authority than can the priest himself. One finds the same thing true in family life. If the older brothers in the family willingly obey and respect their father, their example will be far more effective with the younger children than will be the father's own insistence on his authority.

THE SPECIAL DIFFICULTIES AND NEEDS OF LAY CATECHISTS

The religious teaching of children attending public schools obviously presents a far more difficult catechetical situation than does the ordinary instruction given in Catholic schools. A higher quality of religious teaching is needed if these students are to be given true religious formation, and yet this teaching must be carried out under much less favorable circumstances, and often under positively unfavorable ones.

2.　The lay CCD teacher is, in the vast majority of cases, a voluntary, unpaid worker. But is there not also a field for qualified lay teachers working as adequately salaried, full-time "parish assistants" or catechists (such as already exist in some European countries), who could give their full talents, time and energy to this work? Such lay people could also assist the priest in many material ways, and thus free him for his special priestly work. One does not become less "apostolic" from the fact of receiving the means of subsistence in return for one's apostolic work, or no priest or Sister could lay claim to this title!

Let us consider these difficulties and special needs in somewhat greater detail.

Thus these Confraternity classes demand from the teacher, above all, a higher degree of catechetical concentration on the very essentials of Christian doctrine and Christian life. This concentration should never be mistaken for a mere simplification or abbreviation of the material that must be taught. Simplification makes the lessons "easier" for both the teacher and the students, but only in a very short-range view. Genuine concentration is far more difficult for the teacher to achieve, but it effects true religious formation; it makes each lesson a living seed of Christian truth that can bear lifelong fruit in Christian learning and living.

Again, there is so little time available for these classes—in some places hardly a full hour each week of the school year, with vacations, holidays etc. taking away even from this minimum. For this reason, again, the teacher must be able to center his whole teaching on the essentials of Christian doctrine and to build up a genuine Christian life on these essentials. To be lost in accidentals detracts from any kind of Christian formation, but in these classes it would be disastrous.

Furthermore, these classes need to be made more attractive, more interesting to the students than do the classes in religion given in Catholic schools. If children in Catholic schools find some of their religion classes dull, they will still not usually be allowed to leave school, and one can hope that the Catholic environment of the school and the whole atmosphere of the education given in it may compensate for a low quality of religious instruction. But in the classes for public school children—will the children continue to come, and come regularly if they find the teaching dull? And if they do come, how will they benefit from a class that gives them no religious inspiration? But how difficult it is to make classes truly interesting for such children! Many of them come from families with no religious background. The hour appointed for the class is often, if not generally, not very convenient for them; the place is frequently not too suitable; the teacher does not have at hand the technical helps available to a teacher in a regular school class. In such classes, therefore, more than almost anywhere else, the teaching must bring out as clearly and attractively as possible the values of Christian doctrine and of true Christian living. The children must come to feel that we are *leading them to a real treasury;* our message must truly be experienced as the Good News. Everyone connected with this work, of course, realizes this necessity; the difficulty is to carry out the required kind of teaching in actual practice.

Since the apostolate of lay catechists is so important and, at the same time, so difficult, the catechetical movement in the United States must strive in every way to prepare these teachers as well as possible, and to facilitate their arduous task.

SOME SUGGESTIONS

The apostolic spirit of the Catholic laity in the United States makes it relatively easy to secure the required numbers of volunteer catechists: in some places, it seems, more people apply for the preparatory training than are actually needed. Where this is true, it will be possible to choose among those who apply. The more we appreciate the great intrinsic difficulties of the CCD apostolate, the more we see the need for a clear-sighted selection of candidates even for the preparatory course, and still more when actually appointing teachers. Obviously, not every fervent Catholic possessing sufficient knowledge of Christian doctrine also possesses the capacity to be trained for this particular kind of teaching, or can successfully conduct such classes. The best training course cannot work miracles; and this kind of teaching, as it is needless to say, requires the moral qualities not only of a good Catholic, but also of a good catechist and educator.

Again, training for this kind of teaching needs, obviously, to provide the candidates with the necessary knowledge both of Christian doctrine and of catechetical method. In most cases, therefore, two courses are given, one on doctrine and one on method. As we mentioned above, the classes given to children attending public schools call in a very special way for concentration on essentials, for vitality, and for effective direction in Christian living; they call for a presentation of Christianity which will show the beauty of Christian doctrine and the values of Christian life. In other words, might we not say that the lay catechist needs, above all, to acquire a thoroughly "kerygmatic" mentality and to know how to incarnate the kerygmatic approach in each and all of his lessons? He needs to come to see clearly, for himself, how the fundamentals of Christian doctrine form a wonderful unity, the Mystery of Christ. He himself must come to be enthusiastic about Christian doctrine as being completely centered in Christ; "Christ in you; the hope of glory" (Col. 1:27). Teachers of future lay catechists should not in any way take it for granted that people who have a fairly adequate material knowledge of Christian doctrine, that is, of the individual doctrines in themselves, necessarily also possess this kerygmatic insight into Christian doctrine as a living and life-giving whole. How could they, when in the past the religious training given in Catholic schools has seldom been given this orientation? The courses in doctrine given to lay catechists, then, need to be clearly and inspiringly "kerygmatic" in order to enable them—perhaps for the first time—to see Christian doctrine and Christian life in its true light. And, obviously, this vision will give them most valuable and efficacious assistance in their own spiritual life. Before they are allowed to proclaim the Christian message to others, they should themselves experience the transforming power of the Christian message, rightly proposed. This is precisely what St. Paul meant when he emphasized the "power" *(virtus)* of his preaching: "And my speech and my preaching (the Greek original has *kerygma,* message) were not in the persuasive words of (sophistical) wisdom, but in the demonstration of the Spirit and of power" (1 Cor. 2:4).

In this connection, might we also suggest that the regular retreats recommended for all CCD lay teachers be thoroughly "kerygmatic". In particular, a retreat given at the end of the training course would have great value.[3] Such retreats would show these future teachers in a living way how the fundamentals of Christian doctrine actually are the pillars of Christian spiritual life, how they are to strive to live the message that they are undertaking to proclaim to others.

The course on method given to future lay catechists should make the students acquainted with a very simple but efficient method of religious formation. Here we intentionally use the singular—"method" rather than "methods". For the danger in proposing many methods is that future teachers will not learn to handle even one, and when they go out to teach, after some futile attempts of various kinds, they will return to the obsolete and fruitless, but easy method of explaining the text of the catechism word by word, and then asking the students to memorize this "beautiful" doctrine. Would we not do well to follow the example of Fr. Jungmann; in his *Katechetik* which is written for professional teachers of religion in the very homeland of the catechetical movement, he introduces only one method, "the" catechetic method which is the fruit of the recent efforts in the field of religious didactics, and then he shows how this one method applies to different kinds of religious instruction, allowing for and even requiring appropriate modifications.[4] When we do so, we can be much more hopeful that the students are really understanding the method we are teaching them, and that they are becoming thoroughly acquainted with it by the necessary catechetical exercises. This course on method must also give the future teachers the fundamentals of religious education, for in the

3. In Appendix A (p. 256) are some suggestions concerning "kerygmatic" retreats. But of course, a retreat given to teachers entering upon their catechetical apostolate would need to bring out this apostolic viewpoint much more evidently than is suggested in these outlines for general retreat purposes.

4. Joseph A. Jungmann, S.J., *Katechetik* (2nd ed., Freiburg, 1955), pp. 120 ff.

classes they are to teach they must not only impart knowledge, but truly educate their students.

Everyone connected with the CCD work of training lay catechists realizes, of course, that without a thorough spiritual formation they cannot adequately fulfill their apostolic task. If such formation is necessary for priestly and religious teachers, obviously it is needed for laymen also. And this formation must, for them too, be of such a kind as to teach them how to carry it on for themselves, how continually to deepen and grow in their personal participation in the Mystery of Christ all through their lives. Otherwise, there is obviously far greater danger than with those who are living the priestly or religious life, that these lay teachers may lose their living interest in the message they are proclaiming, and that their catechetical efforts will therefore bear little or no fruit.

May we suggest, therefore, that every future CCD teacher needs most especially to be brought into close and personal contact with *Sacred Scripture* and with the *Liturgy,* and this both for his own sake and for the special kind of teaching he is to do.[5] For his own spiritual vitality, he needs continually to be more completely formed to the image of Christ by the Word of God in Sacred Scripture and by the very life of Christ given us in the Mass and the Sacraments. These are the living sources of Christian vitality, the great means Christ gives us in the Church for growth in His life and union with Him.

And, in addition, the CCD teaching is concerned above all with providing an elementary initiation into the Christian religion, and to make this elementary initiation the fruitful seed of the students' future religious development. Sacred Scripture and the Liturgy are, precisely, at once the most fruitful means of elementary initiation, as we saw earlier in this book, and the perennial sources of growth in Christ. The CCD teacher, then, needs both to lead his students to these sources, and at least in some degree, to show them how to find here the unfailing means to ever-fuller participation in the Mystery of Christ. And how can the teacher do so, if he has not experienced this for himself?

But with regard to the Liturgy also, we should never forget that children in the CCD classes need, even more than others, a full development of the catechetical power of the Mass and the Sacraments. Since their formal religious education is often limited to less than one hour a week, how important it is that every Sunday Mass should become an efficacious means of religious formation. Although a lay teacher can explain the Mass, and prepare his students for better participation

5. This need was specifically discussed in the Workshop in the Lay Apostolate at the CCD National meeting at Buffalo, N. Y. 1956.

in the Mass — the proper celebration of the Mass which makes such participation possible, easy and fruitful is not in his power. Only the priest can do this. Neither a silent Low Mass nor a High Mass, necessarily all in Latin, can have great formative value in the lives of these children. How greatly they would benefit from a well-performed dialogue Mass with fitting hymns at the right places in the vernacular and with vernacular readings and responses, so arranged that the real meaning of the Mass and its structure shine out as clearly as possible! We priests can certainly not require an intensive initiation into the Liturgy from our lay teachers unless we ourselves are ready to provide a celebration of Mass that is catechetically developed.

The basic training given to lay catechists before their appointment as teachers needs to be continued by careful guidance, both spiritual and professional, all during their time of teaching. And, in addition, they need the aid of printed material to help them in their difficult work by giving the hints necessary for the preparation of each class. Until recently there has been a lack of catechetical material completely adapted to the special needs of such teachers. We are happy to say, in this connection, that a group of Sisters, headed by Sister Maria de la Cruz, H.H.S., is working out a course that excels from the viewpoint both of content and of method.[6] Although it is constructed for children attending public schools, this course also deserves the attention of religion teachers in Catholic schools, since it is, perhaps, the first series of texts for use in catechetical instruction which follows the principles of modern catechetics, especially with regard to content, consistently and without any compromise.

And one more important aid to the work of lay catechists would be a catechetical review edited to suit their particular needs. Such a review could do much not only to present helpful new material for teaching and to illustrate by concrete articles the various adaptations of the modern catechetical method, but also to continue and further the educational, kerygmatic and spiritual formation of the catechists themselves.

The great work of the CCD is, first of all, a lay apostolate. But it obviously needs, and is receiving, the active collaboration of the clergy and of religious teachers. Some further suggestions as to the special help that the parish priest can give to his lay assistants in the catechetical apostolate may be found in the chapter on the Priest as the Herald of Christ (p. 229). Religious teachers not only assist in the training of CCD teachers and guide them, but are themselves actively engaged

6. *On Our Way* series, by Sister Maria de la Cruz, H.H.S. (Sadlier, New York).

in the CCD apostolate. In many places, Religious who work hard in Catholic schools during the school year give special courses for public school children on Sundays and in the summer. And Religious who engage in this work affirm that it gives them valuable lights and inspirations for their regular school teaching. Above all, such Religious become eager to use every opportunity to open the eyes of their students in school to the wonderful and urgent apostolate awaiting them in the work of the CCD. And here, may we say, is the most valuable form of assistance that Catholic schools can give to the work of the CCD; to provide their own students with excellent religious formation and with the apostolic spirit. More and more lay teachers are needed and will be needed in the future if the millions of Catholic children in the public schools are to receive any kind of religious training. And the graduates of Catholic schools and colleges should be the first to be ready and willing to answer this urgent call.

In this chapter, we have stressed the work of the lay teacher through the CCD, since this is the special field assigned to them by the Church. But, conditions being what they are, more and more lay teachers of religion will be needed also in Catholic schools themselves. The situation of such teachers is substantially the same as that of religious teachers, and they need, therefore, a similar catechetical training (see the following chapters, especially pages 212-217, 221-226).

Obviously there are many other ways in which apostolic-minded lay people can spread Christ's message, according to their special talents and circumstances. But we are not mentioning them in this book, since it is concerned with the catechetical apostolate properly speaking. But it should always be remembered that the first field for the catechetical apostolate of the married laity is in their own families. The religious teaching and training of their children is the inalienable right and duty of Catholic parents. They are the first messengers of Our Lord to their children before they attend any school; and no school can make up for the lack of a thoroughly Christian education in the family, an education which the school should need only to complement.

CHAPTER THREE

The Catechetical Apostolate of Religious[1]

If St. Scholastica or St. Gertrude or some other great nun of the Middle Ages could visit the countless convents throughout the world today—and especially those in the United States—what would be her reaction? First of all, doubtless, she would be filled wih joyful admiration at the number of religious vocations in the Church today. There were many nunneries in the Middle Ages, but the number of monks then far exceeded the number of nuns. This joyful admiration at the fact that our Lord finds so many faithful brides in the midst of a badly secularized world would, I think, be united to a kind of sacred envy at the wonderful apostolate entrusted to sisters in our times.

Medieval religious would rejoice further at the importance of the Sisters' apostolate in the Church today. In the Middle Ages the possibilities of a direct apostolate for nuns were quite limited. And now? In the United States alone there are 120,000 Sisters teaching in Catholic schools or preparing themselves for that glorious apostolate. Most of them teach religion as well as secular subjects, thus acting in a special way as heralds of our Lord. Everyone knows how much American Catholicism owes to the legions of Sisters in Catholic schools. Where else do Sisters perform catechetical works on such a large scale? And they are doing it with fervor and success.

What a sublime honor it is for the brides of our Lord to share in His divine work of redemption—by prayer and penance, and also by a direct apostolate as heralds of the divine Bridegroom! If we teach in theology, according to St. Thomas (S.T. IIa IIae, Q. 188, a6.) that the combination of the contemplative and apostolic life is the highest form of religious vocation, then evidently we are not permitted to

1. Our experience with Religious teachers in the United States has, by chance, been almost entirely with Sisters and not with Brothers. This is the reason why, in this book, we have limited ourselves to discussing the catechetical apostolate of Sisters. But we hope that Brothers also may find the three following chapters useful, making the necessary adaptations, *mutatis mutandis,* resulting from their status as "men of God."

restrict this statement to the religious life of monks. No doubt St. Scholastica and St. Gertrude would congratulate the Sisters of today who are called to such close and sublime collaboration with Christ.

However sublime their apostolic calling may be—and here we are considering especially the catechetical apostolate—Sisters are always, first of all, brides of Our Lord. However excellent the apostolic vocation of teaching religion, if that teaching is not integrated with and subordinated to the fundamental vocation to be Our Lord's bride, it becomes a monstrosity in religious life. A Sister teaching religion does not have two vocations but only one. Like any Sister, she is, above all, Our Lord's bride. The Lord sends His bride to the children, and all her work for them must be done in that capacity. This fundamental call modifies, inspires, and sometimes also limits the Sister's apostolic activity. Her catechetical apostolate receives its special appeal, value, and efficacy from the very fact that it is done by a fully devoted bride of Our Lord.

OUR LORD'S VOCATION

For a deeper understanding of the Sister's status as both bride and herald of Christ, we may look to the divine vocation of Our Lord Himself. The Father sent Him to us to proclaim His Father's message. He is the divine herald par excellence. Our Lord Himself emphasized again and again that in all His teaching He is acting as the faithful herald of his Father. Reviewing His catechetical activity, He declared at the end of His public life: "I have not spoken on My own authority, but He who sent Me, the Father, has given Me commandment what I should say, and what I should declare . . . The things, therefore, that I speak, I speak as the Father has bidden Me" (John 12:49–50). At the same time as He stresses His mission as herald, He also stresses His divine sonship, since His mission as the divine messenger cannot be understood except in the light of His dignity as Son of God. By proclaiming the message the Father has entrusted to Him, He shows His filial attachment to the Father. His whole teaching receives its special significance, its dignity and value, its unparalleled vigor, from the fact that He is the only-begotten Son of the Father Who sent Him. First of all, He is from all eternity the Son of God the Father; whatever He does by the command of His Father, He does with the spirit and ardor of a fully devoted Son.

THE SISTER'S VOCATION

When a Sister considers herself in the fulfillment of her catechetical task as being the bride of Christ Who gives her a share in His own work, then her Martha activity becomes actually a function of the contemplative Mary at the Lord's feet; her catechetical apostolate becomes a manifestation of genuine bridal love, a means of uniting her heart with the Lord. Then not only the personal spiritual life of the religious teacher is furthered, but also the catechetical apostolate.

We do not need to dwell on the fact that apostolic zeal is the unfailing result of genuine bridal love. And genuine zeal is also the soul of catechetical activity. Without this zeal, the teaching of religion becomes a lifeless routine for the teacher and a worthless mechanism for the pupils. Only religious zeal coming from a loving heart will bring religion to the hearts of the students. Religion is essentially more than a system of reasoning: by its nature, it is life, a life of love.

Only a deep personal love of Our Lord will keep the Sister's heart young and willing to endure the burden of the classroom while practicing an intensive religious life—not only for a few years but for a whole lifetime, even after she has reached the period of life when many others seek and obtain an easier schedule.

The Special Catechetical Apostolate of Sisters

Might we, then, say that the Sisters' vocation as brides of Christ should inspire not only their catechetical apostolate, but should also, to a remarkable extent, give a special tonality to their message itself? At first glance this seems inadmissable. Is not the message we proclaim as heralds of Christ always the same revelation? Even the Holy Father may not change this divine message in any way; he must proclaim exactly the same message as that which was proclaimed by Our Lord in His Father's name and announced by the Apostles sent by Our Lord. How could a Sister ever be permitted to change this eternal message? Of course, there is no question of real change; we are not masters of the message we are to proclaim, but heralds commanded to transmit it faithfully. Yet, we must be willing instruments in the hands of the only herald of the Father, that is, of Jesus Christ.

This comparison shows us how remarkable a modification may exist without real change. Cannot a musician play one and the same melody on different instruments? The instruments do not change the melody, but each instrument renders the melody in its own special tonality. Does this not fully accord with the intention of the musician himself? He knows why he prefers here and now this particular instrument more than that. This is also true of our divine Musician and Herald. Whatever the instrument He uses, He wishes to play the same divine melody, to proclaim the same melody in different tonalities. When He desires to make one point in His message certain and clear for everyone, He uses His big trumpet of Rome; hence this instrument must excel, and does excel all others in authority, exact formulation, and reliable guidance. But this is not His only instrument. If He wishes, especially in our times, to proclaim His message also by melodious violins, who should dare to rebuke Him? But we may ask what might be His divine intention in using the gentle tone of His violins—what may be their special function in the whole symphony? And we may also ask here: what can Sisters as loving brides of Our Lord confer upon the catechetical apostolate, and what should be the characteristic feature of their catechetical work?

A SPECIAL UNDERSTANDING

First of all, Our Lord expects from His brides *a special understanding* of His message. This does not mean special scholastic training. Such training may be useful for Sisters who are to teach religion to upper classes in high school or in college, but Our Lord does not expect from all Sisters charged with catechetical work the scientific analysis and profound speculation of a theologian. He expects rather a genuine religious understanding—the fruit of unselfish love and diligent meditation. He expects a well-developed understanding and deep appreciation of His principal ideas and religious ideals. Who should understand Him if not His brides? Their spirituality must be founded solidly on His fundamental doctrines and nourished continuously by diligent reading and meditation of the Bible, especially of the Gospels. Thank God, the time seems to have gone by when the spiritual life of Sisters was frequently over-loaded with many isolated devotions and was too little formed by the substance of Christian dogma. For the bride of Our Lord, more than for anyone else, His fundamental doctrines should be, in the full sense of the word, the very light of life.

In recent years, many Sisters, especially in the United States, receive special theological training as a better formation for the catechetical apostolate. Would that every Sister who is to teach religion could have special theological training! But such training must be adapted to the particular need of the Sisters. It would be a mistake to have this training imitate the theological training of future priests in a mechanical way, and a still greater mistake if emphasis were put on a misunderstood scholasticism too concerned with the cultivation of abstract reasonings, and too little with a deeper religious understanding and appreciation of Christian dogmas.

How would Our Lord teach and form these Sisters if He were directing these courses? When He taught His disciples, the result was not only a clear conceptual understanding, but deep and solid religious enthusiasm. "Was not our heart burning within us while He was speaking on the road and explaining to us the Scriptures?" (Luke 24:32). If anywhere, certainly in theological courses for Sisters, we must use the kerygmatical approach, that is, we must emphasize the religious value of Christian dogma and its relation to Christian life. "The words that I have spoken to you are spirit and life" (John 6:64–65). Is it not the special privilege of Our Lord's bride to grasp the spirit and life of His doctrine? However, such kerygmatic teaching by no means excludes sound scholastic theology in its rightful place.[2]

FAITHFUL AND ARDENT PROCLAMATION

Love renders the bride pliant to the ideas of her Beloved. In the catechetical field this means that she will introduce her own ideas as little as possible and as much as possible the favored doctrines of her Lord. Her catechetical fidelity will let the Lord speak; she will be His willing instrument. The faithful bride will not dilute the magnificent message of her Lord with her own attempts at embellishment. But at the same time, she can give a remarkable emphasis to the affective element of the divine message. This is genuine Sister catechesis; it is the tonality of the Lord's violins. No doubt He attracts and forms many souls more effectively by the soft melodies of his violins than by the somewhat louder sound of His trumpets. This does not mean, of course, that unbecoming sentimentality should ever be allowed to spoil the magnificent melodies of our Lord. A Sister who in her own spiritual life is not able to distinguish deep, tender, but noble religious emotion from inferior sentimentality will never be able to do so when teaching religion. Here especially, any deficiency in solid spiritual formation inevitably has unfortunate consequences in educational activity.

PROCLAIM THE GLAD TIDINGS

Since the apostolic work of the Sister-teacher is inspired and directed by her love of Our Lord, the Lord is the center of her message, just as He is the center of the message entrusted to His lay catechists and to priests. How greatly, therefore, can Sisters profit from the recent catechetical tendency stressing the mystery of Christ as the central theme of Christian doctrine, and participation in the life of Christ as the chief goal of the catechetical apostolate. What a pity it is that some teachers do not yet seem to have an adequate idea of the mystery of Christ! This mystery which we must proclaim is: Christ sent to us by the heavenly Father as our Leader to bring us back to the Father. It is not Christ detached from the Father, but Christ as the gift of the heavenly Father and as our only way to the Father.

2. See the last chapter in this book.

In proclaiming this mystery of divine love, the brides of Our Lord should certainly possess the right understanding of their message and present it as the joyful tidings of God's eternal love. Hence, Sisters will especially appreciate the kerygmatic tendency of modern catechetics, emphasizing that our message is, by its nature, a real *evangelium,* that is, the good news of God's eternal love manifested to us in Christ, and of how we must respond in Christ by giving love for Love. Sisters by their particular vocation as brides of Our Lord are in a special way called and disposed to understand, to appreciate, and to proclaim this sublime message of divine love.

"THE SPIRIT GIVES LIFE"

Although the brides of Christ are privileged messengers of divine love, it does not follow that, in their instructions, they should use the word love as often as possible. They are worthy messengers of the new covenant, the covenant of love, yet "not of the letter but of the spirit; for the letter kills but the spirit gives life" (2 Cor. 3:6). We proclaim God's love not by tiresome repetition of any word, but by showing what God has done for us, and that for us sinners; how "God, who is rich in mercy, by reason of His very great love wherewith He has loved us even when we were dead by reason of our sins, brought us to life together with Christ . . . and seated us together in heaven in Christ Jesus" (Eph. 2:4–7). This is, in fact, the climax of God's unfathomable love and the core of our message: that the eternal Father "gave his only-begotten Son" (John 3:16), in order to give us rebellious servants forgiveness in Christ, and a share in His life, glory, and happiness.

And what is the right answer to this stirring love that we are sent to proclaim? What could it be except that which Our Lord Himself emphasized as the central point of Christian law and Christian life: " 'Thous shalt love the Lord thy God with thy whole heart, and with thy whole soul, and with thy whole mind.' This is the greatest and the first commandment" (Matt. 22:37-38). Here again we meet with a very fine point in the catechetical apostolate of the Sister. The deeper she understands the greatness of Our Lord's love for us, which we do not deserve, the deeper and more painfully she feels her own incapacity to answer by a similar love—our heart is too narrow. Yet Sisters have the wonderful possibility of compensating in some way for the insufficiency of their own love by the sincere and deep love they are promoting in their pupils. Evidently what our students may give can never dispense us from giving the whole of what we have, but even giving the whole, we know, is a too unequal an answer. We wish to give more and more and we are happy to do so through our students. The love Our Lord asks of us and of our students does not consist in sweet words and feelings, but in progressive union with Him in life, and in progressive transformation into Him.

Thus the Sisters' catechetical apostolate will reach its proper goal: progressive participation in the life of Christ, formation of Christ in souls. Genuine bridal love has to prove itself by its genuine fecundity. How blessed are those Sisters who can prove the sincerity and fecundity of their sublime love by feeling and working as did Our Lord's great Apostle: "My dear children with whom I am in labor again, until Christ is formed in you!" (Gal. 4:19–20).

CHAPTER FOUR

Training Sisters for the
Catechetical Apostolate

No American Catholic ever will deny that the high standard of American Catholicism—simple faith, solid religious knowledge, fervent religious practice, generosity—is, to a great extent, due to the teaching of Sisters. And the visitor who observes their work and notes the esteem in which they are held readily adds his praise. But notwithstanding their past and present success, the Sisters themselves are not yet satisfied, and—what seems to be the finest quality of all—they are eager for a better formation, especially in the field of religion.

Nowhere in the Catholic world have I found in the same degree as in the United States such generous efforts to provide Sisters with a solid theological formation. Many congregations of Sisters include courses in theology even in the novitiate, continuing through all the years of professional training. It is a fact that especially in the United States, Sisters indicate an even greater interest in theology and in further theological formation than do many priests. It is amazing to observe how, summer after summer, thousands of Sisters, after an exhausting school year, are eager to attend theological courses, and how hard they work to garner the full fruit of such courses. The catechetical formation of Sisters is indeed a popular movement—but still there may remain, here and there, difficulties in establishing a program of formation which fully answers the special needs of Sisters assigned to the catechetical apostolate. Hence we are presuming to summarize some guiding principles for an adequate catechetical training of teaching Sisters.

THE NECESSARY ASCETICAL TRAINING

Catechetical training requires essentially more than an additional course in theology. Theological courses to provide Sisters with the necessary religious knowledge are obviously to be welcomed. A Sister who is to teach religion in a high school obviously needs a different and more

210

complete training in religion than does a Sister who is to have charge of the kitchen. Yet it would be erroneous to suppose that additional courses in theology will, of themselves, solve the whole problem of training catechists, or, to suppose that such courses are the most important factor in forming good teachers. Mere theoretical instruction is not sufficient.

If a Sister who did not know how to drive had to be required to drive the convent car, you would give her a course in driving. That, together with sufficient practice, would make her competent. To acquire this skill, it would not be necessary for her to have assimilated the whole ascetic formation of the religious life.

If, however, you are training a Sister for service in a hospital, you can teach her the necessary medical knowledge and techniques of nursing in special additional courses—just as you would teach the skills of driving a car—but is that all she needs for her apostolate of charity? No, your Sister nurses must be trained in a special way, from the very beginning of their religious vocation, for the humble tasks of self-forgetting charity, for the patience and sympathy they will need so much in the service of their patients. They must be formed in the right interior attitude, in the virtues proper to their future apostolate— these principles of Christian spirituality must penetrate the whole formation of religious nurses.

Is this event not more true in the case of Sisters who are being formed for the catechetical apostolate? Religious education, which is the forming of Christian personality, demands, in a special way, that the educator— the catechist—have a personality fully formed and developed according to the message that she must proclaim and the goal for which she must strive. Therefore, *catechetical training must penetrate and color the entire ascetical formation of the religious catechist.*

DEVELOPMENT OF KERYGMATIC SPIRITUALITY

The ascetical training of Sister catechists must, from the beginning be focused on a truly kerygmatic attitude and spirituality for the future messengers of our Lord. What we mean by this was explained in the first chapter of this section. It will suffice here to summarize the characteristics of a Sister who not only acts as a catechist from time to time, but who lives completely her apostolic calling and expresses it perfectly in her own personality. This requires, above all, a humble and joyful consciousness of her sublime vocation to become Christ's privileged instrument in proclaiming His message.

Sisters who are working in the field of religious education exercise the highest form of spiritual motherhood, suffering the pangs of childbirth for the souls committed to them, until Christ is formed within each. (See Gal. 4:19). Since the catechetical apostolate, by its nature, consists in personal and devoted collaboration with the divine Messenger, it postulates, in a special way, close personal contact with Christ, Whose instruments we are. This personal contact means not only union with Christ in our daily exercises of piety, but also in our apostolic work. One of the most characteristic qualities of a genuine herald of Christ is to feel and to act as perfectly as possible as Christ's instrument. This fundamental attitude is not the fruit of some additional catechetical courses given to our young Sisters; it must permeate the whole process of spiritual training. This fundamental attitude will bring with it a rightful understanding of, and eagerness for, the special "kerygmatic" virtues: fidelity, unselfishness, winning manners. A good catechetical formation cannot insist too soon upon the cultivation of these virtues.

Modern catechetics rightly emphasize three points inseparable from our task: 1) catechetical concentration on the very essentials of Christian doctrine; 2) a presentation of our message in keeping with its nature as the joyful tidings of our salvation in Christ; 3) and, finally, that the catechist consistently expresses the doctrine she teaches in her own personality. What do these principles imply in the training of future catechists?

ASCETICAL AND CATECHETICAL CONCENTRATION

Why, for example, does the teaching even of willing and pious catechists so often show a deplorable lack of the necessary concentration? Why is the teaching even of Sisters sometimes too much absorbed in accidentals? The first reason for this rather common defect is a defective ascetical formation. Lack of ascetical concentration necessarily involves lack of catechetical concentration. Give the novices a spiritual formation plainly centered on the essentials of the Christian religion, and you can be sure that afterwards in their apostolate they will focus their teaching upon these same essentials. If the herald of Christ is sent to proclaim a message which is essentially the "Good News", her training cannot begin too early to transform her into a "fellow-worker in joy", to use the fine expression of St. Paul (See 2 Cor. 1:24).[1]

Furthermore it is of great importance that the future Sister catechist see her fundamental vocation as that of our Lord's bride. What a contradiction it would be if a Sister could not integrate and harmonize her work as teacher with her essential status as a spouse of Christ! If the catechist must present her message not only by her words but

1. On this important aspect of the catechetical apostolate see J. Hofinger, S.J., "Fellow-Workers in Joy," *Catholic School Journal for March, 1957.*

still more by her personality, it is evident that her message should influence deeply her whole ascetical training.

In her future catechetical apostolate, the Sister who now is being formed and trained, will be the herald of Christ. The Mystery of Christ will be the central theme of her teaching; the Mystery of Christ is the proper goal of all her catechetical activity. Hence the Mystery of Christ, and not some sentimental "Jesus-piety" must be, from the beginning, the center of her conscious spiritual life. To "live Christ" must be the core and the summary of all her spiritual endeavors—generously, constantly, with all its applications to daily life. Is there not a danger that in the spirituality of Sisters, this Mystery of Christ may sometimes be replaced by various separate devotions, each one of them good and useful, but all together constituting more of a hindrance than a help?

A genuine kerygmatic spirituality, thoroughly based on the "Mystery of Christ", means, above all, a Father-centered spirituality—"the Mystery of God the Father and of Christ Jesus" (Col. 2:22),[2] in other words, how the heavenly Father moved by "His exceeding charity wherewith He loved us" (Eph. 2:4), has called us, and has revealed and given Himself to us in His only begotten Son. In a spirituality based on the "Mystery of Christ" as presented in the Bible and the Liturgy, Christ is always seen as the great gift of the Father's love and as our Mediator and way to the Father. "I am the way . . . No man cometh to the Father, but by Me" (John 14:16). Christ is the way, the Father is the Goal.

Sources of Catechetical Spirituality

It should not be difficult to communicate this kerygmatic spirituality to novices and even to postulants. We need only lead them to the essential sources, and they will be filled with a truly Christian spirit. *The principal sources of catechetical spirituality are the Bible, the Liturgy, and Christian doctrine.*

The Bible

The Bible, especially the New Testament, holds first place among these principal sources; and in relation to our message it is by far the most important document. Its principal author is God Himself. Through the inspired writers, He has composed and transmitted to us these writings as His message, as the bread of our souls. Here we see in the most striking way how, under His special influence, the first great messengers, above all His only begotten Son, understood and formulated

---

2. See the Greek original which with regard to this particular text is often not fully expressed in translations.

the divine message entrusted to them. All historians of our times, even the rationalists among them, admit the undeniable fact that the writings of the New Testament are the classical documents of the spirituality of the primitive Church and of Apostolic preaching. No master or mistress of novices in the whole Catholic world would ever deny these facts, but do all draw from them the conclusions necessary for a sound spiritual formation of the future heralds of Christ? In every religious community, we are rightly eager to lead our novices to the best writings that contain, in their primitive purity, the ideals and spirituality of our own religious group. Is it not even more important to lead them to the first sources of genuine Christian spirituality, composed, ultimately, not by man but by God Himself? Is there not a real danger that in the formation of our young religious we are too much concerned with our "specialities" and too little concerned with the fundamentals of all genuine Christian spirituality? But the novices we train, will, after all, be sent by Christ, through His Church, to spread His Gospel and to communicate His spirit.

The Bible, therefore, must be, in theory and also practice, our most esteemed and most used source of spiritual formation. Even the writings of our founders are, compared with the Bible, only supplementary reading. The young religious must have sufficient time to read and to meditate upon the Bible, and also, they must receive the right guidance to truly Catholic reading of the Bible. Scientific exegetical lectures and studies are not necessary for this purpose. In order that the Bible may really serve to nourish genuine kerygmatic spirituality, it needs to be more lived than discussed, more experienced than analyzed, more prayed than studied. It is our duty to help the young religious to get the true taste of the Bible—not always easy in our times —to find the principal ideas of the Bible and to build up their spiritual life on them, to find the answer to their personal spiritual problems in the Bible. Our own conferences with our young religious must be nourished from the Bible—and this does not mean that we should interlard them with countless quotations: the Bible was given to us by God, not to be a literary adornment for our own compositions, but to guide us, to communicate God's own ideas to us. The spirituality we present must conform to the Bible not only in its individual elements, but as a whole; so that it emphasizes the same fundamentals, presents them from the same dominant viewpoint, stresses the same fundamental attitudes. Thus the young religious will take with them for their whole religious life a deep practical love of the Bible. Is it asking too much, at least of professional messengers of Christ, that once a year they should carefully read the New Testament, the principal document of the Christian message and Christian spirituality?

THE LITURGY

Just as the Bible ranks first among spiritual books, so the liturgy holds first place in the practice of prayer. Here also first place does not mean a merely theoretical evaluation, but something eminently practical—first place in our daily prayer life; first place with regard to careful instruction, guidance, and performance.

Novices who are continuously nourished with the word of God as we have it in the Bible, will, it is true, very easily find the right Catholic attitude to the liturgy—yet they need help, the more so because perfect participation in the liturgy requires the necessary arrangement on the part of superiors. We cannot deal here with details of how young Sisters are to be trained in liturgy;[3] but at least two points call for stress. Participation in the liturgy according to the genuine Catholic spirit—nowadays so much emphasized by the Church—means not only interior participation, but also active exterior participation. The idea to be found, strangely enough, in religious communities, that participation in the liturgy is the more sublime the more it is merely spiritual, that is, interior and silent, is scarcely Catholic; it destroys the Catholic conception of sacramental life and the Incarnation: that divine being and life are communicated to us in visible forms, signs, and actions. Would it not be deplorable and simply wrong if a Catholic girl who in secular life became accustomed to intensive participation in the liturgy found less active participation among the brides of Christ? Why did Christ institute the Mass if not to draw His beloved Bride the Church into His own sacrifice? Who, therefore, in the Church should be most eager for active participation in Christ's sacrifice? One would think that it should be the religious who by their vocation represent, in the most striking way, the Church as Our Lord's bride.

However, in recommending so highly an intense active participation in the liturgy, we do not mean to recommend a daily *Missa cantata* or a daily high Mass. We should not recommend either of these even for seminarians who are being trained for the priesthood. Our most important reason for taking this position is that, since we are training our seminarians for priestly life and work in parishes, they should become thoroughly acquainted with all forms of "popular liturgy". Through

3. Readers may apply to their communities much of what the author recommended in article "Liturgical Training in Seminaries" in *Worship*, July-August, 1956.

practical performance, they should know those forms of the liturgy which facilitate understanding and active participation on the part of the people. We have in mind particularly the different forms of low Mass which allow for various means and degrees of suitable participation by the community, especially a good dialogue Mass with a fitting combination of prayers and hymns. A daily high Mass in the seminary could easily lead seminarians to associate the liturgical movement too exclusively and closely with the celebration and multiplication of high Masses. This would be wrong and would be a real hindrance to the liturgical renewal we now need in our parishes and schools. The Latin high Mass is the most perfect, but also the most difficult, form of Mass liturgy—difficult not so much for the priest and for the choir, but for the understanding and active participation of the people.[4] The application of these principles to an adequate liturgical training of Sister catechists is not hard to make.

Those who are at all familiar with the modern trend in catechetics know what emphasis is placed on the catechetical value of the liturgy. The reason is evident. Liturgy teaches and re-enacts in an unparalleled way the Mystery of Christ. The Mass provides the most perfect participation in the Mystery of Christ that we can receive on this earth. The Mystery of Christ is the central Theme which we heralds of Christ are commissioned to teach. Participation in the Mystery of Christ is the proper goal of all our catechetical activity. In view of the general recognition of the outstanding teaching value of the liturgy, we well may wonder why the catechetical movement in the United States, on the whole, up to the present time, has not stressed the use of the liturgy as has that of other countries excelling in modern catechetics. One reason for our neglect may be that, until recently, it was not possible to convince the majority of Sister teachers of the tremendous catechetical value of the liturgy—probably because this point was neglected in their own preparation for teaching.

CHRISTIAN DOCTRINE

The third principal source of catechetical formation is Christian doctrine. Obviously a training based on Bible and liturgy will of itself lead to a vital understanding of the fundamental Christian doctrines. Yet the fruit the young Sisters should receive from the diligent study and use of the Bible and participation in the Liturgy can be essentially deepened by a special course in Christian Doctrine. This should give them an impressive survey of the subject, which is at the same time fully directed to life: it should show them how our own spiritual life

4. See *Worship*, 1956, pp. 433-434.

must be based on the message we are sent to proclaim. The doctrines to be included in this survey are, of course, the ones we meet continuously in the Bible and the Liturgy; but here they are proposed in a more systematic form, which facilitates a still deeper penetration and concentration. Thus both our message and our spiritual life will be even more consciously seen and experienced as a wonderful unity; the various doctrines will more and more be seen to unite, to form one overwhelming message, "the mystery which hath been hidden from eternity in God" now realized "in Christ Jesus Our Lord" (see Eph. 3:9–11). And in the same way the various duties, aids, and practices will unite to form one central duty and activity, that is, to bring Christ to life in us (see Col. 2:2). Is not this unity what Sisters need most, both for their own spiritual life and for their apostolate?

To accomplish its purpose fully, such a doctrinal survey should fulfill the following conditions. First, it should be solid, but not more scientific than is necessary to achieve the thoroughly ascetical goal of this training—not knowledge making arrogant, but love building up character (see 1 Cor. 8:1). Second, it should be a survey of the whole of Christian doctrine and not merely of some theological treatises; the whole as a whole, but with a special stress on the points that are of greater importance for our spiritual life, omitting less important points and theological controversies. Finally, it should be closely related to the Bible and the Liturgy, even in the formulations that are used; it should help and so aid the Sisters to find and to meditate upon the same doctrines in the Bible and the Liturgy, where they are found in a less systematic form. Since this doctrinal survey must serve and nourish the spiritual life, the only efficient approach to be used is the "kerygmatic".

CHAPTER FIVE

Theological Training for Sisters *

The ascetical training of teaching Sisters, discussed in the previous chapter, should be completed by theological courses in the literal sense of the word. But the formative value of such courses depends to a great extent upon the way in which they are arranged and given. As is so often the case when a new form of training is proposed, some people are too skeptical, and try at once to prove the uselessness of the innovation by the classical argument that it was not used in the good old times; others, on the contrary, expect the new method to produce a magic effect and to be the solution of all difficulties. The appeal to the "good old times" in this case certainly indicates that we need a more complete catechetical formation of teaching Sisters than was necessary in the past. But courses in theology will provide this formation only if they are fully adapted to the special requirements of the students.

For what Sisters need is not "theology" as such, but a solid doctrinal training for their own spiritual life and for their teaching apostolate, which training should include many elements of theology. Not every form of theology, however, is adapted to their special conditions. Since these courses are required by their apostolate, the right ordering cannot be worked out *a priori* from the notion of "scientific" theology, but only from the viewpoint of the Sisters' future catechetical activity. This seems so evident that one is ashamed to mention it; but considering the way in which theological courses are occasionally arranged, it seems useful to state this explicitly. Theological courses for Sisters, then, are wrongly ordered from the outset if they follow in a more or less slavish manner the arrangement used in seminaries with regard to the material to be taught, or the method to be used, or the sequence of the various subjects, or the goal pursued.

* Some of the ideas proposed in this chapter were examined by Rev. J. Henle, S.J., in his article, "Father Hofinger's Theological Courses for Sisters," in *Catholic School Journal*, 1957, 257f. My answer to Father Henle's objections one would find in *Catholic School Journal*, March 1958. We do not think that we have to change anything in this chapter, but it may be useful to note that the chapter is not concerned with the whole question of Sister formation, but only with their theological training. That Sisters who teach in schools need a liberal arts education concluding with an A.B. is beyond question.

What Is the Precise Aim of a Theological Course for Sisters?

To answer this decisive question, let us start from the "good old times". As long as there have been nuns in the Catholic Church, there have been among their number many outstanding personalities possessing extensive religious knowledge and deep understanding of the Christian mysteries. Nevertheless, as a rule, there was no special religious instruction given to the nuns in addition to instructions for their spiritual life. Nuns who were capable of a deeper religious formation obtained it from their own diligent spiritual reading and study. The libraries of ancient monasteries show how much the nuns of past ages made use of this opportunity; as do also the written works of great nuns like St. Gertrude, St. Mechtild, or, especially, St. Teresa—works which indicate the remarkable theological formation of their authors.

The need for a special doctrinal training for all nuns first became evident when religious who had formerly led a purely contemplative life began to participate in the educational apostolate of the Church. Even in the Middle Ages, true enough, nuns undertook some educational work. But the educational activity of that time can in no way be compared with the intensive educational work of today. Only a few members of the community, usually only one or two, had anything to do with education, and they did not need any special theological formation for the very simple kind of instruction which they had to give — if, indeed, any separate catechetical instruction was given. And, in the hypothetical case that they needed such special training, the quiet rhythm of those good old days left them time enough to attain the necessary formation by themselves from the learned books in the library.

But nowadays the situation of teaching Sisters is quite different. Very often the strength of the whole community is absorbed by educational activities. Today even Sisters who teach in an elementary school need a deepening of their religious knowledge. They need it first of all for their teaching as such. In our times, to give a good course in religion in the upper grades requires on the part of the teacher herself a very solid foundation. If she is to do her work well, in religion as well as in other subjects, she must know more than she teaches. No one denies that a fully trained teacher in an elementary school needs more than an ordinary high school training. The school systems of all countries which are at all advanced in modern education require, or at least request of their teachers considerable academic formation. Why should the teachers of religion be the only exception to the rule?

Furthermore, for their own spiritual life, teaching Sisters today need a much more solid doctrinal training than in former times. Modern teachers receive an intensive preparation in secular subjects before they are permitted to teach, and it is, especially for religious, of great importance that their religious formation be kept on the same high plane as their secular formation. A notable inferiority in their religious formation would have unfortunate consequences both for the Sisters' own spiritual life and for their educational apostolate. A Sister whose religious education is not on a level with her general intellectual culture is in danger either of minimizing religion, or of embracing irrationalism and sentimentality in the field of religion.

These new conditions, then, point not only to the general necessity of "theology for Sisters," but also to a fairly exact formulation of what teaching Sisters of our times need for their religious formation. Future teaching Sisters at the beginning of their novitiate usually have no more religious education than that provided in an ordinary Catholic high school. They must, therefore, be given an additional training in Christian doctrine which will give them the developed religious knowledge necessary for their educational apostolate and for the harmonious development of their religious personality. And in working out the details of the syllabus, we should continuously ask: is this what the Sisters need for a well-developed, cultivated, spiritual life, or for the thorough Christianizing of their secular teaching, or for their catechetical apostolate proper? Anything that does not contribute to this threefold goal may have a place in a theological seminary for priests, but for Sisters, it will not be a help but a burden.

In this connection it is well to know that, even in seminary training for the priesthood, the very best authorities recognize the danger of overburdening the student with superfluous material. Some years ago, Father Karl Rahner, S.J., declared in a famous study of this problem: "A large part of the material with which a seminarian nowadays has to concern himself is, in fact, a dead weight from which he ought to be freed."[1] Nor would anyone who is acquainted with Father Rahner's works charge him with advocating a superficial simplification of theological studies.

For Whom Are These Theological Courses?

There should be no controversy on this point. The courses given to the whole group of young Sisters are intended for the ordinary teaching Sister who will teach religion in an elementary or high school: their goal is not to provide philosophical or theological specialization for the

1. Karl Rahner, S.J., *Gedanken zur Ausbildung der Theologen—Gründe, die eine Änderung in der theologischen Ausbildung nahelegen,* in *Orientierung* (Zurich) 1954, 149-152, 165-168. Auxiliary Bishop Dr. Joseph Maria Reuss stresses the same need in his article: "Priesterliche Erziehung heute," in *Wort und Wahrheit* (Wien) 1954, 85-105.

cream of the community. If some of the Sisters need a special formation for a special purpose, this specialization must be given separately. The ordinary course must give the ordinary student what she needs and can acquire with ordinary diligence. Especially in the courses we are discussing, any teaching that is over the heads of the students would prevent the course from benefiting the spiritual life of the Sisters and their apostolate. Such teaching would lead to a fictitious education from which even the gifted students would not obtain the specialization they need, but which might mislead them into spiritual pride. We are concerned, then, only with a course intended for the whole group.

THE BASIC COURSE IN CHRISTIAN DOCTRINE

Obviously a course intended to form more perfect messengers of Christian doctrine will definitely stress those subjects which directly contain the Christian message—dogma, morals, and ascetics. In seminaries, for practical reasons, these subjects are treated separately. In former times, as is shown by the great theological summas of the Middle Ages, especially the *Summa Theologica* of St. Thomas, dogmatic, moral, and ascetic theology were taught as one theological discipline. Such "systematic theology" presented and treated the whole of Christian doctrine as one complete system, in which the more theoretical fundamentals and the more practical doctrines concerned with Christian life formed one whole—the doctrine of the one entire Christian revelation. In a course for Sisters, there is no reason why "what God has joined together" should be artificially separated. On the contrary, teaching Sisters are very much in need of an insight into the essential unity of Christian doctrine. Is not lack of unity a deplorable fault in nearly all forms of teaching religion—from classes in the elementary school to theological studies in the university? Do not take it for granted that future teaching Sisters have, when they enter the novitiate, a clear view of the internal unity of the message they are preparing to proclaim. Their teachers must stress this internal unity constantly, and explain it lucidly. Whenever we begin a new section of Christian doctrine we should, by a brief, clear introduction, show the place of this individual section in the whole Christian message. This is necessary in connection with every important doctrine that we teach.

Keeping our goal in mind, we must put special stress on a thorough exposition of the revealed doctrine. Together with a clear explanation of the *exact meaning*, we must carefully and impressively show the *religious value* of each particular doctrine and its importance for Christian life—the spiritual life of the Sisters and the Christian formation of their future students.

Every Sister should finish the course with an indelible impression of the wonderful unity of Christian doctrine and a joyful insight into the joyful message of Christ Our Lord. She should also have a well developed discernment between essentials and accidentals, since even revealed doctrines are not all of the same importance. According to St. Paul, the *kerygma* is precisely that essential part of Christian revelation which we are to stress in our catechesis. Therefore a solid kerygmatic formation necessarily implies an efficient training in distinguishing essentials from accidentals. If we focus attention on the essentials of Christian revelation, we shall not find much time for those theological deductions from Christian dogma which are of secondary importance, and we shall find much less time for theological controversies which do not contribute to the goal of our basic course.

Moreover we must take the time for giving the *necessary suggestions concerning a good catechetical presentation* of the doctrines we are expounding. Thus, for example, in dealing with the doctrine of the most holy Trinity, we must show not only the meaning of this fundamental mystery of Christian faith and its importance in Christian life, but we must also indicate how it should be presented on different levels of catechetical instruction—lower grades, upper grades, and high school. We should also suggest what might be the best comparisons to use to clarify the meaning of this mystery, and how to use the comparisons. Failing to give such practical help to the future teacher, our course may be excellent in aiding contemplative nuns in their own spiritual life, but of little use in training efficient messengers of Our Lord. In order to answer the real needs of our teaching Sisters, the basic course must be given in such a way that it makes the Christian message understandable to them, and also admirable, prayable, teachable, realizable.

It may be somewhat difficult to find a fitting textbook for such a basic course fully adapted to the special needs of Sisters. The ordinary scholastic textbooks of seminaries cannot be recommended, even if written in English, and still less the *Summa Theologica* of St. Thomas Aquinas. St. Thomas would be the first to acknowledge that his grandiose *Summa* was written for a quite different purpose.[2]

ADDITIONAL COURSES

While it should be clear to teacher and students that the basic course is of supreme importance, other courses may be useful or even necessary.

Study of the Bible

Continuous reading and study of the Bible are highly important for

---

2. It is evident that the catechetical hints given in the author's short survey of Christian doctrine (Part three of his book) are only a small part of the suggestions which teaching Sisters need for a complete catechetical training.

our Sisters, but special lectures on the Bible do not seem to be as necessary as is the basic course proposed above. The Bible should be used constantly in the presentation of the basic course as a means of theological argumentation, and our presentation of doctrine should be imbued with the word and spirit of God as it is found in the Scripture. The Sisters must be stimulated to diligent Bible reading and their study enriched by good commentaries. To this end, it would be desirable to have from time to time, a series of lectures explaining parts of the Bible. These, however, must be specifically adapted to the special requirements of teaching Sisters and not a mere repetition of lectures to seminarians.

Religious Education

A good course on religious education, including catechetical methods, is absolutely necessary. It should be substantial and practical, stressing the guiding principles which underlie any useful method rather than a confusing exposition and evaluation of many methods. It should make clear to the students that a method is an aid to teaching and should not be permitted to overshadow the truth that is being taught. For even the best methods, whether used in teaching or in our own religious self-education, become in reality a hindrance rather than a help as soon as they are used mechanically and slavishly.

Church History

We presuppose that, at some time in their formation, Sisters are given a course in Church history. This course should not be overburdened with historical facts, but should relate impressively the actual life and growth of God's kingdom. It will point out how we, in our own day, can learn from the mistakes as well as from the outstanding efforts and successes of the past. Church history, taught rightly, has definite catechetical value, and, when presented to Sisters, should include methods of teaching in the upper grades and in high school.

The Place of Liturgy

In a well planned novitiate, the Sisters will be familiar with liturgy from the beginning of their religious life; their basic course in theology will offer many opportunities to broaden their understanding and enhance their appreciation of the official prayer-life of the Church; and their course in religious education will show them how to use the liturgy on the various levels of religious education. If these opportunities of correlating liturgy with the other phases of their formation have been used and if the Sisters in their own community cultivate an intensive liturgical life, a *special course in liturgy* may be of minor importance. An occasional course dealing with the place of liturgy in Christian religion and consequently in Christian education could be very helpful, especially in our times, when, at least in the United States, even many Sisters do not yet sufficiently recognize the tremendous educative values of the liturgy. On the other hand, since, as a general principle, we do not favor the multiplication of courses in the training of teaching Sisters, here, too, we maintain that a reasonable formation of Sisters should not imitate the curriculums of seminaries. The dividing up of subject matter into too many separate disciplines certainly is a major reason for the lack of unity in the priestly formation of today.

Philosophy and Apologetics

What about a *special course in philosophy and apologetics?* Does not a solid course in theology strictly postulate a preceding solid course in scholastic philosophy? Must we not, therefore, begin the theological training of Sisters with a thorough initiation into Christian philosophy? We do not think so. If our course were to be a scientific training in scholarly theology, approximating as nearly as possible the complete training of professional theologians, then a preceding philosophical course would seem to be inevitable. But do ordinary teaching Sisters really need such a complete theological training? Is there not great danger that such a complete scholarly training would consume so much time that we would neglect the essential fundamental formation? Is there not a real danger that many Sisters with only a high school background will not be able to get the full fruit of such a study? Philosophy will be rather "learned" than really assimilated. Should we not, also, take a hint from the difficulties so often experienced in the *philosophicum* of the seminaries?

Would it not, therefore, be wiser in the general course for Sisters to deal with the essential philosophical problems, e.g., with the arguments for God's existence, the immortality of the soul, the freedom of the will—all integrated with lessons in Christian doctrine? And then, towards the end of their training, when the Sisters have attained a degree of scientific maturity, they would derive much fruit from a short survey of the most important philosophical problems and the Christian answers to them, indicating clearly the importance of these answers for an entirely Christian view of life. We recommend a similar method for apologetics.

At any rate, we should never burden the Sisters during their novitiate, nor during their second year, with a dry scholastic philosophy, which—

in this form—is of little or no value to their spiritual and professional training. If we stress so greatly concentration on essentials in the study of theology, we must, even more, stress such concentration in regard to philosophy.

PRESENT NEED OF FORMATION

A modernized formation of teaching Sisters is of great importance to the Sisters themselves and to their future apostolate. As all concerned with this problem are well aware, such a vital matter must not be left to chance; it must be planned carefully and carried out resolutely. Priests who take part in the training must work according to the syllabus and follow the program. The best program will fail without qualified teachers and therefore, no sacrifice and expense should be spared to obtain them.

However, even the best training course is *only a good initiation.* The Sisters must have facilities to continue their own formation. To do so efficiently they need three things above all: first, sufficient time for their own development through private reading; second, the right material for this reading, and consequently a well selected library;[3] third, occasional courses in the content and methods of religious education, for Sisters already working in the catechetical apostolate, to acquaint them with current problems and their solutions. Sisters who, during the time of their formation, never had an opportunity to participate in a course giving a kerygmatic survey of the whole of Christian doctrine should be permitted to attend such a course at least in later years.

The careful reader has certainly noted that in this discussion we have avoided as much as possible the term "theology" for Sisters. This is not the place to examine to what extent the timely catechetical training we have recommended could be called "theology." We are not greatly interested in this question, and we do not think that Our Lord is either. He does not expect to see thousands of Sister theologians in the full sense of the word, but, rather, as many excellent instruments as possible to communicate His life to American students. Moreover, we are convinced that the training we recommend will actually provide for the ordinary Sister a more solid and religiously deeper "theological" formation than courses which imitate "scholastic" theology without the necessary adaptation to the special needs of the Sisters.

It is another question whether, in addition to the general training,

3. For further kerygmatic formation, we recommend especially *Lumen Vitae.* This periodical may be obtained in the United States through the Newman Bookshop, Westminster, Md.

there should be an *opportunity for a more thorough theological training
of a real élite*. We answer, definitely, yes. But even this "theology" ought
to avoid any slavish imitation of the academic courses for priestly
theologians. Even such advanced training for Sisters has a final apostolic
goal, and, consequently, it must be given with the kerygmatic approach.[4]

4. See the final chapter in this book.

CHAPTER SIX

The Catechetical Apostolate of the Priest

The Catholic Church in the United States is outstanding in catechetical activity. Religion is taught in Catholic grade schools, high schools and colleges, and the necessary instruction of the millions of Catholic students attending public schools is provided for, largely through the admirable efforts of the Confraternity of Christian Doctrine. This vast catechetical apostolate is characterized by the very large part taken by Religious in the teaching of religion in Catholic schools, and by the unusually large share taken by lay-people in the teaching of students attending public schools. In comparison to the work done by Brothers, Sisters and lay teachers, the contribution of priests is less emphasized, and is sometimes too limited. Thus the important question arises: to what degree does the help afforded by Religious and lay catechists free the priest from his obligation to teach religion?

In the United States, the efficient assistance given to pastors by Religious and lay apostles makes it less necessary for the pastor himself to give religious instruction than is the case in countries where the priest has to teach unaided, or where he cannot hope for so many or such well-trained collaborators. But it would be wrong to assume that even the best teaching Religious or lay teachers could ever render superfluous the catechetical function of the priest himself. To some extent, certainly, their help makes it possible for the priest to teach for fewer hours every week, but it can never dispense him from his obligation to teach religion skillfully and fervently. In a country with a relatively small number of fully trained physicians, the government would be well advised to take all possible measures to increase the number of nurses, and to train them fully. And it would also be most reasonable, in such a situation, not to burden the few doctors with administrative work which could be done by people without any special medical knowledge. By these means, the doctors themselves would be fully able to concentrate on the medical activity proper to them as doctors. But it would surely be strange if, in such a situation, the doctors were to reduce their strictly medical activity and devote themselves mainly to administration, giving as their reason for so doing the large number of well-trained nurses now available. So in the field of priestly teaching. The happy fact that he has many well-trained helpers should not mean that the priest reduces the scope and extent of his proper work as a priest to confine his activity to ecclesiastical administration. Rather, it should induce him to devote his time more exclusively to the activities which are proper to him as priest, and which can therefore not be carried out by anyone else with this special quality of priestliness.

With regard to religious instruction, the effect of having efficient help should be, first, that we priests devote ourselves to those kinds of religious instruction which can properly be carried out only by a priest, and that we develop these forms of our priestly catechetical apostolate to the greatest possible perfection. And, secondly, that, in our whole catechetical apostolate, we priests cultivate as highly as possible the specifically priestly qualities of religious instruction.

What, Then, Are the Most Important Forms of "Priestly" Religious Instruction?

The first place in priestly teaching belongs, obviously, to the *sermon* to be given to the assembled Christian community *at the Sunday Mass.* Its special worth and pastoral importance is shown historically by the fact that in the ancient Church this instruction was given mainly by the Bishop himself — the writings of the Fathers of the Church are, for the most part, the homilies which they preached to their people during Mass. This is indeed priestly teaching *par excellence,* since it forms, together with the Scripture readings, an integral and significant part of the liturgy of the Mass. Its pastoral importance is obvious: here the pastor addresses the flock entrusted to him by Our Lord, to lead them in the Christian way of life, to provide the spiritual food so necessary for their souls in this secularized world, and so to form real Christians. What a great mistake it would be to think that our catechetical task— to initiate the faithful more and more fully into the Mystery of Christ— ends with the religious instruction given in our schools! This progressive initiation must be continued in our pastoral care for the adults of our flock. And we do so primarily by the priestly instruction given at Sunday Mass followed by the people's active participation in our offering of the Eucharistic Sacrifice.

The extensive help we receive from Sisters and lay apostles may excuse us from giving a great deal of religious instruction in our schools. But our generous helpers and our flock have a right to expect that, for our part, we concentrate all the more on improving the quality of the specifically priestly instruction given during Sunday Mass. The magnificent efforts that are being made all over the United States to extend and improve the quality of the religious instruction given in schools will not achieve their full effect unless this instruction is developed and completed by sermons of the same high quality.

After the sermon on Sundays and Feasts, the next most important catechetical task of the priest would seem to be *the guidance and continued formation* of the catechists who teach in his schools and Confraternity classes. This guidance and formation, obviously, should include much more than the work of administration. The teaching given by our catechists—including Brothers and Sisters—would be vastly more effective if they could work under priestly leadership, properly understood. They need real spiritual guidance for the continual deepening of their religious life, since religion can only be properly taught by a deeply religious person, by a teacher who lives his message. And both religious and lay catechists also need help with the problems of method and content involved in their religious teaching.

Obviously, this catechetical task of the priest means that he must continually see to the deepening and enrichment of his own spiritual life, for only in this way will he be able to deepen and enrich the spiritual life of his messengers. And it means also that the priest must be familiar with both the theory and actual practice of modern catechetics, for only so can he guide and further the work of his catechists. How discouraged they would be if their pastor did not understand their efforts, or, even worse, if his catechetical formation were inferior to theirs and, being unwilling to recognize this fact, he were to try to force them to use ways of teaching which they knew to be ineffective! And, on the other hand, how encouraged are teachers of religion who find in their pastor a sympathetic and enlightened guide! But pastors can hardly be capable of giving such guidance without a continuous study of modern catechetics or without actual practise in teaching. If only for this reason, the priest, then, should never completely dispense himself from conducting classes in religion, and this exercise of the art of teaching will also help him to improve the instruction he gives by means of his Sunday sermons.

And, finally, it is his special priestly privilege and duty to *complete the religious instruction given by his assistants*. In order to do so, he needs frequently to visit the various classes conducted by his helpers. And he should do so, not so much to examine the students in order to find out how successful his assistants have been, as to deepen and complete their religious formation by his specifically priestly influence. Surely every visit of the pastor to a classroom should leave behind it a priestly impression, should bear some special fruit of priestly action. Or would anyone say that it suffices to make some witty remarks to the children and to make sure that they are learning the catechism by heart?

And, obviously, besides his sermons in church and his teaching in his schools, the *instruction of converts* is a most important part of the priest's catechetical apostolate, a typically pastoral form of religious teaching.

But in all these forms of teaching, the priest must not only present sound Christian doctrine—we take this for granted—but proclaim his message in a specifically priestly way. Thus we come to the question:

WHAT ARE THE SPECIFICALLY "PRIESTLY" QUALITIES OF RELIGIOUS INSTRUCTION?

The majority of the faithful believe that the priest possesses a special teaching authority simply by virtue of his ordination. But this is, strictly speaking, not true, at least not in the direct way envisioned by many people. The only teaching authorities in the Church are the Holy Father and the Bishops. The Bishop can give other people a share in his task of teaching his flock, by giving what we call a canonical mission to preach. But the Bishop does not have to give this mission to every priest; and he may give it to people who are not priests, even to laymen. The ordination of a deacon, it is true, especially disposes a man for "the ministry of the word"; and this may be even more fully the case with the ordination of a priest. Nevertheless, even a priest does not get any direct teaching *authority* with his ordination. This authority does not seem to be the most specific priestly quality of our teaching —speaking, that is, of the religious instruction given by priests and not by Bishops.

But what is more characteristic of specifically priestly instruction is that it is given by a man who, because of his priesthood, has a special likeness to Christ Who is at once Priest and Teacher. The high-priesthood of Christ and His supreme authority to guide and to teach, together form in Him one wonderful and organic unity, making up the threefold office of His redemptive mission. But of these three, the fundamental office is certainly His Priesthood. It is as the eternal High-priest that He works our redemption, offering for us and with us the most holy and pleasing Victim to the heavenly Father and bringing us divine life. His priestly mission animated, penetrated and directed His whole teaching, for the final goal of this teaching is to communicate to us a living knowledge and loving appreciation of the divine life which, as Priest, He communicates to us, and to form us to take part in the perfect worship of the New Covenant in order that the eternal Father may be adored in spirit and in truth (John 4:24).

Anyone who participates in any way in Christ's mission to mankind as "The" Messenger of the heavenly Father must strive faithfully to transmit this priestly message of Christ. He must strive, in other words, to initiate his hearers into the mystery of Christ. But it is evident that the ordained priest is expected to emphasize most especially this priestly aspect of Christ's message. Thus the great themes of the religious instruction that we give as priests should be: the divine life that we receive from Christ through the sacraments, and the filial worship that we offer through Christ, in Him, and with Him. Christian doctrine is by its nature directed to divine worship; but the priestly teacher has a special call to bring out this "liturgical" character of the Christian message. Might the fact not be that some of the obvious deficiencies of the catechetical apostolate flow from our having forgotten to stress this essentially priestly and, therefore, liturgical character of the Christian message?

As soon as a priest really grasps this priestly aspect of his office as pastor and teacher, he becomes at once a friend and promoter of the liturgical movement. For he sees that its aim is the same as his own: to form his people for a more perfect participation in Christ's own worship.

And such a priest will also realize that it is his special task and privilege to gain his people for divine worship, not only by teaching the liturgy, but by the right performance of the liturgy. Religious and lay teachers can instruct people in the liturgy and in the part they should take in it, but only we priests can provide our flocks with a celebration of liturgical services which makes them understandable, attractive and truly formative. Here we priests in a very special way, "Teach by doing". One of our most urgent tasks, then, even from the purely catechetical point of view, is to provide the faithful with a celebration of the liturgy so arranged and carried out as to make possible and encourage their full and active participation. And such a celebration of the liturgy will also offer the greatest possibilities for catechetical development.

And, finally, our catechetical apostolate as priests is necessarily influenced by our *special theological training*. Both the Bishops who send us out, and the faithful who come to hear us, rightly expect from us *doctrinal clarity and exactitude*. It is in order to fulfill this expectation that we received such a lengthy and solid scholastic formation in the seminary, and it is obvious that we have need of such careful training in order to carry out our catechetical apostolate in the Church. Mother Church herself has so frequently stressed this point that nobody should be in danger of minimizing it in any way.

But we must never forget the fact that doctrinal solidity is not the only quality to be expected in a priest's religious instructions. With equal, and even greater reason, the Church and the faithful expect a priest to give teaching that is truly the "word of life". He is expected to present the faith, not only correctly and clearly, but vitally and inspiringly, so as to display "the unfathomable riches of Christ", and by this to win the faithful for a new life in Christ.

But such a combination of doctrinal clarity and religious vitality needs to be systematically developed in the course of the formation given in the seminary to a future priest. Who would be so rash as to say that scholastic training alone can bring about this desired result? What is needed here above all, in the theological formation of our students, is the harmonious combination of the scholastic method and the kerygmatic approach. Two years ago, during the International Study Week on Religious Education held at Leopoldville in the Belgian Congo, I had the opportunity of speaking with the Rector of a Mission Seminary in Africa. The conversation turned upon the proper priestly education of future missionaries, and, in particular, upon the best way of imbuing them with the Christian doctrine which they are later to proclaim. The Rector became quite vehement: "Father," he said, "I know from my experience in our seminary that a merely rational (that is, a scholastic) approach is not 'formation, but de-formation'." Is this judgment of an experienced educator valid only for Africa, or does it hold good for other countries as well?

A solid theological training should also give the priestly messenger of Christ the priceless advantage of becoming acquainted with *the first and principal sources of Christian doctrine:* the Bible, the Liturgy, the Fathers. But one sometimes receives the impression that priestly teaching as a whole is not much influenced by these primary sources of the Christian message. The quotations from the Bible found in sermons give one the feeling that they have been added for the sake of adornment, and we hear practically nothing of liturgy or the Fathers. What can the reason be for this not uncommon, but yet somewhat strange state of affairs? May it not be traced to the incomplete way in which these primary sources were treated in theological courses given in seminaries?

For it is obvious that a seminarian who becomes accustomed to consider Holy Scripture, the Liturgy and the Fathers too exclusively as means to prove his scholastic theses, can hardly have been given the proper and full appreciation of these inexhaustible sources. He sees enough of them during his tiresome preparation for his examinations; when these are passed, he is happy to bid farewell to them as to his other "text-books." He has never learned how to nourish his own spiritual life from these well-springs: he has never become acquainted with them from the point of view of his own future proclamation of Christ, although they are the fundamental documents of the Christian *kerygma*. But the fact is, that by careful study of these fundamental sources, the future priestly messenger would be prepared in the best possible way for his future priestly teaching. And he would learn how to find in them the continual inspiration and deepening of his own priestly life, so that he can most effectively inspire and deepen the priestly life of his catechetical assistants. The final solution of this question, then, comes back once more to the need for planning how best to use the kerygmatic approach in theological studies and how to combine it most harmoniously and organically with the scholastic method in the seminary curriculum.

CHAPTER SEVEN

Kerygmatic Theology: Its Nature, and Its Role in Priestly Formation

By his ordination, the Catholic priest is called to take part in a special way in the teaching work of Christ. And when his Bishop gives him the canonical mission to preach, he thereby receives an exalted and important share in Christ's own mission to be the herald of the heavenly Father. "As the Father has sent Me, I also send you" is said to the priest in a far fuller sense than to other fellow-workers with Christ in the teaching apostolate.

Since a future priest is thus to be an especially qualified herald of Christ, he receives a special training; Mother Church strictly prescribes a lengthy formation of at least six years in a Major Seminary. The thorough doctrinal training given him during these six years is, as everyone admits, concerned above all with his formation as a priestly teacher. He needs these long and solid studies in order to become a fully equipped priestly herald of Christ. For him, then, this theological training is not an end in itself, but the means to make him a fully trained herald, able to proclaim Christ's message (*kerygma*) to his brothers: "Go, and, making disciples . . . teach them to observe all that I have commanded you" (Matt. 28:19ff).

THE QUESTION OF KERYGMATICALLY ORIENTED THEOLOGY

In the light of the absolutely clear and strict ecclesiastical legislation and the countless utterances of ecclesiastical authorities, there is no question with regard to three points of priestly formation: *first,* that the priestly herald needs a lengthy and solid theological formation; *second,* that the training in the seminary is not an end in itself, but is for the purpose of training the seminarian for his future work as a priest. The training in the seminary is not, primarily, to train professors of theology, but capable pastors. This doctrinal training is, then, in a special way, directed to the teaching function of the future priest. *Third:* for his teaching function, the priest needs a solid rational foundation in Christian doctrine, and this rational training is called scholastic theology. From his training in scholastic theology, the priestly herald will know clearly what the Church teaches, what the individual doctrines of the Church mean, and how they differ from opposing or nearly related errors.

The only question is, then, whether this rational aspect of Christian doctrine is all that the future herald of Christ needs for his complete formation? Or, in the message he will have to proclaim is there also another, more dynamic aspect, which should be taken into consideration, studied and developed together with the rational aspect?

There is no question, therefore, either of minimizing the rational aspect of the Christian message or of replacing this aspect by more effective elements. The question is simply one of eventually complementing this rational aspect by also bringing out the equally important and essential *dynamic* aspect of the Christian message.

The phrase "kerygmatic theology" has recently come to be used, especially in Europe, for a study of theology which explicitly emphasizes this aspect. But, of course, the reality is nothing new. There are, and there always have been, those who teach scholastic theology so as to bring out both the rational and the dynamic aspects of Christian revelation. What we wish to show here is the need and the possibility of making this second aspect an explicitly recognized and formulated part of the theological formation of future priests.

We shall briefly survey, then, the beginnings of the kerygmatic renewal. Then we shall deal with the essentials of its program, thus clarifying the relationship between the kerygmatic and the traditional scholastic approach to theology; and, finally, we shall point out what results are to be expected from the right use of the kerygmatic approach in the formation of priests.

A Brief Survey of the Modern Kerygmatic Renewal

A far-reaching *revival of scholastic theology* began about the middle of the 19th century, with which such famous names are connected as those of Matteo Liberatore, J. S. Gaetano Sanseverino, Joseph Kleutgen, S.J., the Cardinals Tomaso Zigliara, O.P., and Johannes Franzelin, S.J., together with many others. In 1879, Leo XIII published the great Encyclical *Aeterni Patris*, by which this revival was promoted as being one of the great concerns of the Church. From the very beginning, this revival produced excellent results in the preaching of Christian doctrine. In opposition to the influence of the preceding period of the "Enlightenment," the scholastic revival gave a new emphasis to the correct and clear formulation of Christian doctrine; it pleaded for the predominance of the strictly religious, over the moral aspects of religion; and it insisted strongly on the supernatural character of Christian doctrine.

The classic example of this influence is the catechism by Joseph Deharbe, S.J. (1847). But this same catechism is also a typical example of the less happy effects of Neo-scholasticism on the catechetical apostolate. The too exclusively rationalistic approach of scholastic theology thus affected even catechism classes and their texts, producing that very clear, but also very dry textbook of religion, the Deharbe catechism, which soon gained world-wide prominence, and appeared in countless adaptations, one of which was our own Baltimore Catechism.

Characteristic of this famous catechism is its undeniable clarity and absolute orthodoxy. But characteristic of it also is its lack of clear presentation of the central theme and the core of the Christian message (see above, pp. 69-73). How did it happen, then, that for more than fifty years, during which scholastic theology was flourishing in all Catholic universities and seminaries, no scholastic theologian pointed out the obvious logical weakness of this classic "scholastic" catechism? Was this due to a lack of understanding of Christian doctrine as being a "message"? Or was it from lack of interest in the catechetical apostolate? In any case, it would seem to indicate that the scholastic formation of the time did not train priests adequately for the catechetical apostolate. For an analysis of the scholastic textbooks of the time would show the same characteristics as Deharbe's catechism, and there can be no reasonable doubt that the teaching of the professors was largely influenced by these textbooks. And so we can easily understand why it was that many religious and apostolic-minded students complained that they received very little inspiration for their religious life and future apostolate from theology as taught in the seminary.

But scholastic theology need not suffer from such deficiencies; and this was proved in the early years of the scholastic renewal by Matthias Joseph Scheeben, now commonly considered the greatest theologian of the 19th century. His works are outstanding both in theological speculation and in the exact exposition of Catholic teaching, founded in a solid study of its sources. He demonstrated, in classic form, the organic relationship of the Christian mysteries to one another, and the pre-eminence of religious values. (*Mysteries of Christianity, Glories of Divine Grace.*) His writings enrich the reader also from the strictly religious viewpoint: his theology leads to prayer. This dynamic quality of Scheeben's work is due, in great part, to his thorough study and extensive use of the Greek Fathers.

Thus Scheeben's work had shown, early in the course of the scholastic revival, what valuable inspirations Christian contemplation and preaching could receive from scholastic theology, though in his own time, very few theologians appreciated his work. But the twentieth century has brought, step by step, a turning away from the exclusively rational approach. This process has been quite slow, but it has been unmistakable. Since the first World War, there has been an increasing tendency to provide a more complete dogmatic basis for, and formation in, the spiritual life. A classic author of this movement is Abbot Columba Marmion, O.S.B. (*Christ the Life of the Soul, Christ in His Mysteries*). At the same time there was in France and Germany an increasing tendency to stress the connection between Christian dogma and Christian living (e.g. A. Tanquerey: *Dogma and Devotion;* A. Rademacher, *Religion und Leben,* 1921-1926; P. Lippert, *Credo,* 1916-1923).

Along the same line are the various presentations of theology for educated laymen, widely used by priests as well, which appeared from this time on, in Germany to begin with, but also, and in increasing numbers and variety, in France, England and the United States. Such books not only offered a useful "popularization" of scholarly theology, but were also superior to most of the scholastic textbooks in their theological concentration and their orientation to life. More than one priest found that he began to realize the true richness of Christian doctrine only when he happened to read such a popularization.

But the decisive impulse to the kerygmatic renewal was given by *modern catechetics,* as we saw in the first chapter of this book. It began to be seen, some twenty years ago, that our catechetical task involves more than good teaching methods only. We need, above all, a deep understanding of our message itself. And this deeper and fuller understanding presupposes a more kerygmatically oriented training of the messenger. In other words, it requires a more fully kerygmatic orientation of theological training in seminaries.

Both the pressing need for, and the program of this kerygmatic renewal were given a historical basis and clearly set out for the first time in the classic book by Fr. Joseph Andreas Jungmann, S.J., *Die Frohbotschaft und Unser Glaubesverkündigung (The Good News and our Proclamation of it,* 1936). Jungmann's basic ideas might be summed up as follows: a change in methods alone can never solve the catechetical problem. To give to the teaching of religion in church and in school the vital force it should have, all those concerned in such teaching must first explicitly realize what is the essence and the specific character of the Christian message. Present-day defects in preaching and teaching are traceable, in part at least, to the fact that textbook theology has not been greatly concerned with this message, this *kerygma,* as such. Indeed textbook theology has its own non-kerygmatic method, which could not help exercising a far-reaching and unhappy influence on the teaching of Christian doctrine. For scholastic theology and catechetics, although obviously related to one another, differ greatly in both their material and formal object. The proclaiming of the truths of Christianity, even to well-educated people, is essentially different from the strictly scholastic method used in professional theological training. A great effort needs to be made, therefore, far greater than has been done in the past— to supplement scholastic speculation with a thorough study of Holy Scripture and the Fathers in order to bring out the meaning, nature, and character of the Christian message.

In this sense, Jungmann asked for a theology oriented to preaching and teaching *(Verkündigungstheologie)*, and other professors then at the University of Innsbruck made the same point in various works. Hugo Rahner, S.J., in *A Theology of Preaching*, and F. Dander, S.J., in *Christ All in All*, presented a kerygmatically oriented survey of Christian dogma. J. B. Lotz, S.J., in *Scholarship and Preaching*, tried to present the philosophical basis of Jungmann's ideas, and F. Lakner, S.J., in *The Central Object of Theology*, tried to present the theological basis. Both these last men overstressed the need for, and the possibility of a special kerygmatic theology within the framework of seminary training, contrasting such a theology with an "absolute" theology conducted in the traditional scholastic way for those pursuing higher ecclesiastical studies. On this point, they were rightly opposed by H. Weisweiler, S.J., and M. Schmaus, in particular.

After the second World War, Jungmann's ideas were further worked out in a positive way by G. B. Guzetti, who incorporated Jungmann's ideas into the pattern of scholastic theology, which, after all, permits of different emphases.

In the meantime, the belief has been gaining ground that a more pronounced kerygmatic orientation is needed in professional theology if we are to have a kerygmatic renewal in the field of catechetics. And it is a fact that in countries in which the necessity for a kerygmatic renewal in the education of priests has not yet made itself felt, there is, generally speaking, little interest in a more kerygmatic approach to catechetics.

But great uncertainty exists everywhere as to the best way in which to carry out this pressing need for a more kerygmatic orientation in the theology courses given in seminaries and in universities. A textbook by Maurus Heinrichs, O.F.M., written during the second World War for use in mission seminaries in China, incorporates remarkable suggestions for the organic combination of the scholastic and kerygmatic approach. This work is a notable first attempt, but it is not a final solution of the problem.[1] And, furthermore, the combining of the scholastic and the kerygmatic approach needs to be done quite differently at the different levels of theological formation. It is important from this point of view that leading professors of scholastic theology at the Gregorian University in Rome, such as J. Alfaro, S.J., J. Alszeghy, S.J., G. Flick, S.J., J. Fuchs, S.J., have been striving to give to their theological lectures the needed kerygmatic orientation. In mission countries especially two famous theological faculties in India excel in the same line, viz., the Pontifical Seminary in Poona and the theologate of the Jesuits in Kurseong.[2]

The problem, then, has been recognized and is being studied, but a complete and detailed solution has not yet been found.

What Kerygmatic Theology Really Is

From this brief historical survey, we can see that what is now asked for in the training of future priests is a study of theology more definitely oriented to the preaching and teaching of the Christian message, what is called, for purposes of convenience, *kerygmatic theology*. Such a name is, obviously, of no assistance in making popular what it stands for, and it would be most helpful if a good English designation could be found. But at least the Greek origin of "kerygmatic" fits in with the similar origin of the word "theology"; and it indicates clearly what it stands for: that kind of theological teaching which truly fulfills its task in relation to the proclaiming of the *kerygma*, the Christian message.

For genuine theology has as its first purpose *a thoroughly religious understanding and appreciation of divine revelation* . . . not any kind of understanding of Christian dogmas, but a religious one, which causes us to understand more deeply God's perfection and our relation to Him. And since the object of theology is by its very nature of the highest value—this value being an absolutely essential element of it—any true theology must bring out this value and lead to the religious appreciation of the divine doctrine revealed. Christian revelation is, by its nature, *evangelium*, Good News, a message concerned with religious

1.   On this question and this particular textbook, see: Johannes Hofinger, S.J., *Das Problem des Textbuches in Seminarien der Missionländer, in Neue Zeitschrift für Missionswissenschaft*, 1956, p. 46-63.

2.   The suggestions of Jungmann have been followed, though not always without some compromise, in the latest European catechisms (France, Belgium, the Netherlands, Strasbourg, Basel, and, above all, in the New German Catechism of 1955). Among leading catechetical journals, the international *Lumen Vitae* (Brussels), and also Katechetischen Blätter (Munich) are especially concerned with the furtherance of the kerygmatic renaissance. In the missions, the *Mission Bulletin* (Hongkong) and *Clergy Monthly* (Kurseong, India) work in this direction. See, e.g., the significant article of J. Putz, S.J., "The Art of Teaching Christian Doctrine," in *Clergy Monthly*, 1958, 17-23.

values. And any theology which does not present this essential aspect of Christian revelation rightly and impressively is *ipso facto* deficient.

Everyone admits that a good biography of George Washington, for example, must bring out the historical importance of his personality and his work for the United States. All the relevant historical facts must be considered and evaluated in this light. Any history of his life which lost itself in historical details without showing his great personality and his historical importance would, certainly, be a poor one. And would not everyone also admit that a treatise on the Blessed Sacrament, for instance, should, above all, show clearly and impressively the unfathomable divine love shown in this divine gift, and the place of this doctrine in our whole "evangelium". And that, consequently, a treatise which is primarily a cosmological analysis of the meaning and consequences of transubstantiation gives a rather poor "theology" of the Eucharist?

Nor does this mean to belittle the importance of precise theological analysis aided by sound philosophy—any more than a true work of history can do without thorough historical research. But the focus of historical science and of the presentation of history are not the detailed research that go into them: the focus of theology is not scholastic analysis.

True theology has as its *second purpose: efficient help for the correct, and at the same time, efficacious proclamation* of Christian revelation. This is especially true with regard to theological courses given in seminaries. Mother Church has emphasized this more "practical" view in countless documents on seminary education. Or is it only in theology that we must say: "Non vitae, sed scholae discimus"? The scholastic rational approach admittedly is of great assistance in the correct teaching of Christian doctrine, and therefore the Church wisely demands a sound use of this approach in theological training. But correctness is not the only aspect of genuinely Christian preaching. Christ's heralds must proclaim a message which is, finally, not for the mind alone, but for the whole man, for life and action.

As we saw in the first part of this book, the final goal of all our catechetical activity is participation in the Mystery of Christ. Since our message thus calls for action, for men to follow Christ's gracious invitation, we have to show them the motives for so acting. And this means that we must present the values of Christianity, for values alone have motivating power. Theological training must, therefore, bring out these values and develop them, so that the future priest may himself be fully aware of them and able to proclaim them clearly and inspiringly.

Moreover, the future herald of Christ needs to find in his theological formation another aid to his future work. He needs to be shown what are the essentials of his message and what is its interior structure and coherence. Good theological formation in seminaries, then, must bring out the essential points, the right order and the interconnection of Christian doctrines. Are our seminarians not at least occasionally in danger of overlooking the substance of Christian doctrine among the many single theses they have to study, not being able to see the woods for the trees? They can answer individual theses very accurately, and yet they are unable to bring together these various single stones to build up one glorious doctrinal structure. And from this, surely, results the lack of unity and of catechetical concentration in preaching the faith which have so frequently been criticized.

Obviously, every form of theology does not have to serve the work of teaching and preaching in the same way or to the same degree. A great difference necessarily exists between detailed theological studies and a summary presentation of the whole of Christian doctrine. And an even greater difference exists between theology courses for training professional theologians, and courses for lay catechists which are exclusively and directly for the purpose of training for teaching. But the more specialized theological courses also need to be seen and given in the light and vivified by an awareness of the holy service which theology must render to revelation, to faith and to the proclaiming of God's word. Even research needs to be undertaken in the same light and with the same awareness. And this awareness is shown above all by the choice of themes and by the way in which the problems are posed and treated.

Thus we can see that the objections which are still raised from many sides against the idea of kerygmatically oriented theology have their source either in an erroneous concept of the proper task of theology in general, or, more frequently, in mistaken ideas about the nature and goal of "kerygmatic theology".[3]

Erroneous Ideas About "Kerygmatic Theology"

a) Kerygmatic theology is not a *new branch of theology* which is proposed as an addition to the already numerous subjects in the seminary curriculum. What is desired is, rather, the functional orientation of theology, especially of dogmatic theology, moral theology and exegesis, towards the living appreciation, and, as a consequence, to the vital and

3. An example of the latter is *S. Thomas et Theologia "Kerygmatica,"* by Rev. J. Kunicic, O.P. (Angelicum, 1955, pp. 35-51). The "kerygmatic theology" here described does not correspond to that advocated by modern catechetics, and is one against which both St. Thomas and we ourselves would object as greatly as does Fr. Kunicic. Unfortunately the author does not quote any actual authorities on kerygmatics. *Die Verkündigungstheologie* by E. Kappler (Freiburg, 1949) does not present the kerygmatic question correctly, but the author does give, in the first part of the book, a detailed report of great value on kerygmatic literature.

effective teaching and preaching of the faith. Thus, to exclude misunderstandings, it would be preferable to speak of the "kerygmatic approach to theology" rather than "kerygmatic theology".

b) Although the kerygmatic approach is different from the scholastic approach, the *kerygmatic approach is not anti-scholastic*. In the same way, positive theology is not opposed but rather complementary to scholastic theology. What St. Ignatius said, in his rules for having the true spirit of the Church, of the relationship between positive and scholastic theology can also be applied here: "The eleventh rule is to praise both positive and scholastic theology; for, as it belongs to the positive teachers, such as St. Jerome, St. Augustine, and St. Gregory, to stir up our affections to love and serve God in all things, so it belongs rather to the scholastic doctors, such as St. Thomas, St. Bonaventure and the Master of the *Sentences,* to define and explain for our times what is necessary for salvation . . ." *(Spiritual Exercises).* It might be opportune to notice that St. Ignatius considers that scholastic theology of its nature should be kerygmatically oriented: as a message "for our times" it presents "what is necessary for salvation".

c) Thus it is clear that "kerygmatic theology" does not mean a simple practical kind of theological course for seminarians who are unable to follow deep theological teaching of high academic value. On the contrary, the kerygmatic approach strives in a special manner to grasp in the deepest way possible both the religious beauty and the inner relationship of the Christian mysteries, precisely because it wishes to bring out the religious values of Christian doctrine.

Again, this kerygmatic orientation does not consist in making numerous practical applications of the matter studied to the spiritual life, or to use in sermons and so on. It consists rather in a kerygmatic outlook on the whole presentation and organization of material, although its connection with Christian life and preaching should also, at the proper times, be brought out and discussed.

d) And, lastly, "kerygmatic theology" *is not lay theology* as contrasted with the traditional scholastic theology used in seminaries and in faculties of theology in universities. The kerygmatic approach obviously should play a very important part in religious instruction given in high schools and colleges and in the training of lay catechists; but the theological training in seminaries itself can and needs to be given the kerygmatic orientation.

In order to give the kerygmatic approach its due place in the theological training of future priests, we need to see both the differences between these two approaches, and how they may be harmoniously combined.

Most Characteristic Differences Between the Kerygmatic and Scholastic Approaches

Different goals. Scholastic theology aims primarily at an intellectual elaboration of Christian doctrine. It calls, therefore, for formulations that are as precise as possible, for solid argumentation with a manifest preference for syllogistic form and deduction, aiming at a speculative penetration and development of the revealed truths. But "kerygmatic" theology aims at the religious appreciation and the missionary proclamation of the revealed truth. Its principal question is, then: what, out of the abundance of revealed truth, is the essential matter to be meditated and proclaimed; under what aspect is our message to be presented? Christian preaching must proclaim doctrine as "glad tidings"; it must call and direct men to a life altogether new. "Kerygmatic" theology, then, strives to understand Christian doctrine in relation to Christian living, to bring out its religious values.

Different objects. Since their goals are different, both the material and formal objects of these two approaches to theology must be different also. Scholastic theology is, in principle, concerned with the whole of revealed truth (cf. *Summa Theologica*), although its preference is for those parts of revealed doctrine that offer the richest material for its special formal object, that is, for a rational elaboration of the revealed truths that draws heavily on philosophy. But the kerygmatic approach limits its interest more to those aspects of revealed truth which are in a special way meant to be lived and proclaimed. Its formal object is, precisely, the nature of Christian doctrine as God's message to mankind.

The *different values* of the two approaches can now be clearly seen. Scholastic theology offers us a precise formulation of Christian doctrine; it assures orthodoxy; it develops the gift of a clearer discernment between truth and error in doctrinal matters. The kerygmatic approach, on the other hand, develops especially the sense of the substance, the relations and the religious values of Christian doctrine. It gives us the ability to pray, to meditate, to appreciate, to live Christian doctrine. The difference between these two approaches might be compared with those existing between microscopic and artistic photography: which also have different purposes, different objects, different values—and fundamental compatibility.

The very differences between the scholastic and the kerygmatic approaches indicate the possibility and the necessity of completing and complementing the one approach to theology by the other. And since a harmonious combination is so important for the well-rounded training of future priests, let us now give some suggestions towards reaching a practical solution.

How May These Approaches Be Combined?

A harmonious combination does not mean either that the two approaches be given separately, or that they be mechanically combined. We do not want a course in "kerygmatics" that would be a kind of expanded catechetics, in addition to the regular scholastic course in dogma. And neither do we want the dogma course to be presented entirely according to the rational, scholastic approach with some kerygmatic considerations added at the end of each thesis. No. The kerygmatic orientation must pervade the whole.

But this penetration does not mean a revolutionizing of theological training. It does not demand an essentially new structure either of the theology course as a whole, or of the methodical presentation of the individual doctrines.

Therefore there is *no need to change the usual sequence* in which the different treatises are presented, a sequence which is founded on sound scientific reasons. The students should rather be reminded that this scientific order is not that of catechetical exposition, and given the reasons for the difference between the two methods. And the same principle should be applied to the selection of material to be taught.

Thus in a kerygmatically oriented course, we would begin, as is customary, with the treatise on God the One and Triune. But we would show the students why scientific theology demands this ordering and why the catechetical presentation in grade schools requires a different one. By so doing, obviously, we shall not only aid the seminarians in their future apostolate, but we shall at the same time deepen their theological understanding. So, again, to use the kerygmatic approach in no way means that we should omit the section on the Divine Relations in God because we do not use this material in ordinary teaching and preaching. True, we do not: but this study is none the less necessary for a solid and scientific understanding of the doctrine of the Trinity, and it is strictly necessary for answering various objections against this doctrine. And, besides, it can be very useful in giving us a deeper understanding of our own participation by grace in the life of the Blessed Trinity. But the seminarian should be enabled to understand why he should study this rather abstract section of theology; and we should not spend more time on it than is really necessary.

Again, a kerygmatic approach to the presentation of individual doctrines would not mean that the scholastic thesis form should be abandoned. But everything need not be presented in this form, and the structure of the thesis itself might be modified somewhat.

To begin with, it would be highly desirable that *only dogmas of kerygmatic importance* be proposed in thesis form. The other theological material could be better presented in the form of *asserta,* or of *scholia* and *corollaria,* especially in matters of lesser importance. By these means, the seminarians would learn what the essentials of doctrine are, and how to concentrate their attention on them while not neglecting the other material as ordered around these main points.

But for the sake of this proper concentration and ordering, the kerygmatic renewal pleads for a thorough examination of the matter to be taught and for the courageous elimination of everything that is not truly useful for the solid training of the future priest. By "useful", we mean, of course, what serves the formation of a well-rounded, deeply spiritual and solidly trained priest. Such a priest must have what we might call a solid professional education, although he does not need the specialized training of a future professor of theology or research scholar.

This solid education of future pastors and preachers is not served by, for example, the detailed study of all the theological controversies of former times. Even the more important controversies could be presented in a fairly short and substantial way, so that the truth would shine out, and the Catholic answers to objections made clear. But in many of our "traditional" textbooks, do we not find rather that the controversies themselves come to seem more important than the truth revealed by Christ? What importance would Our Lord Himself give to these controversies if He were personally to train His messengers today?

Thus the individual theses should be proposed, first of all, in clear relation to the whole of Christian doctrine. Before beginning on an individual thesis, we should first indicate the main problem which this thesis is to answer. And we should never introduce a new section of theology, much less a new treatise, without giving a brief and vivid introduction which will show the connection of this particular section with the whole, and the special importance of what we are about to study in relation to theology itself and to Christian preaching.

Then the exposition of the thesis itself should be ordered toward an intelligent and well-founded, but also a truly religious understanding and appreciation of the doctrine proposed. And for this purpose, no more scholastic terms, distinctions, divisions and so on should be used than are really necessary.

The customary paragraph(s) on the opponents of this particular doctrine should, of course, be retained. But it should plainly serve the purpose of clarifying the Catholic position, and helping us to understand the opponents of our own times. Let us do away with all defunct adversaries whose objections are of no significance today. But if an opponent is considered of real importance, then let us not simply name him and his works and the dates of his birth and death, but rather give the essentials of his teaching, of how he came to hold his erroneous doctrine, the forms in which this error is still to be met with in the world today, and how best to lead people from this error to the fullness of Catholic truth. It is true that sometimes we have to deal with errors which are no longer of great importance, but which formerly had a great influence on the development of Christian doctrine. Thus for example, in a solid theological course, we must, of course, deal with the great christological controversies of the ancient Church and show how these controversies helped to clarify Christian teaching on Christ.

It would also seem most advisable to set in the very heart of every thesis a brief but substantial theological and religious consideration of the place and value of this particular doctrine in the whole structure of Christian doctrine and life.[4]

Again, Holy Scripture and Tradition should not be used only as means for "proving" each thesis. Their teaching should be given in such a way as to enable the student to begin to grasp the richness and depth of God's own revelation. In the thesis on divine providence, for example, we should not only introduce some classic texts that prove the "tenor" of our thesis. We should give the students some idea of how rich are both Scripture and Tradition with regard to this doctrine, and of how they teach much more than we can express in the tenor of a single thesis.

Again, a kerygmatic orientation would have nothing to do with *merely formalistic objections.* The syllogistic form ought to aid in showing what the real problem is, not to hide it. Here, or perhaps better, in the explanation of the thesis itself, we should ask: how does this particular doctrine *meet with the problems of our times.* One of the weak points in our formation of priests frequently is that their theological training has not equipped them to deal with the special needs and problems of our times, and, particularly with those of the actual people to whom, and the culture in which, they are to proclaim Christ's message. A kerygmatic formation should, then, not only consider divine revelation in itself, but also take into consideration its special relevance to the mentality of the people who are to receive it today.

4. The textbook by M. Heinrichs, O.F.M., *Theses dogmaticae,* mentioned earlier in this chapter, illustrates how such theological considerations could be presented. We would prefer to have these *momenta thesium* in a more systematic form. In China also we published a series of such *momenta thesium* in the *Collectanea Commissionis Synodalis,* Peking, 1944.

If we cannot show that our message answers the problems that weigh on people today, how can we be surprised at the fact that they take no interest in it?

And, lastly, at the end of the thesis, at least occasionally, it would be well to add some suggestions as to practical ways of teaching and preaching this particular doctrine. If the whole matter has been presented with the proper kerygmatic orientation, then such practical notes at the end can be made very brief, and yet most useful.

These, then, are the general lines along which a soundly scholastic, and yet vitally kerygmatic seminary course in theology might be constructed. This would mean no turning away from the true spirit of scholastic theology, for, as it would not be difficult to show, the greatest scholastic teachers ever since the Middle Ages have perennially felt the need for such kerygmatic orientation, and have tried to fill that need in one way or another for their own times.[5]

Thus, while no textbooks constructed according to these principles are as yet in general circulation[6] an experienced seminary professor who is convinced of the need and the value of this orientation would find no insuperable difficulty in giving his courses along these lines, even though he used an exclusively scholastic text. Here it is certainly true that it is the spirit that gives life, and the most ideal text would be of little use without it. For the seminary professor is, obviously, the key figure in this whole question. If he begins to teach along more kerygmatic lines, then the spirit of the kerygmatic renewal will spread out rapidly from the seminary in ever-widening circles, for the renewal of Catholic life and the vastly increased effectiveness of missionary work of all kinds.

CATECHETICAL AND MISSIONARY VALUE OF KERYGMATIC THEOLOGY

For the spiritual life of the priest himself. He would have been trained to see the Christian message not only as true, but as good, beautiful and livable, as something to be so highly loved and appreciated that he cannot help wanting to share it with others. He would have been trained to find the nourishment for his spiritual life in its unfailing and God-given sources, Holy Scripture, the Liturgy, and the Church's greatest commentators on these, the Fathers. Thus he would have the means himself to continue to grow intellectually and spiritually,

5. When, many years ago, I began in China to seek a more kerygmatic orientation of seminary training, and published some material to aid in making this orientation, Fr. Heinrichs, O.F.M., wrote me: "Father, I suppose you realize how much your aims are in line with those of our great Franciscan theologians".

6. On the problem of a textbook, which is especially urgent in relation to mission seminaries, see the article mentioned above, *Das Problem des Textbuches in den Seminarien der Missionländer.*

even in the busiest of lives, and so the means continually to enrich others.

The great *catechetical value* of kerygmatic theology flows from its very nature. Kerygmatic theology is catechetical theology in the true sense of the word, and, in practice, it merges with the catechetic so far as content is concerned. And it is precisely the content that now, in the second phase of the catechetical movement, needs to be developed and perfected first of all. Kerygmatic theology answers *ex professo* exactly those questions which now are the focus of catechetical interest: the right selection of material, the organization of the catechetical material, the special relation to the whole in which the individual parts of the material are to be presented. We should note here the particular importance of the kerygmatic approach to bring about the much-desired deepening of the religious instruction in Catholic schools, and also of the instruction given to Catholic students attending public schools. And the importance of the kerygmatic renaissance is also evident for the mission of the Church within the United States, for the regeneration and deepening of Christian life and for the attraction and instruction of converts.

The specific *missionary value* of kerygmatic theology follows clearly from the specific character of the missionary proclamation. This is essentially:

A proclamation to outsiders, necessitating a special consideration for, and adaptation to, the intellectual attitude to which the missionary is addressing himself. Kerygmatic theology of its nature should effect the cultivation of this consideration and adaptability in the future messenger.

A fundamental proclamation which must lay the solid foundations of a future indigenous church where now no church exists. Kerygmatic theology, being a theology of catechetical concentration, should provide the future missionary with the ideal training for making such a proclamation.

A living and forceful proclamation which will give to new Christians the special impetus needed successfully to overcome the innumerable difficulties of their pagan surroundings and the latent or open persecution they may have to face, and which will enable them to become in turn effective apostles of the Christian faith. As the theology of Christian values, kerygmatic theology should show the missionary how best to give such a proclamation of the Christian message and inspire him to do so fervently and effectively.

In our times, even countries in which the Catholic population is numerically strong have been more and more closely approximating missionary conditions with regard to the preaching of the faith. Our priests today not only have to minister to a docile flock; they must also strive to bring into Christ's fold the many people in their parish who at present are not interested in His message. Only a truly dynamic preaching of this message will attract their attention and effectively bring them to Christ.

In the early days of the kerygmatic renewal, when Fr. G. Delcuve, S.J. was beginning his catechetical apostolate in Belgium, he was once told by Fr. Emil Mersch, S.J., the famous theologian of the *Corpus Christi Mysticum:* "Father, the better teaching of religion that you are trying to bring about in grade and high schools is very important. But don't forget that there is little hope of a far-reaching renewal of teaching in Catholic schools so long as we have not renewed the theological training of our priests". Is this true only for Belgium?

APPENDIX

A – Sample Lesson from the New German Catechism

Lesson 51

The Church Draws Her Teaching from Holy Scriptures and from Oral Tradition.

The holy Apostle St. Paul warns the faithful: "Stand firm, brethren, and hold fast by the traditions you have learned, in word or in writing, from us" (2 Thess. 2:15).

*   *   *   *

What the Church teaches us comes from God Who is the source of all truth. She hands on to us what God has revealed, and what was taught and believed from the very beginning of the Church. St. Paul says: "I have handed on to you the message which was handed on to me" (1 Cor. 15:3). In the course of time the Church, under the guidance of the Holy Ghost, has explained some of these truths in a more exact manner, especially at times when these truths were attacked. For Christ promised: "The truth-giving Spirit will guide you into all truth" (John 16:13).

Many of the things which God has revealed, He has caused to be written down in sacred books. Through the Holy Ghost, He prompted the authors to write these books; and while they were writing He helped them in such a way that they did in fact put down accurately all those things which God desired to tell us through their means. These writings are called "Holy Scripture" or "the Bible" (which means "the Book"). Because Holy Scripture was inspired by God, it has God for its author. It is "the word of God".

Those parts of Holy Scripture that were written before Christ came are called the Old Testament; those parts which were written after Christ had come are called the New Testament.

The Church preserves Holy Scripture as a very precious treasure. Under the guidance of the Holy Ghost she presents Holy Scripture to us, and explains it. The Church wishes us to listen eagerly to the word of God, and we should love to read it for ourselves. That is why there ought to be a Bible, or at least a New Testament, in every Catholic home. But we ought to read only those translations of Holy Scripture which have been approved by the Church.

Not all the truths which God has revealed are written down in Holy Scripture. Many of them were only preached by the Apostles, and were then handed on by the Church as precious traditions. We call these truths "Oral Tradition" because they were handed on by word of mouth. Very soon after the Apostles' time most of these truths were written down by learned and holy men whom we call "the Fathers of the Church."

The Holy Scriptures and Oral Tradition are the two sources of our faith. With the help of the Holy Ghost the Church preserves both of them without error, and draws upon them for what she teaches us.

Things to be thought over:

(1) From where does the Church draw her teaching?
(2) Why is Holy Scripture called "the word of God?"
(3) Why is it not enough if we believe only what is in Holy Scripture?
(4) What do we call those truths which were only preached by the Apostles but were not written down by them?

95. Where does the Church obtain her teaching?
The Church draws her teaching from Holy Scripture and from Oral Tradition.

96. What sort of books are in the Old Testament?
The Old Testament contains historical books, teaching books, and prophetic books.

97. What sort of books are in the New Testament?
The New Testament contains the four Gospels, the Acts of the Apostles, the Epistles, and the Apocalypse (or "Revelations") of St. John.

98. What are the names of the four Evangelists?
The four Evangelists are called Matthew, Mark, Luke, and John.

For my life: I will handle the books of Holy Scripture with great reverence; before reading them I will pray to God that He will help me to understand and obey His word properly. I will buy myself a New Testament, or get someone to give me one, to be a treasure for my whole life.

From the teaching of the Saints: "When you pray, you are talking to God. When you read Holy Scripture, God is talking to you" (St. Augustine). "He who does not know Holy Scripture does not know Christ" (St. Jerome).

Imprimatur: We can know that an edition of the Bible, or of any other book about religion, has the approval of the Church when we see in it the Church's permission that it be printed: "Imprimatur."

Discussion: Some people say "The Bible alone is enough." But we answer: "First, the Bible does not contain everything that God has revealed. St. John tells us: 'There is much else besides that Jesus did; if all of it were put in writing, I do not think the world itself would contain the books that would have to be written' (John 21:25). And St. Paul wrote: 'Hold fast by the traditions you have learned, in word or in writing, from us' (2 Thess. 2:15). Secondly, the Bible does not itself tell us which books belong to it; we can know which they are only by Tradition."

The Books of the Old Testament: 1. Historical books. The most important are the five books of Moses, the Book of Josue, the Book of Judges, the Books of Kings, and the two Books of the Machabees. 2. Teaching Books. The most important are: The Book of Job, the Psalms, and the five Books of Wisdom. 3. Prophetic Books. The most important are the books of the four great prophets, Isaias, Jeremias, Ezechiel and Daniel.

The Books of the New Testament: 1. The Four Gospels, and the Acts of the Apostles written by St. Luke. 2. The fourteen Epistles of St. Paul, and the seven Epistles of the other Apostles (Sts. James, Peter, John and Jude). 3. The Apocalypse (or "Revelations") of St. John.

B – Sample Lesson from the French Catechism

THE FIFTH ARTICLE OF THE CREED
. . . I BELIEVE IN THE REMISSION OF SINS.

The Remission of Sins

As you have seen, Our Lord compared the faithful to His sheep. He said that He was the Good Shepherd Who gave His life for them. He loved them all: the sheep who stayed in the sheepfold, and those who strayed away. And so sinners came to Him, but the Pharisees murmured, saying: "The man welcomes sinners and eats with them."

Then Jesus told them this parable: "What man of you having a hundred sheep and losing one of them, does not leave the ninety-nine in the desert and go after that which is lost until he finds it? And when he has found it, he lays it on his shoulders, rejoicing, and on coming home he calls together his friends and neighbors, saying to them, 'Rejoice with me, because I have found my sheep that was lost.'

"I say to you that, even so, there will be joy in heaven over one sinner who repents, more than over ninety-nine just who have no need of repentence."

Now we can understand why we say: "I believe in the remission of sins".

Jesus has given us the means to have our sins forgiven. You will see how in the lesson.

Answer these questions: What comparison did Jesus use in speaking of the faithful? Why did the Pharisees reproach Him? What does the parable of the lost sheep teach us?

LESSON

142. When did Jesus Christ give His Church the power to forgive all sins?
   Jesus Christ gave His Church the power to forgive all sins on the evening of His Resurrection.
143. How does the Church forgive sins?
   The Church forgives sins principally by the sacraments of Baptism and Penance.

For my life. How many faults do I need to forgive? I will forgive others so that God will forgive me, and I will never hold a grudge against anyone.

Prayer. "Forgive us as we forgive those who have offended us."

God's Word. "The Son of Man has come to seek and save that which was lost" (Luke 19:10).

———

Liturgy—During the Vigils, that is to say, the night-watches before Easter and Pentecost, the blessing of the baptismal fonts takes place. The celebrant blesses the water which is to be used for Baptism, for that sacrament which washes away original sin.

Questions to answer—1. Name the sinners whom Jesus pardoned in the Gospel? 2. Who was astonished that He forgave sins? 3. Who must He have been to forgive sins? 4. To whom did He give the power to forgive sins?

Things to Do—Make a series of pictures or sketches of the parables in which Jesus expressed His ideas concerning sinners, (especially the barren fig-tree, the lost sheep, the lost coin, the prodigal son).

C – Outline for a Three-day Retreat
On Our Adopted Sonship

I. *How Rich and Happy Are We Who Are Sons of God!*

What a pity that we ourselves do not know our own riches. During these days of recollection, we want to learn to know our incomparable riches, and to evaluate and esteem them rightly, and thus *to become thoroughly happy people.* As St. Thomas says: how can a man in mortal sin laugh any longer? Truly, only through abysmal ignorance or horrible levity. On the other hand, how can a man in the state of grace continue to feel any really great sadness? Certainly, only by reason of a deplorable ignorance or neglect of the happiness that is really his. Our religion, according to the teachings of Christ, is a *treasure,* which we must *seek* energetically, which we must *dig for* carefully, which we must *increase* diligently. Especially during these days, let us fervently seek, dig for and increase our treasure.

II. *Baptism—The Foundation of our Happiness.*

The stupendous miracle of baptism: *the Great God—Our Father.* The example of a beggar adopted by a very rich man out of sheer mercy. The special obligation of grateful reverence, obedience, and love. This is also our position in relation to God.

III. *Riches in Our Father's House—"Creatures".*

a) Behold what great riches! The Father is truly good and liberal!

b) *What are all these things for?* That through these gifts, we may know and esteem the heart of the Father; that we may easily and happily live the life of sons of God, and may serve the Father in joy of heart. "Serve the Lord with gladness!"

c) The gifts of this life are but a faint prelude to the future glory of the sons of God which awaits us. Let us now be faithful in little things!

IV. *A Dark Day in the Life of a Son of God—Mortal Sin.*

We can still lose the happiness and dignity of sons, we can still freely reject them by mortal sin. *The inner nature of sin:* the deliberate

256

rebellion of a proud and thankless son. O the horrible malice of sin! The extreme foolishness of sin! But the good Father does not will the death of the ungrateful son, but that he be converted. *Contrition!*

V. *The Ungrateful Son Permanently Rejected—Hell.*

God invites the sinning son to be converted; He arouses him, yet does not force him. If he does not want to be converted, but constantly rejects the Father, he must expect from the Father a final and definitive rejection: hell—the hell of a rebel son who is degraded. We Christians have no other choice but that between a special kind of happiness and a *definite kind of misery.* God, on His part, has already made His choice from all eternity. Despite our multiplied ingratitude, He has destined for us the happiness of sons, if only we wish to accept it. Now it is up to you to make *your choice.*

VI. *The Prodigal Son.*

Behold a picture of ourselves!
a) The folly and malice of sin;
b) The calamity of sin;
c) The taking away of sin—sincere conversion. Its elements: acknowledgment of the dominion of God, His justice and our own injustice toward Him, acknowledgment and hope of mercy.
d) The converted son: joy, gratitude, fervor of the son now returned —"subsequent penance", sincere, grateful, happy.

VII. *Father, I Have Sinned—Confession.*

How well the merciful Father received the prodigal son! Yet, he had to acknowledge his sin with humility and contrition. We must do the same in the sacrament of consolation and peace!

Examination: Show the anti-Christian character of the principal sins against the Ten Commandments.

Contrition coming from a truly filial heart. The Father looks only to the heart.

Confession made to the Father; do not focus attention on the man in the priest.

Firm Resolution to lead a new life as a true son. The happiness of this life.

VIII. *The Greatest Gift of the Father—Incarnation-Redemption* (Rom. 8:32; John 3:16).

"Born for us, given unto us", the Son of the Father, that He might lead us, His brothers, back to the Father. The purpose of the first coming of Christ: to establish the new Kingdom of God — the ideal family of the sons of God. Do you want to have a part in it and to collaborate diligently? *Christ is calling you,* especially now during the retreat. What will your answer be?

IX. *The Ideal Son of God—Christ, the "First-Born Among Many Brethren".*

The Father sent us His only-begotten Son, that we might have a divine model of the ideal son of God. *Here is the goal of Christian life,* to which we are predestined from all eternity; to become conformed to the image of the Son, that He may be the first-born among many brothers, now in obedient and sacrificing love, then later in triumphant love—to suffer with and to be glorified with our "elder Brother". The *innermost spirit* of Christ is the spirit of filial love, which does not ask what it *must* do, but what it *can* do to honor the Father. *Concrete and practical application* of the example of Christ to the life of prayer and work of the retreatants.

X. *The "Eucharist" of the Sons of God—the Sacrifice of the Mass.*

We are overwhelmed with so many blessings. How can we render worthy thanks? Our divine Brother also took care of this need, and gave us a divine solution: He instituted the Sacrifice of the Mass. The inner meaning of the Mass: thanks rendered in common by the sons of God, led by Christ, their Brother. The meaning of the principal parts of the Mass: gospel, offertory, consecration, the dismissal (go and begin generously to do what you have promised: sacrifice of life, apostolate of life).

XI. *The Reign of the Father.*

Here is the principal ideal of Christ, the second Adam: the full restoration of God's dominion: a) *within us* ("Die to sin—live to God"); b) *outside of us* (the Church—the new Kingdom of God), but *through us:* the apostolate of the sons of God. "Thy kingdom come!"

XII. *The Kingdom of the Father Consummated—the Final Stage of the Son of God.*

Now along the road, our divine Brother tells us about our Father's house. Insatiable desire for the heavenly homeland. *Maranatha!* Come, O Lord, come and lead us back into the glory of the Father! The fruit of this heavenly desire; fortitude and constancy on our earthly journey.

XIII. *The Mission (Sending) of the Holy Spirit.*

Christ, before He sent his Apostles into the whole world, communicated His Spirit to them abundantly. But they too had to prepare themselves for this. "The spiritual retreat" of the Apostles. In the same manner, Christ also wants to send us as His apostles into the pagan world. He likewise wishes to communicate His Spirit to us, especially now at the end of the retreat. The Holy Spirit gives us the spirit of Christ. He teaches us 1) to pray in the spirit of Christ, 2) to work in the spirit of Christ. Solemn renewal of confirmation.

XIV. *The Bread of Life.*

Behold the gift of the Father, with which He feeds His sons, lest they faint along the toilsome way to their fatherland. I live, now not I, but Christ, the ideal Son of God, lives in me. The genuine fruit of Communion: a life truly conformed to Christ.

ANOTHER SERIES OF MEDITATIONS

1) How rich we are by Baptism
2) The incomparable Father
3) The paradise of a son of God
4) The prayer of a son of God
5) The rebellion and rejection of the ungrateful son
6) The decalogue of the son of God
7) Father, I have sinned—confession
8) The leading back of a son of God by *the* Son of God—Incarnation
9) The ideal Son of God
10) The hidden life of a son of God (value and sanctification of Christian life)
11) The ideals of a son of God—Sermon on the Mount
12) The sacrifice of a son of God: sacrifice of the cross—sacrifice of the Mass
13) The eternal consummation of a son of God
14) "Viaticum" of a son of God

D – Suggestions for "Kerygmatic" Sermon Topics from the Sunday Gospels

BY REV. J. KELLNER, S.J.

Advent

1. *First Sunday of Advent:* Our Preparation for Christ's Last Coming. 'Lift up your heads, because your redemption is at hand.' (Luke 21:28)
2. *Second Sunday of Advent:* God Speaks to Us Through Holy Scripture. 'This is He of Whom is written . . .' (Matt. 11:10)
3. *Immaculate Conception:* The Singular Privilege of Our Lady and How We Participate. 'Hail, full of grace.' (Luke 1:28)
4. *Third Sunday of Advent:* God Speaks to Us Through Tradition. 'I am the voice . . .' (John 1:23)
5. *Fourth Sunday of Advent:* Our Preparation for the Holy Feast of Christmas. 'Make ready the way of the Lord.' (Luke 3:4)
6. *Christmas Eve:* Christ's Redeeming Love Desires Open Hearts. 'Do not be afraid, Joseph . . .' (Matt. 1:20)

Christmastide

7. *Christmas:* The Mystery of the Incarnation. 'The Word was made flesh.' (John 1:14)
8. *Sunday after Christmas:* Christ, the Ideal of Men. 'And the child grew, and became strong. He was full of wisdom and the grace of God was upon Him.' (Luke 2:40)
9. *Circumcision, New Year:* Christ Is Our Destiny. 'And when eight days were fulfilled for His circumcision . . .' (Luke 2:21)
10. *Sunday after New Year:* Christ Is Our Savior. 'His name was called Jesus.' (Luke 2:21)
11. *Epiphany:* Jesus, the Savior of the Gentiles. 'We have seen His star in the East and have come to worship Him.' (Matt. 2:2)

After Epiphany

12. *First Sunday after Epiphany:* The Christian Family, Another Nazareth. 'He went down with them and came to Nazareth, and was subject to them.' (Luke 2:51)

260

13. *Second Sunday after Epiphany:* The Sacrament of Marriage. 'Jesus too was invited to the marriage.' (John 2:2)
14. *Third Sunday after Epiphany:* The Sixth and Ninth Commandment. 'I will; be thou made clean.' (Matt. 8:3)
15. *Fourth Sunday after Epiphany:* The Church, the Ark of Salvation. 'Then He got into a boat, and His disciples followed Him.'
(Matt. 8:23)
16. *Fifth Sunday after Epiphany:* Human Weakness in the Church Cannot Spoil God's Plan. 'Let both grow together until the harvest.' (Matt. 13:30)
17. *Sixth Sunday after Epiphany:* The Church, the Visible-Invisible Body of Christ. '. . . like to a grain of mustard seed . . . like to leaven . . .' (Matt. 13:31-33)

Pre-Lenten Season

18. *Septuagesima:* Our Great Christian Vocation. 'Go you also into the vineyard.' (Matt. 20:4)
19. *Sexagesima:* The Faith, Our Answer to God's Call. 'The sower went out to sow his seed . . .' (Luke 8:5)
20. *Quinquagesima:* The Mystery of Christ's Passion. 'Behold, we are going up to Jerusalem. . . . And they understood none of these things . . .' (Luke 18:31-34)
21. *Ash Wednesday:* Christian Spirit of Penance. 'And when you fast . . .' (Matt. 6:16)
22. *First Sunday of Lent:* The Spiritual Combat and Temptations. 'Begone, Satan!' (Matt. 4:10)
23. *Second Sunday of Lent:* The Royal Way of the Cross Ends in Glory. 'And He was transfigured before them.' (Matt. 17:2)
24. *Feast of St. Joseph:* The Model of Christian Fatherhood. '. . . being a just man.' (Matt. 1:19)
25. *Third Sunday of Lent:* God's Pardoning Mercy in the Sacrament of Penance. 'And He was casting out a devil, and the same was dumb.' (Luke 11:14)
26. *Fourth Sunday of Lent:* The Virtue of Temperance. '. . . five barley loaves and two fishes . . .' (John 6:9)

Passiontide

27. *First Sunday of Passiontide:* Mortal Sin. 'They took up stones to cast at Him.' (John 8:59)

28. *Second Sunday of Passiontide:* Christ Triumphantly Enters Jerusalem. 'Tell the daughter of Sion: Behold, Thy King comes to thee, meek . . .' (Matt. 21:5)

29. *Holy Thursday:* Christ's Love for Us Unto the End. 'Having loved His own . . . He loved them unto the end.' (John 13:1)

30. *Good Friday:* Love Crucified. 'Behold the wood of the Cross, on which has hung the Salvation of the world' (Liturgy of Good Friday). Christ is crucified Love: Love for us (Gal. 2:20) and Love for the Father in Heaven (Phil. 2:8).

31. *Easter Vigil:* The Re-enactment of Christ's Death and Resurrection in Our Baptism. 'You have died and your life is hidden with Christ in God.' (Col. 3:3)

Eastertide

32. *Easter Sunday:* Christ's Resurrection and Our Resurrection. 'You are looking for Jesus of Nazareth, Who was crucified. He has risen.' (Mark 16:6)

33. *First Sunday after Easter:* The Sacrament of Holy Orders. 'As the Father has sent me, I also send you.' (John 20:21)

34. *Second Sunday after Easter:* The Meaning of the Sacraments. 'I am the good shepherd, and I know mine . . .' (John 10:14)

35. *Third Sunday after Easter:* Heaven: Eternal Happiness in the Father's House. 'Your heart shall rejoice, and your joy no one shall take from you.' (John 16:22)

36. *Fourth Sunday after Easter:* The Holy Ghost, the Soul of the Church. 'He will glorify me, because He will receive of what is mine and declare it to you.' (John 16:14)

37. *Fifth Sunday after Easter:* Christian Prayer. '. . . if you ask the Father anything in My name, He will give it to you.' (John 16:23)

38. *Ascension:* Christ Returns Home to the Father. 'The Lord . . . was taken up into heaven, and sits at the right hand of God.'
(Mark 16:19)

39. *Sunday after Ascension:* The Sacrament of Confirmation. 'And you also bear witness:' (John 15:27)

40. *Pentecost:* The Mission of the Holy Ghost, the Greatest Fruit of Redemption. '. . . the Holy Spirit, Whom the Father will send in My name . . .' (John 14:26)

After Pentecost

41. *First Sunday after Pentecost: Trinity Sunday:* God's and Our Most Profound Mystery. '. . . baptizing them in the name of the Father, and of the Son and of the Holy Spirit.' (Matt. 28:19)

42. *Feast of Corpus Christi:* The Holy Eucharist, the Divine Food for God's Children. 'My flesh is food indeed . . .' (John 6:56)

43. *Second Sunday after Pentecost:* The Mass, the Festive Gathering of God and His people on earth. 'A certain man gave a great supper and he invited many.' (Luke 14:16)

44. *Third Sunday after Pentecost:* The Mercy of God — Manifest in Jesus Christ. 'Now the publicans and sinners were drawing near to Him . . .' (Luke 15:1)

45. *Feast of St. Peter and Paul:* The Primacy of St. Peter and His Successor, the Pope. 'Thou art Peter, and upon this rock I will build My Church.' (Matt. 16:18)

46. *Fourth Sunday after Pentecost:* The Hierarchy of the Church. 'And Jesus said to Simon: . . . henceforth thou shalt catch men.'
(Luke 5:10)

47. *Fifth Sunday after Pentecost:* Christian Charity. The Fifth Commandment. 'Thou shalt not kill. . . But I say to you . . .' (Matt. 5:21f)

48. *Sixth Sunday after Pentecost:* God Is Our Creator and Conserver. '. . . if I send them away . . . they will faint on the way . . .' (Mark 8:3)

49. *Seventh Sunday after Pentecost:* Living Faith. 'Not everyone . . . but he who does the will of my Father in heaven . . .' (Matt. 15:21)

50. *Eighth Sunday after Pentecost:* Right Attitude towards Property. The Seventh and Tenth Commandment. 'Make an accounting of thy stewardship . . .' (Luke 16:2)

51. *Ninth Sunday after Pentecost:* Christian Worship. The First and Second Commandment. 'And He entered the temple and began to cast out those who were selling and buying in it . . .' (Luke 19:45)

52. *Feast of Assumption of Our Lady:* The Queen of Heaven — the Most Perfect Fruit of Redemption. 'He has done great things for me . . .' (Luke 1:49)

53. *Tenth Sunday after Pentecost:* Christian Humility. 'Everyone who exalts himself shall be humbled, and he who humbles himself shall be exalted.' (Luke 18:14)

54. *Eleventh Sunday after Pentecost:* Sins of the Tongue. The Eighth Commandment. '. . . and he began to speak correctly.' (Mark 7:35)

55. *Twelfth Sunday after Pentecost:* The Christian Love of Enemies. 'But a certain Samaritan . . .' (Luke 10:33)

56. *Thirteenth Sunday after Pentecost:* Gratitude towards God and the Prayer of Praise. 'But where are the nine?' (Luke 17:17)

57. *Fourteenth Sunday after Pentecost:* Trust in Divine Providence. 'Do not be anxious . . . for your Father knows . . .' (Matt. 6:31f)

58. *Fifteenth Sunday after Pentecost:* Miracles, Proof of Christ's Mission. 'God has visited His people.' (Luke 7:16)

59. *Sixteenth Sunday after Pentecost:* Christian Celebration of Sundays and Holydays. The Third Commandment. 'Is it lawful to cure on the Sabbath?' (Luke 14:3)

60. *Seventeenth Sunday after Pentecost:* The Basis of All Commandments. 'On these two commandments depend the whole Law and the Prophets.' (Matt. 22:40)

Pre-Advent

61. *Eighteenth Sunday after Pentecost:* Apostolate, the Works of Mercy. 'And behold, they brought to Him a paralytic lying on a pallet.' (Matt. 9:2)

62. *Nineteenth Sunday after Pentecost:* The Joyful Tidings of God's Kingdom. 'The kingdom of Heaven is like a king who made a marriage feast for his son.' (Matt. 22:2)

63. *Twentieth Sunday after Pentecost:* The Sacrament of Extreme Unction. 'Sir, come down before my child dies.' (John 4:49)

64. *Twenty-first Sunday after Pentecost:* God's Punishing Justice, Hell. 'And his master, being angry, handed him over to the torturers . . .' (Matt. 18:34)

65. *Feast of Christ the King:* Bringing the World Back to Christ the King. 'Thou sayest it; I am a king.' (John 18:37)

66. *Feast of All Saints:* The Great Harvest Feast of Redemption. 'Blessed are you . . . Rejoice and exult, because your reward is great in heaven.' (Matt. 5:11f)

67. *All Souls' Day:* Christian Death, the End and the Beginning. 'And they who have done good shall come forth unto resurrection of life.' (John 5:29)

68. *Twenty-second Sunday after Pentecost:* Christian Attitude Toward Public Life. 'Render to Caesar the things that are Caesar's.' (Matt. 22:21)

69. *Twenty-third Sunday after Pentecost:* The Sacrament of Baptism Gives Us Divine Life in the Church. 'He went in and took her by the hand; and the girl arose.' (Matt. 9:25)

70. *Last Sunday after Pentecost:* Watchfulness for Christ's Last Coming. '. . . know that it is near, even at the door.' (Matt. 24:33)

Bibliography

To Part One

OUR TASK

1) *On the Central Theme of Our Message*

JUNGMANN, S.J., Josef A.—*Christus als Mittelpunkt religiöser Erziehung.* Freiburg: Herder, 1939.

LAKNER, S.J., Franz—"Das Zentralobjekt der Theologie", *Zeitschrift f. kath. Theologie*, 1938, pp. 1-36.

MERSCH, S.J., Emil—"Le Christ mystique, centre de la théologie comme science", *Nouvelle Revue Theologique,* 1934, pp. 449-475.

MERSCH, S.J., Emil—"L'objet de la théologie et le Christus Totus", *Recherches de Science Religieuse,* 1936, pp. 129-157.

2) *On Progressive Initiation into the Mystery of Christ through Bible-Liturgy- Catechism.*

FERNAN, S.J., John J.—*Theology—A Course for College Students.* New York Jesuit Educational Association, 1953.

GRIMM, Leonhard—*Praktisches Handbuch zum Katholischen Gottlehrbüchlein für die untern Klassen der Volksschulen.* Freiburg: Herder, 1950.

PICHLER, Wilhelm—*Katholisches Religionsbüchlein.* Erstausgabe: Wien 1913.

PICHLER, Wilhelm—*Katholiche Glaubensfibel.* Lehr- und Lesebuch für die Volksschulen. Salzkotten: Meinwerk, o.J. (1951).

LUMEN VITAE special number XVI: The Bible, History of Salvation, 1955, No. 1.

HOFINGER, S.J., Johannes—"Catechetics and Liturgy—Teaching the good news—The Grade School Child", *Worship,* 1955, Jan., Feb., Sept.

HOFINGER, S.J., Johannes — "Is the New German Cathechism Worthy of Being Studied?" *Catholic School Journal,* 1958, March, 36-38.

JUNGMANN, S.J., Josef A.—"Liturgy and the History of Salvation", *Lumen Vitae,* 1955, 261-268.

JUNGMANN, S.J., J.—*Das Christusgeheimnis im Kirchenjahr*. In the collection of his articles *"Gewordene Liturgie,"* Innsbruck 1941, pp. 295-321.

PEUS, Ferdinand—Kampmann, Theoderich—*Mysterium und Gestalt des Kirchenjahres. Eine Hilfe für Glaubensunterweisung.* Paderborn, 1952, Schöningh.

LUMEN VITAE—Special number XII: *Initiation into the Sacraments,* 1954, No. 1; special number XVII: *The Liturgy, Representation of Salvation,* 1952, No. 2.

LA MAISON-DIEU—No. 42: *Liturgie et Collège,* 1955.

HOFINGER, S.J., Johannes—"The Catechism Yesterday and Today", *Lumen Vitae* 1956, pp. 479-486.

HOFINGER, S.J., Johannes—*Geschichte des Katechismus in Österreich von Canisius bis zur Gegenwart.* Innsbruck: Rauch, 1937.

LUMEN VITAE, Special number II: *Teaching the Catechism,* 1950, No. 2-3; special number III: *The Catechism Text-Book,* 1950, No. 4; special number XVIII: *Doctrinal Teaching, Message of Salvation* 1955, No. 4.

Katholischer Katechismus der Bistümer Deutschlands. Freiburg: Herder, 1955. English edition: *A Catholic Catechism.* New York: Herder and Herder, 1957.

FISCHER, Hubert—*Einführung in den neuen Katechismus.* Referate des Katechetischen Kurses zu München vom 16.-18.6. 1955. Zweite verbesserte Auflage. Freiburg: Herder, 1955.

GOLDBRUNNER, Josef—*Katechismusunterricht mit dem Werkheft.* Drei Teile. München: Kösel, 1956.

Handbuch zum Katholischen Katechismus. Herausgegeben von Franz Schreibmayr und Klemens Tilmann. Until now only part I (of 3). Freiburg: Herder, 1956.

To Part Two

THE STRUCTURE OF OUR MESSAGE

BUSCH, Wilhelm—*Der Weg des deutschen Katechismus von Deharbe bis zum Einheitskatechismus.* Freiburg: Herder, 1936.

HOFINGER, S.J., Johannes—"De apta divisione materiae catecheticae", *Collectanea Commissionis Synodalis,* Peking 1940, pp. 583-599, 729-749, 845-859, 950-965.

JUNGMANN, S.J., Josef A.—"Die Gliederung des Katechismus in geschichtlicher Beleuchtung", *Katechetische Blätter,* 1941, pp. 89-97.

RAHNER, S.J., Karl—"Über den Versuch eines Aufrisses einer Dogmatik", *Schriften zur Theologie* I, pp. 9-47. Einsiedeln: Benziger, 1954.

To Part Three

THE CONTENT OF OUR MESSAGE

BIRNGRUBER, O. Cist., Sylvester—*Das Göttliche im Menschen.* Eine Laiendogmatik. Graz: Styria, 1948.

JUNGLAS, Johannes P.—*Die Lehre der Kirche.* Eine Laiendogmatik. Bonn: Buchgemeinde, 1936.

GRIMM, Leonhard—*Der katholische Christ in seiner Welt.* 2 Bände. Freiburg: Herder, 1939-40.

HENRY, O. P.—*Initiation Théologique.* 4 vol. Paris: Cerf.

HILDENBRAND, August—*Handbuch christlicher Unterweisung.* 2 Aufl. Freiburg: Herder, 1954.

SCHEEBEN, Matthias J.—*The Mysteries of Christianity.* Translated by Cyril Vollert, S.J. 3rd Impression. St. Louis: Herder, 1947.

SEMMELROTH, S.J., Otto—*Gott und Mensch in Begegnung.* Ein Durchblick durch die katholische Glaubenslehre. Frankfurt: Knecht, 1956.

SHEED, F. J.—*Theology for Beginners.* New York: Sheed and Ward, 1957.

VAN DER MEER, F.—*Katechese.* Köln, 1954 (Translation from Dutch).

WILLIAM, M.—*Unser Weg zu Gott.* Innsbruck: Tyrolia, 1951.

To Part Four

THE MESSENGER AND HIS FORMATION

1) *On the training of Sisters and Priests.*

HENLE, S.J., J.—"Father Hofinger's Theological Courses for Sisters," *Catholic School Journal,* 1957, pp. 257-258.

HOFINGER, S.J., Johannes—"What Kind of Theological Courses Do Sisters Need?", *Catholic School Journal,* March, 1958.

HOFINGER, S.J., Johannes—"What Kind of Formation Do Our Catechists Need?" in *Shaping the Christian Message,* edited by G. Sloyan. New York: Macmillan, 1958.

HOFINGER, S.J., Johannes—"Catechesis in the United States Today," *Lumen Vitae,* 1956, pp.246-258.

HOFINGER, S.J., Johannes—*Lebensvolle Glaubensverkündigung.* Special Edition of "Missions-Korrespondenz" Kaomi near Tsingtao, 1945.

RAHNER, S.J., Karl—"Gedanken zur Ausbildung der Theologen" *Orientierung,* 1954, pp. 149-152, 165-168.

REUSS, Josef M.—"Priesterliche Ausbildung heute", *Wort und Wahrheit,* 1954, pp. 85-105.

The Doctrinal Instruction of Religious Sisters. Being the English version of *Formation Doctrinale des Religieuses.* Westminster: Newman Press, 1956.

2)   *On Kerygmatic Theology*

ARNOLD, F.—*Dienst am Glauben das vordringlichste Angliegen heutiger Seelsorge.* Freiburg: Herder, 1948.

ARNOLD, F.—*Grundsätzliches und Geschichtliches zur Theologie der Seelsorge.* Freiburg: Herder, 1949.

ARNOLD, F.—"Renouveau de la Prédication Dogmatique et la Catéchèse", *Lumen Vitae,* 1948.

BELLARD, James—*Meditations on Christian Dogma,* 3rd edition. Westminster: Newman, 1948.

BEUMER, J.—*Theologie als Glaubensverständnis.* Würzburg: Echter, 1953.

DANDER, S.J., Franz—*Christus Alles in Allem.* Innsbruck: Rauch, 1953.

DeCONINCK, S. J.—"La Theologie Kerygmatique", *Lumen Vitae,* 1948, pp. 103-115.

GUZETTI, G. B.—"The Theology of Preaching," *Theology Digest,* May, 1952, pp. 2-4.

HEINRICHS, O.F.M., Maurus—*Theses Dogmaticae,* 3 vol., ed. secunda, Hong Kong (70 Kennedy Road, 1954.

HITZ, C.SS.R., P.—"Theologie et catéchèse", *Nouvelle Revue Théologique,* 1955, pp. 897-923. Condensed in English: "Theology and the Ministry of the Word," *Theology Digest,* Winter, 1958, pp. 3-7.

HOFINGER, S.J., Johannes—"De Deo Creante et Elevante: Momentum Theologicum et Kerygmaticum Tractatus 'De Deo Creante et Elevante,' " *Collectanea Commisionis Synodalis.* Peking: 1944, fasc. 1-3.

HOFINGER, S.J., Johannes — *Lebensvolle Glaubensverkündigung.* Special edition of *"Missions-Korrespondenz."* Kaomi near Tsingtao: 1945.

HOFINGER, S.J., Johannes—"Das Problem des Textbuches in Seminarien der Missionsländer", *Neue Zeitschrift für Missionswissenschaft,* 196, pp. 46-62.

HOFINGER, S.J., Johannes—"They Call It Kerygmatic Theology", *The Priest,* 1956.

HOFINGER, S.J., Johannes—"Missionary Catechesis in Mission Lands and Dechristianized Regions," *Lumen Vitae*, 1955, pp. 547-556.

HOFINGER, S.J., Johannes—"Teaching the Good News", *Worship*, 1955.

JUNGMANN, S.J., Josef A.—"Theology and Kerygmatic Teaching," *Lumen Vitae*, 1950, pp. 258-263.

JUNGMANN, S.J., Josef A.—*Die Frohbotschaft und unsere Glaubensverkündigung*. Regensburg: Pustet, 1936.

JUNGMANN, S.J., Josef A.—*Katechetik*, 2nd ed. Freiburg: Herder, 1955. In English: *Handing on the Faith — A Manual of Catechetics*. Trans. by Anthony N. Fuerst. New York: Herder and Herder, 1958.

KAPPLER, E.—*Die Verkündigungstheologie*. Freiburg: Schweiz, 1949.

KÖSTER, SVD., Hermann—*Vom Wesen und Aufbau katholischer Theologie*. Kaldenkirchen.

LAHITTON, Josephus—*Theologiae Dogmaticae Theses ad Usum Seminariorum et Verbi Divini Praeconum*, 4 vol. Paris: Beauchesne, 1932.

LIÊGE, A.—"Pour une thélogie pastorale catéchètique", *Revue des Sciences philos. et théol.*, 1955, pp. 3-17.

MURRAY, S.J., John Courtney—"Towards a Theology for the Laymen," *Theological Studies*, 1944, pp. 43-75, 340-376.

PUTZ, S.J., J.— "The Art of Teaching Christian Doctrine," *Clergy Monthly*, 1958, pp. 17-23.

RAHNER, S.J., Hugo—*Eine Theologie der Verkündigung* 2. Aufl. Freiburg: Herder, 1939.

RETIF, A.—"Qu'est-ce que le kérygme?", *Nouvelle Revue théol.*, 1949, pp. 910-922.

RETIF, A.—*Foi au Christ et mission d'après les Actes des Apôtre*. Paris 1951.

REUSS, Josef Maria—"Priesterliche Ausbildung heute", *Wort und Warheit*, 1954, pp. 85-105.

SCHMAUS, M.—"Brauchen wir eine Theologie der Verkündigung?", *Die Seelsorge* 16 (Hildesheim 138), pp. 1-12.

SCHMAUS, M.—"Ein Wort zur Verkündigungstheologie", *Theologie und Glaube*, 1941, pp. 312-322.

SCHÜRMANN, H.—*Aufbau und Struktur der neutestamentlichen Verkündigung*. Paderborn: Schöningh 1949.

TANQUEREY, Adolphe—*Doctrine and Devotion*. Tournai: Desclée, 1933.

Index